Typographic
Design
in the

Design
Concepts

David A. Amdur

THOMSON

DELMAR LEARNING

Australia • Canada • Mexico • Singapore • Spain • United Kingdom • United States

Typographic Design in the Digital Studio: Design Concepts

David A. Amdur

Vice President, Technology and Trades ABU:
David Garza

Director of Learning Solutions:
Sandy Clark

Senior Acquisitions Editor:
James Gish

Product Manager:
Jaimie Weiss

Editorial Assistant:
Niamh Matthews

Marketing Director:
Deborah S. Yarnell

Marketing Manager:
Guy Baskaran

Director of Production:
Patty Stephan

Production Manager:
Larry Main

Content Project Manager:
Mary Beth Vought

Technology Project Manager:
Linda Verde

Library of Congress Cataloging-in-Publication Data
Amdur, David A.
  Typographic design in the digital studio : design concepts / David A. Amdur.
      p. cm.
  Includes bibliographical references and index.
  ISBN 1-4018-8093-2
  1. Graphic design (Typography) 2. Type and type-founding--Digital techniques. I. Title.
  Z246.A56 2006
  686.2'2--dc22

2006020758

NOTICE TO THE READER

Publisher does not warrant or guarantee any of the products described herein or perform any independent analysis in connection with any of the product information contained herein. Publisher does not assume, and expressly disclaims, any obligation to obtain and include information other than that provided to it by the manufacturer.

The reader is expressly warned to consider and adopt all safety precautions that might be indicated by the activities herein and to avoid all potential hazards. By following the instructions contained herein, the reader willingly assumes all risks in connection with such instructions.

The publisher makes no representation or warranties of any kind, including but not limited to, the warranties of fitness for particular purpose or merchantability, nor are any such representations implied with respect to the material set forth herein, and the publisher takes no responsibility with respect to such material. The publisher shall not be liable for any special, consequential, or exemplary damages resulting, in whole or part, from the readers' use of, or reliance upon, this material.

Typographic Design in the Digital Studio

Design Concepts

Contents

Preface ix

Typography Influences Us Everyday ix

Typographic Skills Needed by Designers x

Who Is this Book for? xii

For PC Users xii

How To Use this Book xii

Chapter by Chapter xiv

Acknowledgements xvii

About the Author xviii

Questions and Feedback xviii

Contributors xix

Dedication xxi

CHAPTER 1   Getting Started with Typography
in the Digital Environment   1

Working in the Digital Environment 1

Two Ways That Computers Represent Images 7

Types of Computer Graphics Programs 9

Design Concepts Study Guide Chapter 1 12

CHAPTER 2   The Voice of Type   15

Can You Hear the Type? 15

Introduction to the Anatomy of Letter Characters 18

Type Family: Variations on the Theme 19

Don't Faux It 21

Placing Type Over Pictures 22

Design Concepts Study Guide Chapter 2 24

CHAPTER 3   Observing Abstract Form in Type Design   27

Learning to See Feelingly 27

Words Are Tools 28

Three Types of Terms 28

Elements, Qualities, and Principles in Letterforms 29

Composition: Putting the Parts Together 31

Design Concepts Study Guide Chapter 3 35

CHAPTER 4   Exploring the Fundamentals:
             Making Display Type Work   41

Focus on Fundamentals 41

Stacked Display Type and Line Breaks 42

Putting the Stack in Order: Alignment 42

Fine-Tuning Alignment and Punctuation 44

Capitalization Formats 45

Text within Boxes 46

Adjusting the Spacing of Letters: Tracking 46

The Space Between Lines: Leading 48

Adjusting How Letters Fit Together: Kerning 50

Save the Kerning for Last (Almost Always) 51

Design Concepts Study Guide Chapter 4 53

CHAPTER 5   Structure and Measurement   59

Six Categories of Type Structure 59

Type Measurement and Specification 61

Designing Typographic Logotypes 63

Design Concepts Study Guide Chapter 5 66

CHAPTER 6   Resources of Style, Sources of Inspiration:
             The History of Typographic Design   73

Before the Alphabet 73

The Phonetic Alphabet and the Forms of Letters 76

Early Letter Spacing, Punctuation, and Layout 80

Medieval Manuscript 80

The Typographic Revolution 83

The Origin of Roman Type 84

The Modern Impulse 88

Victorian Type: An Aesthetic of Enrichment 91

The Arts and Crafts Movement:
A Bridge from Victorianism to the Future 95

Art Nouveau 97

Typography of the Machine Age 98

Design at Mid-Century 106

Holes in the Armor: Postmodern Typography 110

Design Concepts Study Guide Chapter 6 118

CHAPTER 7   **The Nitty-Gritty of Body Copy: Keep'n It Readable**   **133**

Choosing the Right Typeface 133

Type Color 134

Type Size 135

Columns 135

Leading Body Type 136

Tracking and Word Spacing 136

Rags: Bad, Good, and Special 138

Hyphens 138

Unwanted Widows and Lonely Orphans 139

Manual Interventions: Patching Up Blemishes 139

Paragraphing 140

Changing Type to Create Emphasis 140

Doin' the Numbers 142

Lists 142

Design Concepts Study Guide Chapter 7 145

CHAPTER 8   **Making Information Accessible**   **153**

Two Principles of Information Organization:
Hierarchy and Grouping 153

Strategizing for Communication: The Design Brief 154

The Grid: A Tool for Structure 156

Put It on the Tab 161

Tables 162

Design Concepts Study Guide Chapter 8 165

CHAPTER 9   **Type in Publications**   **173**

It Pays to Advertise 173

Elements That Sell the Publication 174

Elements That Sell the Stories 176

Elements That Help Navigation 179

Grid Systems in Publications 184

Design Concepts Study Guide Chapter 9 187

CHAPTER 10   Type Effects—The Good, the Trite, and the Ugly   201

The Designer's Judgment 201

Drop Shadows and Embossed Letters 202

Text on a Curved Line 202

Shaped Text Blocks 203

Text Wraps 204

Beware of Ghosts 205

Pictorial Effects 205

Interaction of Type and Image 208

Design Concepts Study Guide Chapter 10 210

CHAPTER 11   Off the Page—Type in New Media   211

Type On Screen—Through the Glass, Haphazardly 211

Show and Tell: Type in PowerPoint Presentations 214

TTTTWWW: Taking Type to the World Wide Web 215

Type Elements in Web Design 216

Live Text vs. Type Images 218

Applying Attributes to Live Text 219

Print-Friendly Web Content 220

Type in Flash Animations 220

Designing a Web Site 221

Design Concepts Study Guide Chapter 11 224

CHAPTER 12   A Closer Look at Type Design   233

Detailed Anatomy of Letterforms 233

Optical Adjustments in Typefaces 235

'R' You Seein' the Type? 235

A Close Look at Serifs 236

Design Concepts Study Guide Chapter 12 238

APPENDIX: Type Specimens 247

GLOSSARY 273

SELECTED BIBLIOGRAPHY 289

INDEX 293

Preface

Typography Influences Us Everyday

We are affected by typography during almost every waking hour. Early in the morning type greets us from the packaging of the food we eat for breakfast. Throughout the day, it beckons from just about every can, bottle, or box we see. Type calls to us from newspapers, calendars, magazines, books, and other printed materials; from billboards, buildings, and signs on the streets and highways; from the television, movies, and computer screens—even from t-shirts and other clothing. We are a culture of information junkies, and type has proven to be the most adaptable, economical, and effective way to convey information.

But, verbal messages—the words that the type spells out—are only part of the story. To see what I mean, try to imagine a world where all type looks the same. It would look monotonous and sterile—like an aisle of generic products at a discount grocery. On the other hand, if you take the time to look at and think about the type all around you, you'll discover that well-designed type adds personality, feeling, and some measure of beauty to printed messages.

Most people are influenced by typography without giving it much thought. But, you are now on the point of entering the small elite company of those who understand how type can be used to communicate in vivid, rich, and subtle ways.

A world where all type looks the same would look like an aisle of generic products at a discount grocery.

Typographic Skills Needed by Designers

All of the many kinds of communication that were mentioned on the previous page were created by graphic designers. As you can see, this field covers a broad range of endeavors. These include many kinds of publications, advertising, and promotional display; packaging, signage, and environmental design; logo design and related graphic expressions of corporate and brand identity; as well as motion graphics and interactive media. The mission that underlies all of these enterprises is the need for engaging communication. It should be clear that knowing how to use type is essential to this mission.

To succeed as a graphic designer, you need to develop competence in both typographic design and execution. Competence in typographic design begins with observing how type is used and analyzing how well it works—or doesn't work. This investigation can be helped by learning the concepts, terminology, and "rules of thumb" that professionals use to get desirable results.

Competence in execution means learning to use the tools that are needed to get professional results. The methods of typographic execution have changed a great deal since the start of desktop publishing twenty-odd years ago. Before that time, designers didn't set type. Most headlines in ads and magazines were lettered by hand. All typesetting had

Corporate identity from A to Z; Corporations use distinctive typography to create easily recognizable logos that instantly communicate ideas about who they are. How many of these letters do you recognize? *Courtesy Kit Hinrichs, @issue:magazine*

to be sent out to experts who used expensive equipment—so the job was slow and costly. It wasn't practical to have this work done until the designers could be sure of just how they wanted their final layout to look. To make this judgment, they had to test trial layouts by accurately sketching in the type by hand. Therefore, type rendering was an essential entry-level skill for the design profession. Thankfully, the substantial time and effort that students devoted to mastering this manual skill also brought important side benefits: Drawing was (and always will be) an excellent way to make observations and literally "get the feel" of letterforms. By the time students became fluent in drawing many styles and sizes of letters, they possessed a great deal of background and sensitivity that could be applied to problems of design.

Nowadays, type rendering is no longer a key survival skill. Instead, a relatively small investment can buy a digital studio with a vast assortment of beautiful type. With digital applications, designers can easily set their own type and experiment with endless variations of layout ideas. Of course, even today, most students are still encouraged to at least try their hand at type rendering. Some choose to develop talents in calligraphy, custom lettering, or typeface design. But relatively few students approach type rendering with the kind of commitment that used to be commonplace.

However, now that designers set their own type instead of having it done by experts, skills in the fine points of typography have never been more important. Without the rigorous apprenticeship of the past, students need better guidance than ever to gain competence in typographic design and execution. The ease of digital tools is deceptive; they don't guarantee good design any more than a shop full of power tools can guarantee fine woodworking (but, of course, they are safer for your fingers).

This textbook is designed to teach today's students with today's digital tools. These tools have unprecedented ease, speed, and precision. They will be used to guide you in observing the characteristics of type, choosing the type that's appropriate for a given job, and placing the type in attractive and effective ways.

Who Is this Book for?

This guide was written so that students with no previous experience with either graphic design or computers can get the information they need to develop abilities in both of these areas together. At the same time, it was designed so that more advanced students can easily distinguish between information they need and what they can skip.

This book is ideal for an integrated introduction to typographic design and design applications, or it may be used in courses that are taught in tandem or in sequence. It also can be useful to those who need to transition between QuarkXPress and Adobe InDesign.

It won't appeal to those who favor mannerisms of gratuitous verbiage! I've worked to present this material with clear, concise language and a familiar tone.

For PC Users

Most graphic designers use Macintosh computers because the Mac has superior abilities to handle type and color. However, if you own a PC, don't despair. It is quite possible to execute professional quality design on a PC.

Although this book is primarily orientated toward the Macintosh, PC users will be able to use most of the material. The Design Concepts volume is equally relevant to both platforms. With the exception of the two Mac Skills Modules, all of the Application Skills Modules should be easily adaptable to the PC. The applications work very much the same on both platforms. The most significant difference is in keyboard commands. Throughout the Skills Modules, three icons are used to stand for the major modifier keys. PC users should interpret the icons this way:

⌘ = Control key

⇧ = Shift key

⌥ = Alt key

How To Use this Book

This textbook takes an "integrated approach," meaning that lessons in design concepts and digital tools are tied together. It is a carefully sequenced guide: As you work through the book, new lessons build on the earlier ones and reinforce them so that skills and concepts are mastered and remembered. At the end, you will have the resources to meet a broad range of creative challenges.

The Design Concepts Book

Each chapter of the Design Concepts book introduces certain fundamental ideas. These ideas are made clear by guiding students to make first-hand observations and reflect on their previous experience. At the end of each chapter, a concise study guide is provided to reinforce the main points. Then, a few exercises that employ the new concepts are described. Some of these exercises are short and simple, whereas others are more complex and encourage more creative involvement. When appropriate, some of the exercises make use of hand-rendering. Many of the other exercises can be adapted to traditional media if students have limited access to computers.

Application Skills Modules

After finishing a Design Concepts Chapter, in most cases you will be directed to go to the accompanying Application Skills Modules book There, you will find explainations of the software skills that you will use in executing the exercises. Then, a study guide and detailed directions for the exercises follow. Directions are formatted and indexed to make them easy to refer back to. Each Skills Module builds on the last so that, when you have finished them all, you will have good working knowledge of a digital application.

The first Skills Module introduces the basics of the Macintosh Operating System X (or "OS X"). Thereafter, the Skills Modules book is divided into four separate sections. Each section is dedicated to one of four digital applications. You will have your choice between working with QuarkXPress or one of these programs from the Adobe Creative Suite: Photoshop, Illustrator, or InDesign. Most students will want to follow the sequence for only one of these applications at a time. After you have worked through the sequence for one application, you can go back to learn any or all of the others.

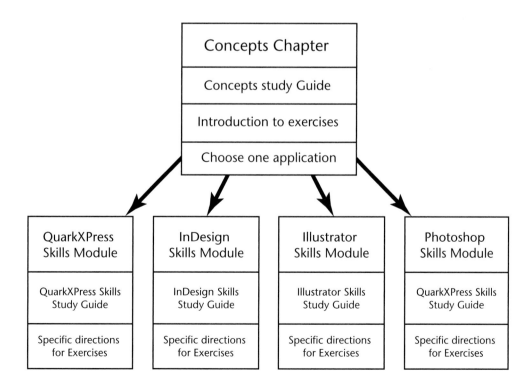

Knowledge Delivered as Needed

Most textbooks are organized much like a grocery store. In a grocery, there's one department with all the vegetables, another with all the canned goods, and another with all the meat products. Likewise, most textbooks put all of the information about each topic in its own particular chapter. But, could you imagine shopping at a store that required you to take all of the vegetables before you went on to the meats? Most of us prefer more variety in our meals.

This textbook is organized more like a tool kit. Rather than weighing you down with an exhaustive survey of every aspect of a particular design concept or software tool, concepts and skills are introduced as they are needed to accomplish certain sorts of tasks. As you move forward, new tools are be added to your kit so you are able to accomplish progressively more sophisticated tasks.

Exercises

The exercises are not intended as ends in themselves. Rather, they should be seen as opportunities to begin practicing design concepts and technical skills. I encourage students and instructors to apply lessons to additional creative problems if time allows.

Application Skills Modules DVD

The DVD in the back of the Application Skills Modules contains:

- **Exercise Resources:** For Exercises from Chapters 2, 7, 8 & 9

- **TypeSpecs.pdf:** A digital copy of the Type Specimens from the Appendix has been provided so that the fine points of samples can be observed at high magnification.

- **Skills Module Demos:** Quicktime movies that demonstrate many of the lessons from the Skills Modules.

Chapter by Chapter

Chapter 1: Getting Started with Typography in the Digital Environment

This chapter introduces the main features that are common to all personal computers, how computers represent type, and the kinds of computer programs used by graphic designers. The related Mac Skills Modules provide an introduction to Macintosh OS X and tell how to manage digital fonts.

Chapter 2: The Voice of Type

How type can express ideas and feelings, the basic parts of letter characters, and how type families work are presented in this chapter. Basic considerations when placing type over pictures are also presented. The Skills Modules introduce the basics to get started with the chosen application.

Chapter 3: Observing Abstract Form in Type Design

This chapter looks at how elements and principles of design relate to typography. The Skills Modules cover working with boxes, guides, and layers.

Chapter 4: Exploring the Fundamentals— Making Display Type Work

Setting display type provides a meaningful context for an in-depth examination of letter spacing and other issues related to readability. The Skills Modules cover the tools for fine letter spacing.

Chapter 5: Structure and Measurement

Now that students have had some experience making decisions about typographic design, they are ready to take on more specific information about how type is structured and measured. Designing logotypes provides a context for exploring type contrast, stacking, fitting, alignment, and overlap. InDesign and Illustrator Skills Modules introduce tools that can be used to modify the shapes of letters.

Chapter 6: Resources of Style, Sources of Inspiration— The History of Typographic Design

It may appear logical to put a historical overview at the beginning of the textbook, but, like the previous chapter, this chapter will be more meaningful after students have had some close-range experience with type.

Past styles are a resource that can be used solve creative problems today. Understanding the origins of typographic styles make them more distinctive, meaningful, and memorable. Larger questions of composition become clearer, too, because unfamiliar styles provide fresh chances to see how the principles of typographic design operate. Also, seeing how designers in the past have adapted to change can help students prepare to meet new challenges. (There are no Skills Modules for this chapter.)

Chapter 7: The Nitty-Gritty of Body Copy— Keep'n It Readable

This chapter introduces factors that help make body text easy to read: typeface, size, spacing, alignment, hyphenation, line measure, and effective paragraphing; how to create emphasis in body text; using figures (numbers) in text; and recognizing and repairing problems that crop up in body text.

The student also learns marks used to correct layout and typesetting. InDesign and QuarkXPress Skills Modules introduce importing and cleaning up text, then setting it neatly into columns.

Chapter 8: Making Information Accessible

This chapter introduces the principles for organizing typography so readers will be attracted to the text and be able to find the information they need. It includes an introduction to the design brief, principles of hierarchy and grouping, introduction to the grid, using tabs, and creating tables. InDesign and QuarkXPress Skills Modules concentrate on using tabs and creating tables.

Chapter 9: Type in Publications

This chapter introduces elements that are used to make long texts more accessible to readers. These elements convey the publication's identity, get readers involved with the text, and help them to find the information they are looking for. Also, students are shown how to use a grid in multiple-page publications. The InDesign and QuarkXPress Skills Modules introduce tools that automate the production of multiple-page documents, such as styles, master pages, and libraries.

Chapter 10: Type Effects— The Good, the Trite, and the Ugly

This chapter presents several special effects that may be used to enhance type and how to use them effectively. Skills Modules introduce these type effects: drop shadows, text on a curved baseline, shaped boxes, text wraps around outlined pictures, distorted type, picture as letter, letters filled with pictures, and various other effects.

Chapter 11: Off the Page—Type in New Media

Problems and solutions for using type effectively in presentations and on the World Wide Web are discussed. Students learn to recognize problems inherent to type on screen and learn strategies for getting readable results. This chapter also introduces strategies for effective type in projected presentations and basic type elements used in Web design.

Chapter 12: A Closer Look at Type Design

The last chapter focuses on the fundamentals of type design. It presents detailed vocabulary to describe parts of letterforms and identifies fine points of design in letters. The exercise is design of capital letters. The Illustrator Skills Module describes how to draw letters so they could be used to create a font.

Appendix: Type Specimens

Samples of body type with short notes that provide background information and point out elements that affect readability. After the text type specimens, samples of display type are provided.

Acknowledgements

As a teacher and author, I am most thankful to those I have learned from. In particular, I am indebted to certain authors that have helped me to understand the field of typography and have taught me by example how to present its concepts to others in turn. Foremost of these are Ellen Lupton, Erik Spiekermann, Robin Williams, Leslie Cabarga, the late Philip Meggs, Emily King, Stephen Moye, and Jim Felici. Students are well advised to look for their books listed in the bibliography, find them, and become enlightened by them. Those who are familiar with these works will readily recognize evidence of my debt to them throughout the pages of this volume.

Next, I would like to acknowledge the generosity of contributors who provided the outstanding examples of typography reproduced in these pages. In the interest of brevity, I refer readers to the list of contributors at the end of this preface.

I would also like to thank my colleagues at Brown College for their help and guidance, particularly Richard Weil for his thorough reading and copious constructive comments.

Thanks are also due to Chris Lehan, who first showed me how to use the Pen tool and how to create type effects in Photoshop. The team at Thomson Delmar Learning also deserve special mention: senior acquisitions editor Jim Gish, who first recognized the value of this project; product manager Jaimie Weiss, who shepherded it through the developmental process; art and design specialist MaryBeth Vought, who supervised design and production; and Tom Stover, production editor. I'd also like to thank the staff at GEX Publishing Services, and Gina Dishman, who supervised the nuts and bolts of final layout and typography.

Thomson Delmar Learning would like to join me in thanking the following reviewers for their valuable suggestions and expertise:

John Chastain
Herron School of Art and Design
Indianapolis, Indiana

Lisa Fontaine
Art and Design Department
Iowa State University
Ames, Iowa

Ron Labuz
Art Department
Mohawk Valley Community College
Utica, New York

Susan Thompson
Graphic Design and Multimedia
    Department
Westwood College
Euless, Texas

Janine Wong
Design Department
University of Massachusetts—
    Dartmouth
North Dartmouth, Massachusetts

Lastly, my greatest debt and deepest gratitude go to my beautiful wife of 22 years, Lynn Wadsworth, and my fabulous daughter, Zara, without whose extraordinary patience this project would have foundered long before its realization.

David A. Amdur
2006

About the Author

David A. Amdur is a Professor of Visual Communications at Brown College, where since 1999 he has taught digital design applications including QuarkXPress, Illustrator, Photoshop, and InDesign, as well as typography, drawing, principles of design, the history of art and design, design conceptualization, and design for advertising and publication.

Since 1981 he has taught art and design at all levels, from pre-K to graduate school, serving as adjunct faculty at St. Cloud State University, Hamline University Graduate School, Minnesota College of Computer Imaging, Anoka Ramsey Community College, and in public and private schools.

He has received awards from the Council for Basic Education, the Getty Center for Education in the Arts, the Minnesota Center for Arts Education, and the Minnesota Humanities Commission to research and develop curriculum in art and design.

He holds a Master of Fine Arts degree from Queens College and was awarded a full scholarship for a year of postgraduate study at the New York Academy of Art. In addition, he studied methods of education at Brooklyn College.

Questions and Feedback

Thomson Delmar Learning and the author welcome your questions and feedback. If you have suggestions that you think others would benefit from, please let us know and we will try to include them in the next edition.

To send us your questions and/or feedback, you can contact the publisher at:
Thomson Delmar Learning
Executive Woods
5 Maxwell Drive
Clifton Park, NY 12065
Attn: Media Arts & Design Team
800-998-7498

Or the author:
David A. Amdur, Professor
Department of Visual Communications
Brown College
1440 Northland Drive
Mendota Heights, MN 55120
Email: amdur@usgo.net

Contributors

The author would like to acknowledge the generosity of contributors who provided the outstanding examples of typography reproduced in these pages. Every reasonable effort has been made for correct ascription of copyright of all material used in this book. Please inform the publisher of any suspected error or omission and it will be rectified in later editions.

American Institute of Graphic Arts (AIGA), 6–74
Art Resource/Artists Rights Society, NY, 2–16, 2–17, 6–11 (Photo: Erich Lessing)
Avenues, 3–13 Photo: Brad Staufer, 9–3
Alicia Babatz, 3–20
Merrill C. Berman Collection; Photo: Jim Frank, 6–51
Marieke Blokland (bloknote.nl), 5–6
Lisa Braithwaite, 6–102
Brinkmann and Bose, Berlin, 6–67, 6–69
Neville Brody, 6–86, 9–2
John Burns, John Burns Lettering and Design, 5–19, 5–22, 5–24
Leslie Cabarga, 12–7
David Carson 6–87
CHANK! (chank.com), 4–16, 6–93
Art Chantry Design Company, 6–84, 6–85
College of Continuing Education, University of Minnesota, 9–4
Rob Douw designer, photo provided by Municipal Archives of The Hague, 6–83
Dover Press, 6–44
Richard Eckersley, University of Nebraska Press, 4–3
Editions Gallimard, Paris, 6–80
Emigre, 2–9, 6–88, 6–89, 6–90, 6–91, 6–92
Jakob Fischer (pizzadude.dk), 5–5
Mark Fox, Black Dog Inc., 5–22
Carin Goldberg Design, 6–100
April Greiman, Made In Space, Inc., 6–88
Ida Griffin, 6–82
Pat Hansen, Hansen Design Company, 5–16
Kit Hinrichs, preface figure 2
Huntington Library, San Marino, California 6–42
International Typeface Corporation/Monotype, 6–78, 3–9, 4–9, 4–10, 4–11, 4–12, 6–96
Jada Ken, 5–25
Chuck Kenan, 6–101
Kieselbach Gallery, Budapest, Hungary and Artists Rights Society, NY, 6–60
Doug Lattery, 3–18
Linotype GmbH, 6–72, 6–96
George Lois, 2–1
Louisiana Museum of Modern Art, Humlebæk, Denmark and Artists Rights Society, NY, 6–59
Herb Lubalin Study Center of Design and Typography at The Cooper Union School of Art, 4–29, 6–75, 6–76, 6–77, 6–79

Getting Started with Typography in the Digital Environment

This chapter gives you the background you need to begin designing with type on a computer.

OBJECTIVES

¤ To introduce the main features common to all personal computers

¤ To explain the formats for encoding visual information

¤ To survey the kinds of computer programs used by designers

Working in the Digital Environment

Those of you who are new to personal computers may find yourself feeling a bit lost once in a while. The digital realm can seem like a foreign city with a strange language. It can be hard to remember what things are called or how to get what you need. Fortunately, the designers of these digital tools have tried to make them easy and intuitive to use. During the eight years that I've taught these digital applications, I've seen beginners quickly overcome initial frustration and gain confidence time and again.

The following section presents the main features that are common to all personal computers. If you are able, try them out on a computer as you read about them.

Hardware and software

Computers are different than most other tools. Most tools are physical objects that we take in our hands. The physical components of a computer are called **hardware**. But when we work with computers we don't

"Personal computers enable desktop publishers to perform publishing tasks that would otherwise require complicated equipment and extensive human effort."

—U.S. Department of Labor
Occupational Outlook
Handbook

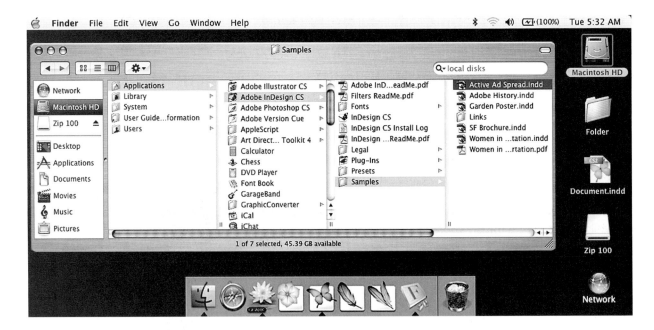

Figure 1-1 A computer desktop

usually focus too much attention on the physical hardware. Instead, we look into the monitor screen and work with virtual (or simulated) tools that are used to display, modify, and organize information in the form of pictures, text, symbols, and sometimes sounds. The digital information that the computer hardware uses to create these tools is called **software**. These tools are so multifaceted that their designers have chosen to organize them into a simulated environment that is loosely based on an office space. When we describe how to use these tools, we often talk as though we are working with things and are going places.

Desktop, applications, and documents

The first screen that you see after the computer has started up is called the **desktop**. (See Figure 1-1.) From the desktop you can open software tools, get digital files, and store these files. The software tools that are used to get work done are called **applications**. Any digital file that is produced or modified by an application is called a **document**. Getting around in the digital environment is referred to as **navigating**. (Don't ask me why they temporarily departed from the office metaphor and embarked to sea!)

Using the mouse

Before describing more of the digital work environment, a key piece of hardware must be explained. This device, called a **mouse**, is the virtual substitute for the user's hand in the digital environment. In other words, the mouse is used to act upon the things that are shown on the screen.

The user holds the mouse in one hand and drags it over a flat surface to move a pointer (or *cursor*) across the screen. One or more push-buttons on the mouse can be used to control the computer software. To **click on** something means to position the cursor over it, then press the button down and immediately release it. To **double-click** means to press and release the button two times quickly. To **click-drag** means to press the button and to continue to hold it while moving the cursor across the screen to a certain place before releasing. Click-dragging to move something to a new place is called **drag and drop**. (PCs and some Macs have two buttons on the mouse, so these can be "left-clicked" or "right-clicked." Unless a right-click is specified, assume that a left-click is indicated. On a Mac with a single-button mouse, holding down the Control key while left-clicking is usually equivalent to a right-click.)

Icons, folders, disks, and windows

You can navigate from the desktop by using the mouse on icons, windows, or menus. An **icon** is a small graphic symbol. You can see five kinds of icons from the desktop in Figure 1-2 and Figure 1-3: application icons, disk drive icons, a folder icon, a document icon, and a network server icon. (Other sorts of icons are used to represent tools or other things.)

A digital **folder**, like an actual file folder that's used in an office, is used to hold related items together and keep them organized. Disk drives are used for recording and storing information. Network servers are computers with very large hard drives that are hooked up to many computers.

If you click on an icon, it changes color, indicating that it is selected to receive a command. Double-clicking on either a folder icon or a disk icon opens a **window** that shows its contents. (If there are more things in a window than can be seen all at once, **scroll bars** appear that you can click-drag to move hidden items into the window. See Figure 1-4.) Double-clicking on an application icon starts the application. Double-clicking on a document icon usually opens the document in its application.

File organization

Because disorganization wastes time and causes frustration, folder structure is used to keep the digital working environment orderly and uncluttered. Files that are related to one another are grouped together into one folder. If a folder gets cluttered with too many files, order can be maintained by organizing the contents into subfolders. For instance, you can see in Figure 1-4 that the Hard Disk is selected in the far left window. The contents of the Hard Disk is shown in the next column to the right: the Applications folder, Library folder, System folder, and Users

Figure 1-2 Application icons

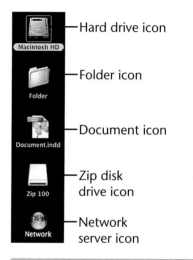

Figure 1-3 Various desktop icons

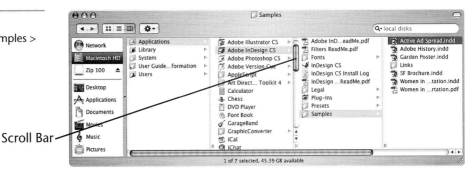

Figure 1-4 Macintosh HD > Applications > InDesign > Samples > Active Ad Spread.indd.

Scroll Bar

folder. (The icon that appears second to the bottom is an alias—more on that later.) The Applications folder is selected and you can see its contents in the next column to the right. You can see that the InDesign folder has been selected. In the next column, the Samples folder has been selected, and from inside that folder a document named "Active Ad Spread.indd" has been selected.

Files and folders can be moved from one location to another by dragging and dropping.

Notation of navigation paths

Throughout this textbook, pathways through windows, menus, and dialog boxes will be noted by listing each selected item in order with the > symbol between them. For example, the path from the desktop to the document "Active Ad Spread.indd" shown in the window in Figure 1-4 would be noted this way: Macintosh HD > Applications > InDesign > Samples > Active Ad Spread.indd.

Menus

A menu is a list of commands to the computer software. (See Figure 1-5.) Menus are usually hidden, but they can be opened by clicking on a word or a symbol (or, in Mac OS X, by Control-clicking). When the menu is open, you can **execute** a command (put it into action) by clicking on it or by click-dragging down to it. When a command can't be executed at a particular time, it will appear gray in the menu instead of black.

Dialog boxes

Dialog boxes are small windows that give information or ask for it. A command in a menu that is followed by an ellipsis (...) opens a dialog box that asks you to choose settings, pick commands from a menu, click on checkboxes or radial buttons, or type information into fields. A navigation dialog box can be used to open a document or to save it to a location. (See Figure 1-6.)

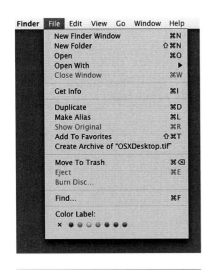

Figure 1-5 A menu

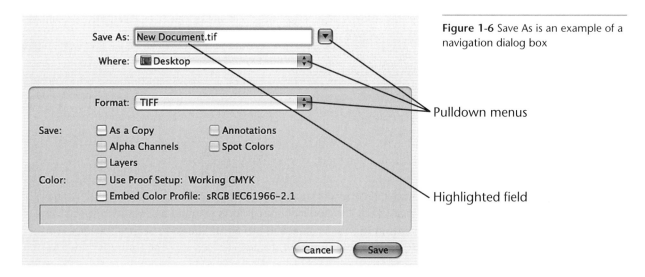

Figure 1-6 Save As is an example of a navigation dialog box

Pulldown menus

Highlighted field

Generally, when you open a dialog box, one field will be highlighted. This indicates that you can type new information into this field. You can toggle from one field to the next by pressing the Tab key on the keyboard. Or, you can click on a field to enter a blinking text cursor into it, or you can click-drag to highlight text inside the field.

Computer memory

RAM means Random Access Memory, but don't worry about that. It's easiest to understand RAM as the "live" short-term memory that is held in the circuitry of the computer. If the computer stops working at any time, all of the information that is in the RAM will be lost without leaving a trace. That's why it's best to protect your work by saving it frequently.

A **Save** command directs the computer to record (or "write") the document information onto a storage device that you choose through a navigation dialog box.

A **disk drive** is an electromechanical storage device that writes information onto a spinning piece of metal or plastic. **Hard disks** are the real workhorses of the breed. These metal disks are built for constant spinning and can hold huge amounts of information. On the other hand, some drives have smaller **removable disks**. If you save to them too often, these disks can wear out and you can lose all your information!

Compact disk drives use a laser to "burn" information onto two kinds of disks. **CD-R** disks let you burn information only once; the "R" is for "read"—after the first time you write to them, they become "read only." On the other hand, **CD-RW** (read/write) disks can be written over with new information about a hundred times. **DVD drives** function virtually the same as Compact disk drives, but they have a much higher capacity. A DVD can typically store 4.7 GB, compared to 700 MB on a CD.

Flash drives are small, inexpensive, storage devices that work without any moving parts. Instead, they save information onto a solid-state chip. These are best for moving files from one computer to another or for a secondary backup.

Backing up your work

They say that you shouldn't put all your eggs in one basket—I'm here to tell you not to save all your hard work on just one disk. Disks break or they get lost or they get left in the trunk of a car that explodes! I know—students have told me. Each time, I've asked them if they backed up their work. If they haven't, I can only offer my sympathy. Don't let this happen to you! Make a habit of always backing up your files by saving copies to more than one storage device.

Because the hard disk is the quickest and most reliable storage device, it's best to save your documents to this disk while you are working on them. The desktop is a good place to put the document because seeing it there will help you remember to back it up. If you want to work on a document that you have previously saved on another disk, copy it to the desktop before you open it. When you are done with the work session, make back-up copies of your work onto more than one storage device. Perhaps you can put one copy onto a removable device, save another to a network server, and move the original off the desktop into a folder on the hard drive that's more out of the way. That way, if something happens to one or more of these storage devices, you're still covered.

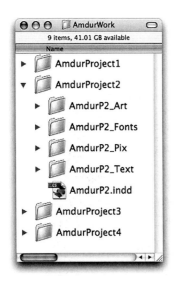

Figure 1-7 A work folder with a separate folder for each project. Within the project folder, resources are kept in separate subfolders.

Keeping your work organized

It saves time and aggravation if you keep your work organized in a systematic way. In general, you don't want to have more items in a folder than you can see on the screen at one time. When this happens, it is best to consolidate items into subfolders. It usually works best to maintain a separate folder for each class or each client and then create subfolders within this folder for each project. Within these folders, you might include separate folders for various resources such as images and fonts. (See Figure 1-7.)

Come up with a systematic way of naming files and folders so that, if they get misplaced, you can tell which project they belong to. I always recommend to students that they include their own last name within the name of any documents that they create. That way, if they mistakenly save the file to some out-of-the-way place, they can easily find it with a find file utility.

Units for measuring information

The smallest unit of information is called a **bit**. It is based on a switch that can only have two alternatives: off or on. This is used to represent the digits 0 or 1. A row of 8 bits can create 256 possible alternatives. This amount of information is called a **byte**—it's enough information to encode one letter or number.

There are 1,024 bytes in a **kilobyte** (**K**). A font file that encodes an entire typeface might take up about 80–100 K of disk space.

1,024 K equals 1 **megabyte** (**MB**) or "meg." The old floppy disks used to hold about 1 to 1.4 MB. Old zip disks used to hold about 100 MB; the new ones hold about 250 MB. A CD holds 700 MB. 1,024 MB equals 1 **gigabyte** (**GB**). DVDs can hold more than 8 "gigs" on one side. Recently, most Macintoshes have been shipped with 180-GB hard drives. Over the past 15 years, the size of hard drives has doubled about every 18 months.

File name extensions

File name extensions (or **dot extensions**) are added to the end of document file names. They consist of a period followed by between two and four letters (usually three). Both Mac OS X and Windows systems need file name extensions to know in which application to open a document. They are hidden by default, but it is recommended that you make them visible by going to Finder menu > Preferences > Advanced > Show all file extensions. This will help you manage your files. The dot extension for an InDesign document is .indd. For a QuarkXpress document it's .qxd. An Adobe Illustrator document is .ai, but these are often saved in a format called Encapsulated PostScript, or .eps.

Two Ways Computers Represent Images

There are two formats for encoding visual information in the computer: the raster graphic format and the vector graphics format.

In the **raster** graphic format, the image is broken up into a mosaic of squares called picture elements or pixels. (See Figure 1-8.) Pixels are arranged side by side in a grid; the image is formed by assigning different color values to each pixel. As you can see in Figure 1-8, the raster grid system has a problem describing curved and diagonal edges. These boundaries take on a jagged stair-step quality that is called rastering, or **aliasing**. However, if the size of the pixels is fine enough, aliasing isn't noticeable.

The size of the pixels in an image is called **resolution**. It is measured in **pixels per inch** (**ppi**). Resolution for input devices, such as scanners, and output devices, such as printers, is measured in a similar unit called **dots per inch** (**dpi**). Resolution for screen display was

NOTE

The term **default** means an option that is automatically chosen by the system if the user doesn't choose a different one.

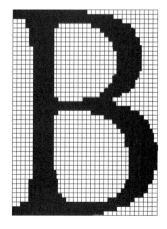

Figure 1-8 A raster image shown at 16 ppi

At low resolution raster type can't render clearly.

Figure 1-9 Enlarged raster type

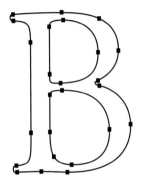

Figure 1-10 A vector image

traditionally 72 dpi, but today's displays can be almost twice that fine. Photographs are usually scanned for commercial printing at 300 dpi. For ink-jet printers, files at 200 ppi are sufficient. Type is typically rendered for commercial printing at 2400 dpi. At that scale, aliasing isn't a problem, even on the small shapes of letters.

As the resolution of an image is increased, the file size expands geometrically. For example, consider an 8.5 × 11-inch image where each pixel can only be black or white, without any shades of gray. (This is called **bit map color** because the color choices are limited to two alternatives; as you learned, this is 1 bit of information). At 72 ppi, the file size would be about 60 K. At 300 ppi it would be about 1 MB, and at 2400 K it would be 64.3 MB. A full-color picture this size at 300 ppi would be 32 MB; at 2400 ppi it would be a couple of gigs—practically unworkable. (Fortunately, precise edges aren't important in photographic images.)

A raster image cannot be enlarged very much without a noticeable loss of quality. (See Figure 1-9.)

The **vector** graphics format, on the other hand, is **resolution independent**. That means that no matter how small or large an image is scaled, it will maintain fine detail and the file size never changes. This is because, instead of being made out separate elements, vector images are described as geometric relationships. Mathematical formulas describe these relationships, so, once you put in one measurement, all the rest automatically follow.

What is a vector?

Vector applications use calculus formulas to track the paths of curved lines. You may not know it, but calculus was originally invented to kill people. No, not students. Soldiers. It was invented to predict the trajectory of cannonballs. As a cannon is fired, two forces work on the ball: 1) the force of the cannon, which pushes up at a diagonal, and 2) the downward force of gravity. (See Figure 1-11.) "Vector" is the name given to these straight–line forces. The curved path of a cannonball can be calculated by resolving the relative force of the vectors. (Well, uh, I couldn't do it—but it's really easy for the computer!) Since its invention, calculus has been used for any number of benevolent and constructive purposes including architecture, optics, mechanical engineering, aerodynamics, navigation, and economics. In the 1960s, the French car designer Pierre Bézier applied calculus to the problem of drawing appealing curves. He developed the system used by all-vector drawing applications, where lines that run between "anchor points" are diverted into graceful curves by the vector force of "handles" that pull on them.

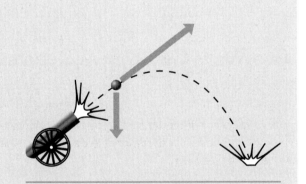

Figure 1-11 Vectors are the lines of force that determine the path of an object in motion.

Figure 1-10 represents the letter "B" as a vector outline. You can see that it is established by a set of points and the line segments that run between them. The word "vector" means the force that is applied to the curved line segments to bend them (see sidebar). The outlined shape can be filled with any color, or a combination of blended colors, or a pattern—so vector graphics can make sophisticated images.

Before vector images can be printed or output on the screen, they must be **rasterized**; that is, they must be translated into a pattern of dots. When this is done for printing, it's called **raster image processing** (**RIP**).

Types of Computer Graphics Programs

Although you could drive a nail with a crow bar, it's definitely much easier to use a hammer, right? As a graphic designer, you will usually use several different kinds of digital tools for different tasks in the same project. It's important to understand the differences between them so you can choose the right tool for each job. Here is an overview.

Image editing

Image editing applications are mainly used to work with photographic images. Such images are called **continuous tone**, or **c.t.**, because they are mostly made up of colors that blend together to describe three-dimensional forms. These images are encoded into the raster format. Adobe Photoshop is the dominant application in this category. It can be used to repair images and improve their colors. Colors within pictures can be changed entirely, or parts of images can be taken out of their original context and recombined in creative—or devious—ways. Digital filters and tools that simulate painting can be used to create special effects or original illustrations. Photoshop is also used by Web page developers to prototype the layout of a proposed design for a Web page.

Images that are developed for print tend to be quite large, but these programs can also produce lower resolution images for the Internet.

Photoshop CS2 has sophisticated type typographic tools, but the raster format cannot render small type clearly. However, large headline type can be rendered with reasonable clarity, and exciting special effects can be applied to them.

Paint programs

Paint programs are raster format applications that simulate traditional painting and drawing media. Corel Painter is the dominant product in this category. It can be used to produce creative effects for headlines or titles, but it is usually best to create the type in a program that has more sophisticated type tools and then import it.

It's important to understand the differences between digital tools so you can choose the right tool for each job

Illustration programs

Illustration programs are vector-based applications, such as Adobe Illustrator and Macromedia Freehand. These applications were originally developed to create what was traditionally called "line art": hard-edge spot illustrations or logos made up of flat, colored shapes. Since that time, many enhancements have made these tools capable of producing far more sophisticated images, but many professionals still refer to the documents produced by these programs as **art files**. Art files are usually much smaller than raster (c.t.) files and can be scaled to any size without losing image quality.

The real strength of these programs for typography comes out of their ability to modify and combine letter forms. (However, some font licenses do not permit such modifications.) It is possible to create multiple-page documents in Illustrator, but page layout programs such as QuarkXPress or InDesign are far better tools for those jobs.

Page layout programs

Page layout programs, such as QuarkXPress or Adobe InDesign, are primarily used for preparing documents for print. They can place type, images, and other graphic elements with great precision. They have the best tools for working with type and many tools that can automate production of multiple page documents. Because these are vector programs, the file sizes of documents are quite reasonable.

Web page development programs

Web page development programs, such as Dreamweaver or Page Spinner, are used to create pages for the Internet. QuarkXPress 6 introduced a system for codeveloping pages for print and for the Web.

Web browsers hardly support even the most basic degree of control over typography. If a designer wants a title or headline in a Web page to appear in a predictable way, it must be developed in another program and linked to the page.

Animation and interactive design programs

Programs for **animation and interactive design** can be used to develop computer-based presentations that put type and images into motion and integrate sounds. They can also provide ways for viewers to control or respond to what they see and hear.

These programs offer more control over type than Web page tools, but display type is usually best developed in another program and imported as a graphic.

Presentation programs

Presentation programs, such as Microsoft PowerPoint, are primarily used to create slide shows to accompany lectures and presentations. These shows can integrate animation and other audiovisual elements.

Like animation programs, these applications only have very basic type tools. Fine or creative typography must be developed in another program and imported as a graphic.

3-D Programs

3-D programs conceptualize complex three-dimensional forms as vector constructions that are informally called "wire frames." Raster textures can be applied to the surfaces of these forms, different sorts of lighting can be applied, the objects can be visualized from different points of view, and they can be animated to simulate motion.

These programs can be used to create "motion graphics" that put type and other graphic elements into motion.

Font editing and creation programs

Font editing and **creation programs** can be used to change font specifications and convert formats, to change characters or add new ones, or to create an entirely new font set. Fontographer and FontLab are the preeminent applications in this category.

Utilities

Utilities are small applications that help you perform specific tasks, such as managing fonts or printing.

Chapter Summary

Some of you came with a great deal of experience with computers—others, none at all. But after working through this chapter and the related Mac Skills chapters the playing field will be more level. Now you are familiar with the main features that are common to all personal computers. You understand the formats used in graphics programs. And, you have an overview of the kinds of computer graphics programs that are used by graphic designers. In the Mac Skills chapters you will get detailed information about Macintosh Operating System X and how to manage fonts. Then, you will be ready to begin applying these tools to creative typographic communication.

Design Concepts Study Guide Chapter 1

After you have read the previous chapter, fill in the blanks with the letter of the correct answer within each section.

1. _____ The physical components of a computer are called

2. _____ The digital information that the computer hardware uses to create virtual tools is called

3. _____ The software programs that are used to get work done are called

4. _____ Any digital file that is produced or modified by an application is called a

5. _____ To "double-click" means

6. _____ To "click-drag" means

7. _____ "drag and drop" means

A. to press the mouse button and continue to hold it while moving the cursor across the screen to a certain place before releasing

B. to press and release the button two times quickly

C. document

D. click-dragging to move something to a new place

E. software

F. hardware

G. applications

- -

8. _____ "Default" means

9. _____ If you click on an icon

10. _____ A menu is

11. _____ When menu commands can't be executed at a particular time

12. _____ A command in a menu that is followed by an ellipsis (...)

13. _____ You can toggle from one field to the next in a dialog box

14. _____ It's easiest to understand RAM as

A. will open a dialog box that will allow you to choose settings, pick commands off of a menu, click on checkboxes or radial buttons, or type information into fields

B. they will appear gray instead of black

C. by pressing the Tab key on the keyboard

D. a hidden list of commands to the computer software that can be opened by clicking on a word or a symbol

E. the "live" short-term memory that is held in the circuitry of the computer

F. it will change color indicating that it is selected

G. an option that is automatically chosen by the system if the user doesn't choose a different one

- -

15. _____ A disk drive is

16. _____ Hard disks are metal disks that are

17. _____ The smallest unit of information is a

18. _____ A row of 8 bits can create 256 possible alternatives—this is called a

19. _____ 1,024 bytes is a

20. _____ 1,024 K is a

21. _____ 1,024 MB is a

22. _____ File name extensions (or dot extensions) consist of

A. bit

B. a period followed by between two and four letters (usually three)

C. megabyte (MB) or "meg"

D. byte

E. built to save constantly and can hold huge amounts of information

F. kilobyte (K)

G. an electromechanical storage device that writes information onto a spinning piece of metal or plastic

H. gigabyte (GB)

○ GETTING STARTED WITH TYPOGRAPHY IN THE DIGITAL ENVIRONMENT ○ ○ ○ ○ ○ ○

23. _____ The graphic format in which the image is broken up into a mosaic of squares called "pixels" is called

24. _____ A jagged stair-step quality on the boundaries of shapes is called rastering or

25. _____ Resolution of a raster document is measured in

26. _____ Resolution for input devices, such as scanners, and output devices, such as printers, is measured in

27. _____ Images that are described as mathematical relationships between points and line segments and may be filled with a color, or a combination of blended colors, or a pattern are called

28. _____ This type of image, no matter how small or large it is scaled, maintains fine detail and never changes the file size:

29. _____ Translation of vector images into raster images so they can be printed is called

A. aliasing

B. raster image processing (RIP)

C. dots per inch (dpi)

D. resolution independent

E. raster

F. pixels per inch (ppi)

G. vector graphics

○ ○

30. _____ Applications primarily used to work with photographic continuous tone (or c.t.) raster images are called

31. _____ Raster format applications that simulate traditional painting and drawing media are called

32. _____ Vector-based applications that were originally developed to create hard-edge spot illustrations or logos called "line art" are called

33. _____ Applications primarily used for preparing documents for print are called

34. _____ Applications used to lay out pages on the Internet are called

35. _____ Applications used to develop computer-based presentations that put type and images into motion and integrate sounds are called

36. _____ Applications used to create slide shows to accompany lectures and the like are called

37. _____ Applications used to create objects that can be visualized from different points of view and are animated are called

38. _____ Small applications that help you perform specific tasks such as managing fonts or printing are called

39. _____ Programs that can be used to change font specifications and convert formats, change characters or add new ones, or create and an entirely new font set are called

A. page layout programs

B. 3-D programs

C. illustration programs

D. presentation programs

E. paint programs

F. utilities

G. font editing and creation programs

H. image editing programs

I. Web page development programs

J. animation and interactive design programs

○ ○

The Voice of Type

This chapter begins by asking you to consider how you are influenced by the emotional expression of type. Then, it introduces technical information that will help you work with type more mindfully.

OBJECTIVES

- To observe how type can express ideas and feelings
- To identify basic parts of letter characters
- To describe how type families work
- To learn about faux type styles and other distortions
- To introduce basic considerations when placing type over pictures

Can You Hear the Type?

Spoken language doesn't express ideas and feelings with words alone; an important impact is also made by tone of the voice, volume, and the speed of delivery. Written communication, of course, can't use these means of expression, but typographic design can give voice to words.

Consider the classic ad that George Lois created for Allerest allergy remedy shown in Figure 2-1. The contrast between two typefaces makes it easy to imagine two different voices. The first voice is clear and authoritative—it may be the voice of a doctor. The The responding voice is given graphic expression through the use of bloated letters and phonetic spelling. It coveys a wretched "stuffed-up" feeling. Can't you "hear" it?

> "**A**nyone looking at a printed message will be influenced, within a split second of making eye contact, by everything on the page: the arrangement of various elements as well as the individual look of each one. In other words, overall impression is created in our minds before we even start reading the first word."
>
> —Erik Spikermann

Figure 2-1 George Lois, 1961
(Courtesy Papert Koenig Lois)

Danger!

DANGER!

Figure 2-2 Two typeface settings of the same word

Figure 2-3 Does this type inspire confidence?

Didot

Culz

DESDEMONA

Edwardian Script ITC

Lucida Blackletter

MESQUITE

Figure 2-4 A variety of typefaces

In Figure 2-2 you can see two different settings of the same word. Which conveys a stronger warning?

Take a look at Figure 2-3. Do you think that the look of the type would inspire confidence in the doctor's professionalism?

Type can also convey a sense of context. See, for example, the typefaces listed in Figure 2-4. Which typeface would work best for a Western-themed steakhouse? Which for a wedding invitation? Which might work well in a button-down corporate environment? Which might be good for a party invitation? Which could be used in a Medieval theme park? Which calls to mind the Jazz Age of the 1920s?

Type also can express emotions. Consider the very emotional pictures shown in Figure 2-5. Below these pictures are four distinctly different type settings of a single word. Which typeface do you think would best match the feeling expressed by each picture? Of course. there isn't an absolutely right or wrong answer for such a question. But, as you look at

OH! **Oh!** *Oh!* **OH!**

and think about the pictures, you will develop a logic for your choices—and chances are that your choices will be similar other people's. After you've made your choices, you can compare them to mine in the exercise section at the end of the chapter.

As you look at typefaces, analyze their forms, learn about their history, and learn how to use them in layouts, you will expand your ability to make type "speak" in expressive ways.

Figure 2-6 The basic elements of letter characters. More features are presented in Chapter 12.

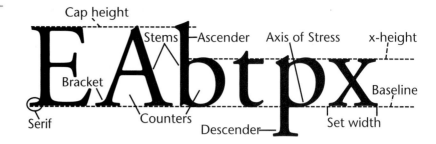

Introduction to the Anatomy of Letter Characters

Knowing the names of these character parts will help you to recognize characteristics of type that express ideas and feelings. Figure 2-6 shows some of the key features of letter characters. Other terms will be considered later.

Learn to identify these features:

Stem	The main stroke of a letter
Baseline	The implied line on which most the characters rest
Descender	The part of a lowercase letter that extends below the baseline on letters like *p* or *q*
Ascender	The tall stem that reaches upward on lowercase letters such as *b*, *d*, or *l*
Cap height	The height of capital letters in a particular typeface; note that this may be different than the height of the ascenders.
x-height	The height of most of the lowercase letters in a particular typeface (excluding the height of the ascenders); the line of the top of the x-height is called the mean line or waist line.
Counter	A shape inside of a letter
Set width	The width of a character

The following are elements of some typefaces only:

Serif	small cross-stroke at the end of a main stroke
Bracket	A curve from the serif to the main stroke
Axis of stress	The direction of an implied line that passes through the thin parts of the round shapes in letters
Swash	A decorative extension at the beginning or end of a letter. Swashes on capital letters are designed to begin words; therefore, it usually looks clumsy to use two swashed capitals in a row. (See Figure 2-7.)

Figure 2-7 It usually looks clumsy to use two swashed capitals in a row.

Figure 2-8 A few difficult letter combinations are shown on the top row. The second row shows the replacement ligatures.

Figure 2-9 Zuzana Licko designed some unusual ligatures for her elegant typeface Mrs Eaves Italic. (Courtesy Emigre)

Ligature	Two or more letters that have been redesigned to join together into a compound character; this usually is done to avoid clumsy fitting between characters. (See Figure 2-8 and Figure 2-9.) Many applications can automatically substitute ligatures for certain letter combinations.

Type Family: Variations on the Theme

If you have any previous experience using type on computers, you've probably discovered that most kinds of type have alternative styles available, such as Bold or Italic. A set of related typefaces that share a common name is called a **type family**. Times and Helvetica are names of popular type families. Each alternative style within a family is referred to as a separate **typeface**. Both of these terms are often used interchangeably with the word "font." But these three terms have distinct meanings that must be understood to avoid confusion.

The meanings of technical terms often change as technology changes. In the days of metal type, the term "font" meant the complete set of all the cast pieces that made up a typeface (including all numerals, punctuation marks, and any other symbols) *at one particular size.* Today, the term **font** now refers to the encoded information that describes the entire typeface and the digital file that contains this information. Most of today's digital fonts can be scaled to any size, so size is no longer seen as a characteristic of those fonts.

So, to summarize, the font tells the computer how to draw the typeface. Several related typefaces comprise a type family. In practical terms, the only time most people actually deal with a font is when they load it into a computer system or when they collect the elements used in a layout so it can be prepared for publishing (*see side note*). When designing layouts, we generally choose one or two type families. We can create some variety in our design by choosing different typefaces within the same family.

For the most part, the typefaces in a family will contrast in three ways: weight, proportion, and structure.

In terms of weight, *regular*, *roman*, or *book* faces are designed for long runs of body text. In addition, a type family usually includes a contrasting *bold* face and often a *light* one. Finer variations may include *demibold* or *semibold*, which aren't as heavy as *bold*. *Extrabold* and *black* are more extreme. The lightest weight may be called *ultra light*. Variations in proportion can be more *condensed* (narrow—see Figure 2-10) or, on the other hand, more *extended* or *expanded* (wider).

NOTE

The professional agencies that RIP a designer's layout documents and prepare them for printing are called **service bureaus** or **prepress houses**.

Helvetica Neue 25 Ultra Light
Helvetica Neue UltraLight Italic
Helvetica Neue 45 Light
Helvetica Neue 46 Light Italic
Helvetica Neue Regular
Helvetica Neue 56 Italic
Helvetica Neue 75 Bold
Helvetica Neue 76 Bold Italic
Helvetica Neue Condensed Bold
Helvetica Neue Condensed Black

Figure 2-10 Some examples from the Helvetica Neue family

aefkmyz
aefkmyz

Figure 2-11 The first line is a true italic, whereas the lower line is regular type that has been made oblique on the computer. The italic is more condensed and its calligraphic qualities give it a feeling of speed. (Adobe Garamond)

ITALIC CAPITAL LETTERS
REGULAR CAPITAL LETTERS

Figure 2-12 Italic and regular capitals have much less structural difference than lowercase letters do. Actually, most italic capitals are simply oblique. (Adobe Garamond)

Oblique typefaces are slanted. This creates a structural contrast with the regular style and usually is used to emphasize certain words. **Italic** faces, which have calligraphic qualities of cursive writing, are a much more radical structural variation. (See Figure 2-11 and Figure 2-12.) For the most part, Oblique typefaces don't have serifs, and italic styles have been designed for most serif families.

Another fundamental structural contrast is the difference between roman (serif) type and type without a serif (known as **sans-serif**). Although it isn't common, some designers have recently created type families that include both. (See Figure 6-97.)

All of the stylistic variations I've just described can be compounded so that, for instance, you may use an *ultra light condensed italic* font. A single type family may have more than 50 members. The terms that describe these variations are not standardized so that, for instance, one family's *bold* face may be lighter than another family's *book*.

An important factor to consider in a type family is how well the different style typefaces work together. You'll find that some type families are better coordinated than others. To understand the reason why, it helps to consider how a type family is created. Sometimes the process is very piecemeal. Consider this scenario: First, letters are commissioned for a particular project such as a magazine nameplate. If the design is distinctive yet flexible enough to create sufficient demand, the designer may be contracted to complete the rest of the alphabet. Later, the other characters are developed to complete the font. Perhaps years later this font has proved popular enough to warrant the design of a bold version, and, still later, other members are added to the family. Sometimes, the later designs are executed by different designers. It is difficult to maintain a consistent look, and often the sizes of x-heights, cap heights, ascenders, and descenders vary. The original version of the immensely popular Helvetica type family was the product of many different hands; as a result, it suffered from the sorts of problems I've just described. The Linotype foundry addressed these problems by commissioning the systematically coordinated revision called Neue Helvetica in 1983 ("neue" means "new" in German).

Occasionally, finding fonts can be tricky because they are named in an unexpected way. Although the family name usually comes first, sometimes it is preceded by the initial of its style, so that "Times Bold" may be listed as "B Times Bold." While some computer applications list members of the same family together, in others you have to look for *bold* typefaces in the *B*s and Italics in the *I*s.

Don't Faux It

Faux (pronounced "foe") is a French word that means "false" or "fake." Many applications offer you the option of styling a regular font into a faux bold or italic. I strongly recommend that you resist this option for two reasons. The first is technical; many times the faux styles will not print out properly. Moreover, if you bring a document containing faux styles to a prepress house to prepare for professional printing, chances are that it won't process properly; correcting this problem will cost time and money.

The second reason is aesthetic. Type designers are very talented and dedicated artists that take great pains to design beautiful typefaces. How could you expect a dumb computer to replicate this effort with the push of a button? See for yourself: Figure 2-13 compares a faux bold with a real one. A lowercase serif faux italic will look like the oblique sample in Figure 2-11.

Most applications will also let you scale (or stretch) type. But be careful: most typefaces won't suffer too much when scaled from 97% to 103%, but if you go far beyond this range the distortion might get obnoxious. (See Figure 2-14 and Figure 2-15.)

Clarendon
Clarendon
Clarendon

Figure 2-13 Clarendon Regular is on top, below it is a computer-generated faux bold, and the last line is Clarendon Bold. The faux bold has crude details: the counters on the *a* and the *n* are too closed, the *a* has a stubby tail, the *r* has a bloated arm, and *n* and *d* have swollen joints. (Aspirin won't help: Choose a real font!)

AaBbCc
AaBbCc

Figure 2-14 On top is Univers 63 Bold Extended. Below, Univers 65 Bold has been scaled horizontally about 160% to match. If you compare them carefully, you'll see that the balance of characters on the second line is destroyed by extra-fat vertical stems and curved strokes.

AaBbCcDdEeFfGg
AaBbCcDdEeFfGg

Figure 2-15 On top is Univers Ultra Condensed. Below, Univers Roman has been scaled horizontally to about 50% and faux bold has been applied so the proportions and weights roughly match. However, once again, the balance of the characters on the second line is upset, but this time, it is the vertical strokes that are too light and the horizontals too heavy.

Figure 2-16 This public awareness poster, created by Swiss designer Carlo L. Vivarelli in 1949, promoted care for the elderly. It features strong contrasts of light and dark, between form and space, and between smooth geometric letterforms and the heavily textured photograph. *Courtesy Art Resource*

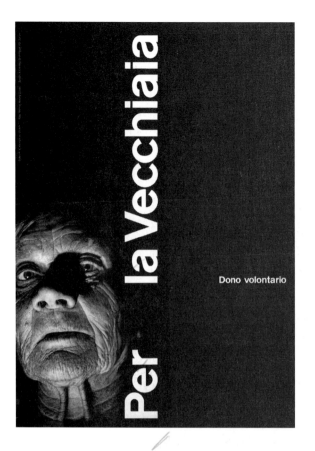

Placing Type Over Pictures

The exercise at the end of this chapter involves placing type over a photographic image. Whenever you do this, care must be taken to make sure the type remains clear and has enough visual impact. Type easily can get lost when it is placed over rugged textures, strong lines, or highly contrasting shapes. It's most legible when it's placed over relatively smooth areas. Of course, bolder, simpler, and larger type can put up with more competition than type with more delicate shapes.

It is important to consider the color of type in relation to the background. Of course, black type is most effective when it is set over as light an area as possible. Conversely, the color of type can be switched to white when it is set over a dark area. On the other hand, sometimes you may want a more subtle relationship that makes the type "sink in" to the image somewhat. (See Figure 2-16 and Figure 2-17.)

The best advice in these matters, as in all areas of visual design, is simply to *look*. Put yourself in the place of a viewer who doesn't have any particular interest in seeing your message. Try looking at the layout at a small magnification. Or, better yet, print it out and look at it from across the room. Then, see if it grabs you. If you cannot *not* see it, then it's working.

Figure 2-17 Another classic Swiss public awareness poster, this time created by Josef Müller-Brockmann in 1960. In the original, the type shouted out its message "Less Noise" in bright red. The type was placed so that it seems to squeeze the poor woman's head like a vice. Printed in black and white, the type is not nearly as bold. See how the final "r" at the end of the first word almost gets lost into the dark shadow under the women's chin? On the other hand, the "a" in the second word fairs better; it's bold enough to survive the strong contrast beneath it. *Courtesy Art Resource/Artists Rights Society*

Chapter Summary

This chapter introduced the idea that type expresses feelings. It gave you a basic vocabulary to describe parts of letter characters. You have learned how type families work and the problems with faux type styles and other distortions.

Basic considerations concerning the placement of type over pictures were also introduced, so that you are prepared for the exercise, which involves matching the emotional expression of type and pictures. The related application Skills Module will get you started placing pictures and setting type in your chosen application.

Design Concepts Study Guide Chapter 2

After you have read the previous chapter, fill in the blanks with the letter of the correct answer within each section.

1. _h_
2. _F_
3. _L_
4. _G_
5. _C_
6. _B_
7. _K_
8. _M_
9. _E_
10. _A_
11. _I_
12. _d_
13. _J_

A. x-height
B. ascender
C. counter
D. ligature
E. set width
F. serif
G. stem
H. cap height
I. baseline
J. swash
K. descender
L. bracket
M. axis of stress

- -

14. _H_ A set of related typefaces that share a common name is called a

15. _F_ Usually, different typefaces in a family contrast in one or more of these ways:

16. _E_ The term "font" refers to

17. _I_ The professional agencies that RIP designer's layout documents and prepare them for printing are called

18. _K_ Demibold and semibold

19. _J_ Extrabold and black

20. _D_ Condensed type is

21. _A_ Extended type is

22. _B_ Italic faces

23. _C_ The difference between roman, oblique, or italic and the difference between serifs and sans-serif type are examples of

24. _G_ It is strongly recommend not to use

A. wider
B. have calligraphic qualities of cursive writing
C. structural contrast
D. narrower
E. the encoded information that describes the entire typeface and the digital file that contains this information
F. weight, proportion, and structure
G. faux type styles
H. type family
I. service bureaus or prepress houses
J. are heavier than bold
K. aren't as heavy as bold

- -

Exercise

Type expression

This exercise has been designed to reinforce the concepts that were presented in this chapter. In the related Application Skills Modules you will be given detailed instructions that will allow you to complete the exercise in QuarkXPress, InDesign, Illustrator, or Photoshop.

Overview

In this exercise, you will explore how type can express emotion. First you will choose four raster images that express extreme states of emotion. The emotions expressed by each picture should be very different from all the others. Over each image you will set the same one or two words. The challenge is to find the appropriate typeface, size, shade, and position that makes the type as expressive as possible.

The second objective of the exercise is to practice setting type over a picture. When you do this, you must be sensitive to the color and texture under the type. It can be hard to recognize letters when they are placed over rugged textures, strong lines, or highly contrasting shapes. So, it's best to place type over as smooth an area as possible. Another consideration is how dark or light the background is. Of course, black type will be most effective when it is set over as light an area as possible. Conversely, the color of type can be switched to white when it is set over a dark area.

Objectives

- To observe type and use it as a means of expression.
- To get experience setting type in relation to a picture.

Specifications

You will create four letter-sized (8.5" × 11") layouts. Each will be filled with a different raster picture that expresses an intense emotion. Over each picture, you will superimpose the same one or two words. In each composition, the words should be set so that they are easy to read, have strong visual impact, and express an emotion parallel to the one expressed by the picture.

Procedure:

1. Choose pictures

For this exercise, you need four images that express very different states of emotion. **Pictures that you can use have been provided on the DVD in the back of the Application Skills Module book (However, please note that these images are copyrighted material and using them for any**

purpose other than this exercise is expressly prohibited.) Alternatively, you can use your own photos—but it may be a good idea to check with your instructor to make sure they are appropriate for the exercise. (Again, please bear in mind that if you use images borrowed from published or online sources, any work derived from such images may violate copyright—they must never be used for published work.)

2. Create folder

Create a folder to store the exercise (by clicking on the Desktop and pressing ⌘ ⇧ N). Name the folder: "x1_[your last name]". Put your picture files into it. Store all files related to this exercise in this folder. When you are done working, back up this folder on more than one storage device.

3. Write copy

Choose one or two words to use in all four layouts. It should be neutral or flexible enough to take on different emotions from the picture, type, and placement that you use in your compostion.

4. Choose fonts

Use Font Book to search for fonts that may work for this exercise. (If you don't have this utility, go to one of the Application Skills Modules now.) Open Font Book by clicking its icon on the Dock (or by going to HD > Applications > Font Book). Choose Preview menu > Custom. In the window at right, highlight the type and enter your words. You may want to try different capitalizations of the words. It's easy to try out different fonts by selecting them in the Fonts column. (More complete directions for this utility are given in Mac Skills Module 2.) Write down the names of a few different possibilities for each emotion—you can't tell which will work best until you see it in a layout.

5. Skills Modules

Choose one of the application Skills Modules 2 to continue.

CHAPTER 3

Observing Abstract Form in Type Design

In this chapter, the vocabulary of elements and principles of visual design are applied to type and typesetting.

OBJECTIVES

¤ To recognize the importance of observing visual characteristics in type design

¤ To begin to use a vocabulary of visual elements, qualities, and principles as tools in typesetting and type design

Learning to See Feelingly

The quote at right hits on a basic truth that applies not only to pictures, but to all kinds of visual design: To understand and appreciate any sort of design composition, we need to use our eyes differently than the way we usually do. Most of the time we are simply looking for some purpose at hand: maybe to find the car keys, or to read some kind of information, or whatever. . . And yet, even though we may not be aware of it, we are also affected by the feel of what we are looking at—the sensual qualities of things and how they are arranged. Each of us has had some conscious involvement with these concerns: perhaps when admiring a sunset (or even a picture or a good work of design), maybe when arranging furniture in a room, or deciding which shirt will "go with" which pants. But to create compelling and sophisticated designs, designers need to develop a more refined ability to observe and reflect on the feel of what they are looking at. Designers have created a special vocabulary to help them to do this.

"I'll show you how to look at a picture. . . Don't look at it. Feel it with your eye."

—Gulley Jimson

The fictional artist hero in Joyce Cary's novel *The Horse's Mouth*

Words Are Tools

Two scientists, Edward Sapir and Benjamin Whorf, developed an influential hypothesis about the way people use language. They asserted that the words people use determine how they see things and think about them. As an example, they reported on the traditional languages of the people popularly known as "Eskimos." These languages have many specialized words to describe different conditions of snow. Those words helped their speakers to recognize different kinds of snow that could be used for many different purposes, including making shelter, hunting, and transportation.

This is easy to understand if you consider that avid skiers also have many special words to describe conditions of snow in relation to their sport. Likewise, musicians learn a vocabulary that helps them to distinguish relationships of tone and rhythm. And, connoisseurs of fine wine have a rich array of terms that help them to recognize subtle nuances of flavor.

Just as a musician must develop special skills in hearing and structuring sounds, a designer must develop a refined feeling for visual relationships. This is just as true in typography as in any area of design.

The vocabulary that we are about to consider is part of a set of tools that will help you to focus your attention on visual structure. These words will remind you to pay attention to how you do things. They will enable you to discuss your work with others and will help you to make better design decisions.

Some of the words may seem so simple that you'll have trouble taking them seriously. Others may seem like they come from a foreign language. But the usefulness of a tool is only revealed as the tool is mastered. If you keep these terms in mind as you work and discuss your work with others, your mastery of them will grow. As it does, so will your ability and understanding.

Three Types of Terms

As you approach this vocabulary, it may be helpful to keep in mind the differences between three kinds of terms.

The word **elements** is used to describe the parts used in a design. The abstract elements of design include: format, point, line, texture, shape, space, color, and others. These terms are also known as the *formal* elements because they describe the fundamental parts that are used to form any visual design, from a building, to a picture, to a letter character. Whereas these formal elements are used in all areas of design, there are also other sorts of elements that are specific to other areas of interest. For instance, in Chapter 2 we looked at elements of letter characters and later we will look at elements of typographic layout.

If they cause you to try out a new solution they're doing their job.

Qualities are adjectives that are used to describe the "feel" of elements. These include everyday terms such as rough or smooth, but there are also important words that aren't so common, such as organic or geometric, which will be explained below.

Principles of design describe how elements work together. It is a mistake to think of these principles as absolute rules. Instead, it is more productive to think of them as "guidelines" or "rules of thumb" that help you to develop more powerful designs. They give you a way to identify, think about, and speak to others about how a design is working. If they cause you to try out a new solution they're doing their job.

The next section introduces some of these terms and shows how they can help us understand the design of letterforms. Then, we see how they can help us put designs together.

Figure 3-1 A black shape on white paper. We recognize that it is an "o" and not some other letter because of its specific shape. (Times)

Elements, Qualities, and Principles in Letterforms

The element of shape is of fundamental importance in letterforms. However, it turns out that the word "shape" is hard to define without using near synonyms like form, contour, or silhouette. And, of course, the word has a couple of different meanings. For our purposes, let's define **shape** as a two-dimensional area that is separated from those around it by differences in color or by an outline. The outside boundaries of a shape can be straight or round. Shapes can have equal proportions, like circles and squares, or they can be longer in one direction—having an **oblong** quality. An oblong shape tends to pull the eye along the direction of its length. Shapes are always perceived in relation to the areas that surround them and come in between them; these areas are called **negative shapes**. As we've seen, the negative shape inside of a character is called a **counter**.

The differences between the shapes of different letters is the key to legibility because it is through these differences that we recognize one letter from another. (See Figure 3-1 through Figure 3-6.)

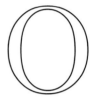

Figure 3-2 An "o" that's defined by outline. (Times)

Figure 3-3 A letter shape filled with texture and one filled with a repeating pattern.

Figure 3-4 Letters with different directions: centered, vertical, and oblique. (ITC Kabel Bold, Plaza, Gill Sans Bold Italic)

Figure 3-5 This reversed letter shows the importance of negative shapes within and around a character. (Gill Sans)

ou mw

Figure 3-6 Some typefaces don't have such clear differences of shape between letters—this makes them harder to read. These are the letters *o*, *v*, *m*, and *w* in Fractur font.

Because the alphabet began with handwritten script, the shapes of letters are made up of lines. Lines, like oblong shapes, tend to pull the viewer's eye along their path—and this can be a smooth ride or a bumpy one. The surface quality, or **texture**, of the edges can be smooth or rugged. They can be crisp and hard or soft and fuzzy. Smooth and regular shapes that are derived from basic shapes, such as circles, triangles, or rectangles, are said to have a **geometric** quality, whereas shapes that have the irregular and flowing quality of living things are said to be **organic**. Lines that do not vary in thickness are called **monoweight**. Lines that vary between thick and thin are said to have a **calligraphic** quality because they look like they were formed by a brush or flat-nibbed pen. Such qualities of line and shape can suggest feelings, such as a sense of speed, or even, as we saw in the last chapter, express an emotional feeling. (See Figure 3-6 through Figure 3-10.)

When we speak of differences between elements or qualities, we invoke the principle of **contrast**. Any elements or qualities can be made to contrast: shapes, textures, colors, line thicknesses, proportions, distances, and so on. Without contrast, of course, everything would look the same; we wouldn't be able to recognize anything from anything else. On the other side of the coin, when we increase contrast it can make things stand out and create visual energy.

In spite of the contrast between the shapes of letters, a quick look at the samples of type shown in Figure 3-6 through Figure 3-10 will show that the letters within a particular typeface seem to share an overall "family resemblance." This is because similar shapes and qualities of line have been reused throughout all the letters in the typeface. In other words: The principle of repetition has been used to create a feeling of unity throughout the typeface. **Repetition** means reusing similar visual elements. Like the principle of contrast, repetition can be used with just about any sort of element or quality. The quality of **unity** is experienced when separate parts seem to tie together to make up a whole. The human mind has a natural instinct to recognize similarities; repetition of similar elements and qualities throughout a typeface creates a unified identity for it—what designers call a "look."

The principles of design can also expresses feelings. **Rhythm** is an example. This term means creating visual interest by setting up intervals

abc abc

Figure 3-7 Geometric and organic characters (Futura, Sand)

Cheltenham Book Italic

Figure 3-8 A sense of speed is suggested in this font by quick turns of line and calligraphic variation of weight

Avant Garde

Figure 3-9 The monoweight lines and geometric qualities of this face give it a cool, mechanical character.

Figure 3-10 An irregular distressed line can convey a feeling of nervous agitation. (Font by Daniel Voshart)

of both repetition and variety. A visual rhythm, like a musical one, can be more regular or more syncopated. (See Figure 3-11.)

In general, the principles of design remind us of an important lesson: not to merely think of things in themselves but instead, to recognize the importance of relationships. This is particularly true of the principle of balance. **Balance** is a principle of compensation. A good way to understand it is to think of each element as a visual force—an action—which demands an equal and opposite reaction. Shapes need to be balanced by negative shapes; weights need to be balanced by counter-weights. Figure 3-12 shows a typeface that suffers from severe imbalance.

Composition: Putting the Parts Together

Principles of design are often called principles of composition. The word **composition** means to put separate parts together to create a new whole. For instance, a musician puts together notes and rhythms to form a musical composition. A writer puts together words to form a literary composition. And designers are concerned with how the elements they use work together to form visual compositions.

The first element a designer considers when starting a composition is the **format**. This means the outside shape, size, and proportion of the design composition. As you've seen, a vertical format is called a **portrait** format, whereas a horizontal format is called a **landscape** format. The format of a design is often dictated by where the final product will appear—billboards are usually oblong landscape formats, whereas full-page magazine ads are usually in a portrait format. When making quick "thumbnail" sketches to get ideas for a composition, beginners often make the mistake of forgetting to stay true to the proportion of the format of the final design.

The typeface Didot's regular rhythm conveys a business-like feeling.

The more irregular typeface Caslon feels more casual.

Figure 3-11 These typefaces convey distinctly different feelings.

THIS IS AN Old-time Face

Figure 3-12 This typeface suffers from imbalance: the heavy parts overwhelm both the light parts and the negative shapes. (Brad Staufer)

Figure 3-13 The format is like the stage for a composition. The dramatic impact is most powerful if the entire format is activated. (Photo courtesy *Avenues*)

LESS CAN BE MORE

Bruce Rogers, one of the most influential book designers of the 20th century, wrote that "…the ultimate test, in considering the employment or rejection of an element design or decoration, would seem to be: does it look as if it were inevitable, or would the page look as well or better for its omission?"

Re**p**etiti**o**n **o**f any s**o**rt **o**f element **o**r **q**uality can **p**ull the viewer's eye ar**o**un**d** a c**o**mp**o**siti**o**n creating rhythm an**d** unity

Figure 3-14 Repetition pulls the viewer's eye around the composition. (GillSans)

In working on a composition, it is vital to see the whole, not just the parts. Think of a composition as a drama or a dance that takes place on a stage. The format is the stage. The dramatic impact of the action will be most powerful if all the space on the stage is activated. (See Figure 3-13.)

If you were to look at this page from the distance of a full arm's length, it would be easy for you to perceive the text you are now reading as a general shape filled with gray texture. Such shapes are called **text blocks**. Your ability to recognize these shapes is an example of the principle of closure: the mind's tendency to put together small, disconnected things into larger and more general packages.

In between the text blocks and illustration boxes on this page are negative shapes, which designers call **white space**. White space adds clarity to the composition and helps the readers to focus their attention. Compositions without white space tend to feel confusing and crowded.

When different elements line up, like the edges of text blocks do, you could say that they create the impression of an implied line. When elements share an implied line, we say they are in **alignment**. Alignment is one of the main principles that can be used to create unity in a composition.

The quality of **unity** is of major importance in composition. A composition that has overall unity will hold a viewer's attention longer, whereas, without unity, the viewer's attention will more quickly slip away. Besides using alignments, unity can be established by using repetition and balance of weight.

As has been previously noted, the human mind has an instinct to recognize similarities. So, when similar visual elements are repeated in different parts of a composition, the viewer's attention is drawn from one to the next. This can be used to pull the viewer's eye around the composition, strengthening unity and creating a feeling of movement.

Another important consideration in a composition is overall balance of weight. The simplest way to achieve this is with a **symmetrical** arrangement. This means that each element on one side of the central axis of the composition is echoed by a similar element at an equal distance on the other side. This type of arrangement is sometimes called **formal balance**. It can impart a feeling of stability and "class"—think of wedding invitations. **Asymmetrical** balance is when the weight of elements on one side of the composition is compensated by different elements on the other side. It is important to understand that it is not only dark shapes that have visual weight; white space also has weight. Asymmetrical balance is less predictable and more energetic than formal balance.

Symmetry is an example of one kind of **static** relationship. Static relationships produce the feeling of stability or lack of movement. A static feeling can also be created when an element is aligned with other elements. Likewise, when elements are placed in horizontal or vertical orientations, or when they are put in parallel or perpendicular to each other, the result is static. When an element is placed in the center of the format the result is usually too static—maybe that's why they call it "dead center."

The term "static" is sometimes misunderstood by people because they think of "static electricity" as the shock they have experienced when touching a light socket on a winter day. Actually, static electricity is the state of charge that was built up before the moment of the shock. The shock itself was **dynamic**. Dynamic relationships create a feeling of energetic movement by placing elements in diagonal orientation, off-center placements, or in contrasting directions. (See Figure 3-16 a–e.) Balance of static and dynamic relationships in a composition can create a feeling of sustained excitement.

You are cordially invited
to admire the
Formal Balance of this
symmetrical arrangement.

Please be so kind as to
take note of the way
it encourages your eye
to proceed in a
downward path.

Figure 3-15 A classic example of formal balance (Zapf Chancery)

Figure 3-16 Asymmetrical balance is achieved in this composition by balancing the weight of the heavier characters on the left with the weight of the larger spaces on the right. (GillSans)

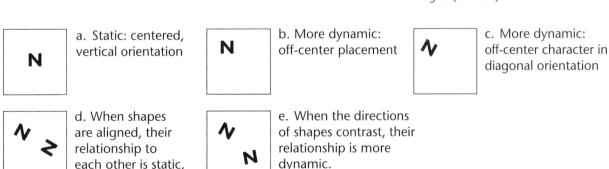

a. Static: centered, vertical orientation

b. More dynamic: off-center placement

c. More dynamic: off-center character in diagonal orientation

d. When shapes are aligned, their relationship to each other is static, but in this case the orientation to the format is dynamic.

e. When the directions of shapes contrast, their relationship is more dynamic.

Figure 3-17 a–e From static to more dynamic (Gill Sans Bold)

CHAPTER SUMMARY

This survey of visual vocabulary has provided you with a "starter toolbox" of terms that can be used to understand type design and composition. Your mastery of these terms will be reinforced in the Study Guide and Exercises that follow. These terms will be used throughout the rest of this book, and later, they will be augmented by other equally valuable terms.

The related application Skills Modules introduces skills in placement and transformation of items. It also introduces the use of Layers. These skills represent the next step in your introduction to typography in your chosen application.

Design Concepts Study Guide Chapter 3

After you have read the previous chapter, fill in the blanks with the letter of the correct answer within each section.

1. _____ The parts used in all kinds of visual design are called

2. _____ Adjectives used to describe the feel of elements are called

3. _____ A two-dimensional area that is separated from those around it by differences in color or by lines is called a

4. _____ The surface quality of a shape or line is called

5. _____ Smooth and regular shapes that are derived from basic shapes such as circles, triangles, or rectangles are said to be

6. _____ Shapes that have the irregular and flowing quality of living things are said to be

7. _____ Shapes that are longer in one direction are

A. texture

B. organic

C. abstract or formal elements

D. geometric

E. oblong

F. qualities

G. shape

- -

8. _____ A line or oblong shape tends to pull the eye

9. _____ Shapes that come in between other shapes and surround them are called

10. _____ The quality of unity is experienced when

11. _____ The general shapes made by lines of small type are called

12. _____ The mind's tendency to put together small, disconnected things into larger and more general packages is called

13. _____ Negative shapes that come in between text blocks and illustration boxes on a page are called

14. _____ When letters are shown as white shapes against a dark background we call them

15. _____ Lines that vary between thick and thin are called

A. text blocks

B. reversed

C. closure

D. calligraphic

E. separate parts seem to tie together to makeup a whole

F. negative shapes

G. along the direction of its length

H. white space

- -

16. _____ Lines that do not vary in thickness are called

17. _____ When different elements line up, you could say they create the impression of a(n)

18. _____ The principles of design describe how

19. _____ Differences between elements or qualities are called

20. _____ The outside shape, size, and proportion of the design composition is called its

21. _____ The vertical format is often called the format

22. _____ The horizontal format is often called the format

A. contrast

B. portrait

C. monoweight

D. implied line

E. format

F. balance

G. landscape

H. elements work together

23. _____ The principle of compensation between elements is called

24. _____ When each element on one side of the central axis of the composition is echoed by a similar element at an equal distance on the other side, it is called

25. _____ When the weight of elements on one side of the composition are compensated by different elements on the other side, it is called

26. _____ Relationships of elements that imply stability or lack of movement through central placement, symmetry, parallel shapes, horizontal or vertical orientations, or placing elements at right angles are called

27. _____ Relationships of elements that create a feeling of energetic movement by placing elements in diagonal orientation, or through contrasts in direction, or in off center placements are called

28. _____ Reusing similar visual elements is called

29. The organization of elements to create visual interest by establishing intervals of both repetition and variety is called

A. dynamic

B. rhythm

E. static

F. symmetrical or formal balance

H. repetition

I. asymmetrical balance

Exercises

The following exercises have been designed to reinforce the concepts that were presented in the preceding chapter. In the related application Skills Modules you are given instruction to expand your repertoire of basic skills in QuarkXPress, InDesign, Illustrator, or Photoshop. Before beginning these exercises, read Skills Module 3 for your chosen software and complete the related Study Guide. You will find detailed directions for each exercise after the Study Guide.

Compositions of Reversed Characters

Overview

This exercise gives you an opportunity to get a fresh look at letter characters. You will focus your attention on just a few characters at a time, they'll be at a larger scale than usual, and they won't be used for their familiar purpose of spelling out words. What's more, they will be in reverse (white on black) and parts of characters will become lost as they extend beyond the black background. All of these circumstances will help you to see the shapes and negative shapes of letter characters as if it were for the first time. You will also have the chance to use the elements and principles that you just read about to create simple abstract compositions. These compositions will emphasize a creative balance of negative and positive shapes.

Objectives

- To observe character shapes and negative shapes
- To practice use of elements and principles while creating abstract compositions

Specifications

Each composition will consist of two or three white letters against a black 2" × 2" square background. The compositions will be placed 1" apart, so six will fit on a page. Choose characters from a variety of fonts. Use both capital and lowercase letters. Try different styles such as bold, italic, or condensed. Each character will go outside of the square on at least one edge, so part of the shape that makes up the character will be lost.

At the same time, you will be practicing some basic skills with your chosen application. See the Application Skills Module for your chosen software for more detailed instructions.

Figure 3-18 Compositions by Douglas Lattery

See the Application Skills Module for your chosen software for more detailed instructions.

Figurative Typography

Overview

This exercise, like the last one, gives you an opportunity to get a fresh look at the shapes of letter characters by employing them in unfamiliar ways. Figurative typography means using characters as shapes to create illustrations instead of words.

Objectives

- To observe character shapes.
- To practice basic skills with your chosen application.

Specifications

Create three different illustrations out of letter characters. You can scale, rotate, and overlap the characters in any way that you want. When you have completed three illustrations, scale them to fit on one page in an interesting way.

Composition Using Pi Characters

Overview

This exercise gives you an opportunity to get acquainted with Pi Characters, which are nonalphabetic symbols or decorative figures. The most common Pi fonts are Symbol and Zapf Dingbats, but there are many different sets available. Several Pi characters are included in regular fonts—they can be found in the Edit menu > Special Characters…, as described in Mac SM 2.

Working with Pi characters will give you a good chance to work with the principle of repetition. You will also be experimenting with variety of tone in this exercise. The challenge will be to create a composition that is complex but doesn't feel cluttered.

Objectives

- To be introduced to Pi characters
- To practice use of elements and principles
- To practice basic skills with your chosen application.

Specifications

Create one composition, 6" × 6", using a variety of Pi characters in a variety of tones.

The challenge will be to create a composition that is complex but doesn't feel cluttered. At the same time, you will practice some basic skills with your chosen application.

Figure 3-19 Figurative type illustration by student Alicia Babatz

Figure 3-20 Figurative type illustration by designer Bradbury Thompson

Figure 3-21 Figurative type illustration by student Elizabeth Page

to take extra care with it. For these reasons, display type provides the perfect context to begin investigating the basic considerations that make type attractive and readable. (See Figure 4-1.)

Stacked Display Type and Line Breaks

Titles and headlines can be set on a single line or they can be broken into two or more lines. The second option, called **stacked** type, has several advantages. Stacking makes it possible to set the type larger than if it were all on one line. It can also enhance readability by breaking up a sentence into meaningful groups of words. And, stacking can make the display type into a compact design element, so that it can be placed on the page in ways that are more interesting than just running across the top. (See Figure 4-2.)

When you break a headline or title into separate lines, try to keep phrases together in a way that makes it is easy for readers to grasp the text's meaning. It is important to read through the text—maybe even read it aloud—to understand which words depend on each other to make sense. One clue is to keep modifier words, like adjectives and adverbs, together with the noun or verb that they modify. Another hint is to keep phrases that start with a preposition such as *in, to, of, from,* and *with* all on one line. Usually, you won't want to split a person's first name from their last name. Likewise, if a company or a product has a name that is more than one word long, keep these words together. Hyphens in display text are usually an undesirable distraction. Lastly, try to put the words that are most important to the message at the beginning of a line. (See Figure 4-3.)

All of the recommendations in the preceding paragraph—in fact throughout the entire book—must be balanced against your own sense of the style and purpose of the communication that you are designing. It is not uncommon for designers to break some "rules" to achieve a novel look or to express a feeling. But, successful designers are their own harshest critics—they look hard and make many revisions to make sure that their design works. When breaking one "rule," they inevitably employ several others—whether consciously or not—to produce a successful design. This book, in fact, is not teaching you "rules" at all; it is pointing out things to which you need to pay attention to make visual communication work. If you focus on the communication, the "rules" will be obvious.

Putting the Stack in Order: Alignment

There are several ways to set lines of type in relation to each other. The most common format is called **flush-left alignment**. This means that the beginnings of the lines of type align along a left-hand edge. (See the

---

Display Type Stands Out on the Page

Body type is for longer runs of text that convey a longer and more detailed message. Whereas the headline is design to standout and make maximum impact, the body type seems to be a even block of gray color. Once the reader begins reading body text, no one part will stick out to distract the reader's attention from reading. Beatrice Warde once remarked that good body type should be like a crystal goblet through which the reader can see the author's message without distortion.

Figure 4-1 Two functions of type: display type and body type (Gill Sans)

Stacked headlines can be set larger. The word groups can be read faster.

Figure 4-2 Stacked text (Gill Sans Bold)

headline shown in Figure 4-4.) In this format, the right sides of the lines don't align—they are left **ragged**. This is the most readable alignment format because when the reader reaches the end of a line, the neatly aligned left edge makes it easy to find the beginning of the next line. Flush-left format also has other advantages. The aligned-left edge helps to unite the separate lines that make up the headline. It also creates an implied line that can be aligned with other elements. Of course, this format puts more visual weight on the left, introducing a dynamic element to the page that calls for a balancing element on the right side—creating a lively asymmetrical balance on the page.

Both **flush-right** and **centered** (see Figure 4-5 and Figure 4-6) type tend to slow down the reader by making the beginnings of lines harder to find. This is less of a problem if the line lengths are fairly equal. Otherwise, it is best to use these formats only for shorter headlines or titles. There are also some design advantages to these formats. Because flush-right headlines are relatively unusual, they create a little extra emphasis. Like flush-left, flush-right headlines create opportunities for alignment and dynamic balance. On the other hand, centered type is static, so it can create a feeling of stability and "class."

The most static format is called **justified**. This is when type is aligned flush on both the left and right sides. (See Figure 4-7.) Body text is often set justified in newspapers and magazines; it gives a neat, clean look, and it's quite readable. However, because stacked headlines usually have relatively few words on each line, it is pretty hard to keep the lines the same length without making heavy-handed manipulations of the spaces between letters or words.

Figure 4-3 This title page, designed by Richard Eckersley, flaunts hyphenated breaks, but judicious spacing and alignments make it a very handsome and expressive display. *Courtesy University of Nebraska Press*

This headline is aligned flush-left

Figure 4-4 (Gill Sans Bold)

This headline is aligned flush-right

Figure 4-5 (Gill Sans Bold)

This headline is centered

Figure 4-6 (Gill Sans Bold)

This headline is justified

Figure 4-7 Notice how the spacing spreads to fill the bottom line. (Gill Sans Bold)

This headline is not conventionally aligned

Figure 4-8 (Gill Sans Bold)

This Headline Does Not Have Visually Fine-Tuned Alignment

Figure 4-9 (Avant Garde Gothic)

This Headline Does Have Visually Fine-Tuned Alignment

Figure 4-10 (Avant Garde Gothic)

There is only one possible remaining choice for alignment, and that is not to align at all. (See Figure 4-8.) Instead, lines can be placed where the designer feels they create an interesting rhythm in relation to each other. When you try this, remember to go with strong contrasts of position; if they're too close, it could just look like a mistake. And, look at the entire page—you may choose to align some part of the headline with some other element.

Fine-Tuning Alignment and Punctuation

In Chapter 3, you began to observe the great variety of shapes in letter characters. This variety is the key to legibility because we recognize letters from one another by their differences of shape. But, this same variety also creates many challenges for designers when we try to set type into neat arrangements. We'll see several examples in this chapter. The first of these is the need for fine-tuning in alignment.

If all letters were rectangular, a neat appearance of alignment would be an easy matter. But our alphabet has round characters such as "C" and "O," diagonal characters such as "A" and "V," and the capital "T" with its wide horizontal top. In flush-left headlines, lines that *begin with these letters will look a little bit indented compared to the other lines.* (See Figure 4-9.) To maintain the look of precise alignment they'll need to be moved just a bit to the left. (See Figure 4-10.) How much? You can only trust the judgment of your eyes. Often it helps to get back from your work some distance when making this kind of assessment.

Of course, similar problems crop up in flush-right settings. And likewise, centered type sometimes requires adjustments to stay nicely balanced.

Because most punctuation marks are smaller and lighter than letter characters, they can seem to create conspicuous indentations in an alignment. Because punctuation marks usually come at the right end of a line, this problem is particularly common in flush-right settings. But in practice, because the flush-left format is so much more common, you are most likely to confront this problem when a quotation mark is at the beginning of a line set flush-left. (See Figure 4-11.) In either case, the solution to such problems is to **hang the punctuation**—to make it hang out beyond the aligned edge. Of course, this won't be necessary with centered headlines, but, once again, you may need to adjust the balance when there are punctuation marks at the beginning or end of a line.

The typewriters of the past used to set straight quotation marks (or ditto marks) that looked like this: ". Today's digital applications have the ability to set curly "typesetter's quotation marks", or "6s & 9s." These are also known as "smart quotes" because computers are smart enough to know that they should curl up like "6s" for opening quotes and down like "9s" for closing quotes. They look far more professional than straight ditto marks.

When setting display type, it's often a good idea make the punctuation marks a few point sizes smaller than the letters. This is because, in most fonts, the punctuation marks are designed to be large enough to be easily legible at the small size of body text; but when type is enlarged to display sizes the punctuation marks can seem to overwhelm the words unless they're reduced. (See Figure 4-12.)

In general, it's best to keep punctuation to a minimum in display type. You might not need periods unless there's more than one sentence. Exclamation marks don't really get anyone excited, and they might be momentarily mistaken for an "I" or a "1." Likewise, contractions should be avoided because they also can confuse a reader: "He'll" can look like "Hell."

Capitalization Formats

Another factor that affects readability is the style of capitalization. SETTING TYPE IN ALL CAPITAL LETTERS (also known as uppercase letters) SLOWS READERS DOWN. This is because small, or lowercase, letters have much greater contrasts in shape than uppercase. In fact, experienced readers don't read the separate letters in common words that are set in lowercase—they save time by recognizing the overall shapes of words. (See Figure 4-13.) The most readable format for capitalization is called **sentence style** or **down-style**. This is the way we usually set body text: Only the first letter of the first word and proper names are capitalized. In **up-style**, also known as **leading caps** or **headline style**, all the major words are capitalized, but not the prepositions, articles, and any conjunctions that have four fewer letters. While leading caps is a more readable format than all caps, it is slower than sentence style because readers tend to pause with each capital letter.

"In this Headline Quotation Marks were *not* Reduced or Hung"

Figure 4-11 (Avant Garde Gothic)

"In this Headline Quotation Marks were Reduced and Hung"

Figure 4-12 (Avant Garde)

ALL UPPERCASE

Leading Caps

Figure 4-13 Style of capitalization affects readability because readers save time by recognizing the overall shapes of words. (Adobe Garamond)

PICKY, PICKY, PICKY...

Is all of this fine-tuning really worth it? It depends. Just as some restaurants take more care with how they prepare food than others, and just as some musicians are more skilled than others in how they play a tune, some publications and some designers have higher standards in the details of typography than others.

A publication that is aimed at a more exclusive clientele will take pains to achieve the most professional look possible, whereas a neighborhood newsletter might not have enough budget to make this kind of attention worthwhile. As a student of design, you are preparing your work for an extremely exclusive audience: potential employers. Don't you want to communicate to them that you have mastered these skills? Take heart: While all of this might seem like a lot to keep track of now, with some practice it will eventually become just like second nature.

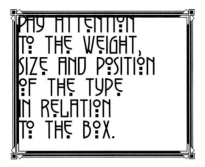

Figure 4-14 (Greyhound)

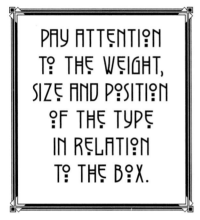

Figure 4-15 (Greyhound)

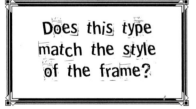

Figure 4-16 (Hoosker Doo by CHANK!)

> Black Type
> Set Over
> a 40% Tint
> Looks Mushy.

Figure 4-17 (Bookman Old Style)

Text within Boxes

Setting text within a box that is filled with a color or surrounded by a frame will unify it, add emphasis, and can add a decorative effect. However, these kind of boxes can also block the reader's eye flow to and from the text. The decoration can make the page look too busy. So, when you choose to do this, be careful to consider both the function and the effect of your decision.

Whenever you set text inside a box, you'll want to pay attention to the weight, size, and position of the type in relation to this container. (See Figure 4-14 and Figure 4-15.) The weight of one element shouldn't overpower the weight of the other. The size of the type should balance with the spaces around it. The text will be most readable if there is a margin that separates it from the edges. During the 1990s, crowding text against an edge became very fashionable—probably just because it had been such a "no-no" previously. This trend seems to be on the way out. As a designer you may occasionally have to choose between novelty or expression on the one hand and the reader's comfort on the other.

When a frame is used, look for a good match between the styles of the type and the frame. (See Figure 4-16.)

When using a colored box, remember that black type loses clarity when it's set over a heavy tint. The exception to this rule is the color yellow—its jarring contrast with black can actually enhance readability. But, in most cases, you won't want to use a tint stronger than 30% under black type. (See Figure 4-17.)

Adjusting the Spacing of Letters: Tracking

Now that we've covered the basics of display type, we have a meaningful context to investigate the fundamental issues of letter spacing. First we'll consider **tracking**: the overall adjustment of letter spacing throughout entire words and longer runs of text.

Display type almost always requires adjustment of tracking. This is because, as the size of type is increased, the spaces between the characters look as though they grow even larger. (See Figure 4-18.) Therefore, it is common to tighten up the tracking in display type.

A classic look is achieved when the tracking is left open enough to balance the forms of characters with the white spaces between them. (See Figure 4-19.) But, since the 1960s, many designers have chosen to impart a feeling of urgency by setting headlines with very tight tracking. (See Figure 4-20.) On the other hand, sometimes display type is given a decorative effect by setting the tracking very wide. This effect, called **letterspacing**, makes readers slow down and see the separate letters before they can read the words. It can create a strong emphasis, but can easily wear a reader down if it's overused. (See Figure 4-21.)

An old rule of thumb said that letterspacing should be applied only to type set in all capitals letters. This is because capital letters are all uniform in height, so they align neatly. These days, however, letterspacing lower-case letters has become more common. (See Figure 4-23.)

Spacing
Spacing
Spacing
Spacing
Spacing
Spacing

Figure 4-18 An optical trick: As the size of type is increased, the spaces between the characters look as though they have grown even larger. (Adobe Garamond Semibold)

MANUALE

TIPOGRAFICO

Figure 4-19 A classic open setting by Giambattista Bodoni

TNT: Tight Not Touching

Figure 4-20 (Baskerville)

L E T T E R S P A C I N G
disrupts the natural tendency to read the shapes of words

Figure 4-21 (Gill Sans)

LETTERSPACED TYPE WITH WORDSPACING TOO TIGHT

LETTERSPACED TYPE WITH CLEARER WORDSPACING

Figure 4-22 Letterspaced lowercase

Figure 4-23 (Gill Sans) When applying letterspacing, be careful that the wordspacing stays clear.

Lead Type

Leading

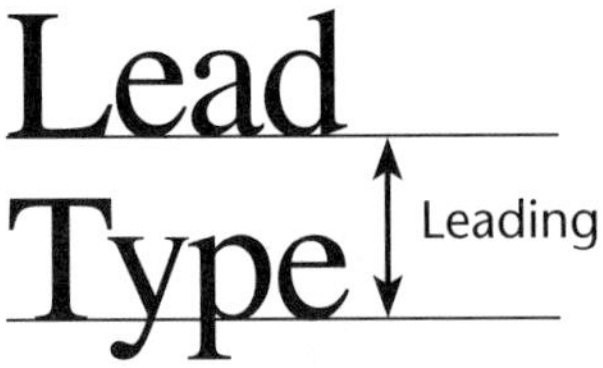

Figure 4-24 Leading, the distance between lines of type, is measured from baseline to baseline. (Times)

This Type is Set Solid

Figure 4-25 The leading is equal to the point size of the type. (Century)

This Type has Negative Leading

Figure 4-26 The leading is less than the point size of the type: Ouch! The "y" is stubbing its toe on the "i"! (Century)

This Type is Set with Auto Leading

Figure 4-27 The leading is 120% of the point size of the type. (Century)

The Space Between Lines: Leading

Space between lines of type is called leading. This term is a holdover from the days of lead type: the distance between lines of type was adjusted by putting strips of lead between them. More precisely, leading is defined as the measurement from baseline to baseline. (See Figure 4-24.)

As with tracking, the choice of leading in display type is influenced by several factors, such as the particular characteristics of typeface that is used and the feeling the designer seeks to convey. It can also be influenced by trends of fashion.

When the measurement for leading is equal to the point size of the type, we say the type is set solid. (See Figure 4-25.) You might think this term makes it sound like letters in different lines would actually touch, but they don't because the font's bounding box includes a little extra space above the ascenders and below the descenders. When the type is set so tight that these parts could actually touch or overlap, we say that the lines are set with negative leading. (See Figure 4-26.) The default setting for "auto"-leading in most digital applications is 120% of the point size of the type. (See Figure 4-27.) Most designers currently set display type tighter than this. (See Figure 4-28 and Figure 4-29.)

Although leading is usually kept consistent, occasionally the line spacing of a headline needs fine-tuning. This, again, is something that only can be done by feel. The headline shown in Figure 4-30 is set with equal leading, but it looks uneven. This is particularly true between the second line, which has no descenders, and the third, which has no ascenders. In Figure 4-31, the headline is adjusted so that the lines appear to be an equal distance apart.

Figure 4-28 Jan Tschichold, one of the dominant theoreticians of early 20th-century design, advocated open letterspacing to create balance between form and space in type composition. *Courtesy University of California Press*

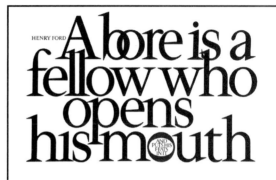

Figure 4-29 Herb Lubalin, an outstanding designer of the 1960s and 1070s, exalted in tight tracking and negative leading. The copy reads, "A bore is a fellow who opens his mouth and puts his feats in it." *Courtesy of The Herb Lubalin Study Center of Design and Typography at The Cooper Union School of Art*

We may need to tweak some spaces to make all look equal

Figure 4-30 All lines are set to 19-pt. leading. Does the leading *look* equal? (Baskerville)

We may need to tweak some spaces to make all look equal

19

17

19

18.5

Figure 4-31 After fine-tuning: The leading values for each line are listed to the far right. (Baskerville)

Adjusting How Letters Fit Together: Kerning

At last we come to kerning: the adjustment of how each letter fits together with its immediate neighbor. Kerning separates the pros from the hacks. The discerning professional recognizes that letters can fit together into word-groups with balance and unity, or the groups can feel disconnected and sloppy.

If all letters were rectangular, a desirable fit could be accomplished by simply spacing them at equal intervals. But, as we saw earlier, many characters aren't rectangular. Letter combinations such as "To," "Av," and many others, can create unsightly gaps that threaten to break up the visual unity of a word. These combinations need to be drawn together. Others, like "Th," can't come closer, so to maintain balance we may want to spread the other letters slightly. The most desirable fit cannot be found by simple measuring. Good kerning is a matter of careful visual judgment. (See Figure 4-32 and Figure 4-33.)

Back in the days of metal type, kerning was a slow process that was done by filing down the sides of type blocks where the space between characters was too wide, or, by adding very thin lead spacers where gaps were too narrow. For the most part, only display type was given this kind of attention.

Today, the designers of digital fonts help us with kerning. They look at many pairs of characters and decide on good fits. Then, they record their judgments in complex kerning tables. This information is encoded into the digital font where it can be used by layout programs to kern type automatically.

down or down? turn or tum?

Figure 4-32 Some pairs look like other letters when they are spaced too close, for instance, *cl* can be confused with *d*, and *rn* can be confused with *m*. (Adobe Garamond)

This type is not kerned.
This type is kerned.

Figure 4-33 Compare these examples carefully. Can you see in the top line that some letter pairs within words feel like they're not hanging together? In the second line, each word is unified—but no letter is too crowded. Look at it from the letters' point of view: They need to work together as a team, but each wants an equal amount of personal space. (Adobe Garamond)

Most of the time auto-kerning works well enough for running body type. But it's not without problems. For one thing, some fonts have worse kerning tables than others—some excellent fonts have very poor kerning tables. Most kerning tables only plan for the most important 2% of the total possible combinations of characters. Both QuarkXPress and InDesign allow users to customize kerning tables, but this takes much time and requ.ires a high level of skill. And, auto-kerning can't handle problems that arise in special situations, such as when the text switches from regular to italic, or when numbers are included in running text. Still, it is very rare for designers to take the time to manually kern body type, except when they see a problem that really sticks out. However, just like in the old days, a good designer will find that, even with auto-kerning, display type requires special attention. Thankfully, manual kerning is much easier with today's tools than those of the past.

Save the Kerning for Last (Almost Always)

Save the kerning for last if you can, after you've chosen all the fonts and their sizes, after you've chosen the styles of alignment and capitalization, after you've adjusted the leading and tracking and the sizes of punctuation, and, of course, after you've checked the spelling (don't ever forget that!). *Last.* Because any of these factors can change the look of all your kerning. . .and you've got better things to do than to do it twice.

Well, kerning comes last *almost* always. One exception is created when you hang punctuation in QuarkXPress. We'll look at that in the Skills Module. Other exceptions concern special effects—so we'll wait until Chapter 10 for those. OK?

Here's a practical approach to manual kerning of display type: Look over the entire text and find the pairs of letters that produce the widest gaps (like "Th" or "vw," for instance). Pull them together as much as you can, but you'll probably want to stop just before they touch. One of

Figure 4-34 A piece of traditional lead type. As you can see, the shape of the letter is raised above a flat surface called the base or platform. The position of the letter within the area of the base was an important part of letter design because it established the basic spacing between letters.

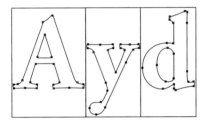

Figure 4-35 With digital type, the default space is established by an invisible bounding box that surrounds each letter. The bounding box defines the area that would surround the letter if it was set with solid leading and no adjustment of tracking or kerning (including auto-kerning). The left and right boundaries around a character are called the letter's sidebearings. Poorly designed sidebearings can make an otherwise good font practically unworkable because kerning problems become colossal.

the main ideas of kerning is to make the type look even, so you'll want to make the toughest cases blend in as much as possible. After you can't make them any tighter, the only solution is to make the other characters a bit looser. But don't overdo it. In most text, some irregularities will be inevitable unless you're willing to set the type very loose. Some unevenness is OK—it helps to give the type a sense of rhythm. But, try to minimize how much the gaps stick out, and get the other parts to feel even. (See the sidebar "Getting a Good Look" for viewing strategies that can help you assess the overall evenness of display type.)

Another litmus test for kerning is to look at how well each word hangs together as a group. Look for the spots where the words seem like they're separating and tighten them up.

After you've adjusted the kerning, look at the spaces between the words and adjust them if they feel too large or uneven. Once again, this is a matter of judgment; it depends on factors such as the overall tracking and the feeling that you want the headline to express to the reader.

It is critical to be consistent in kerning. Once you have kerned a pair of letters, make sure you use the same value whenever the same pair occurs.

CHAPTER SUMMARY

This chapter concentrated on display type—the large type that forms a reader's first impression. We looked at how stacking the type makes it possible to set it larger, break it into meaningful word groups, and unite it into a compact design element. Capitalization and punctuation in display type were explained. We also examined factors to consider when setting text within boxes.

Our examination of dislay type created a meaningful context for introducing several fundamental issues in type setting: alignment, leading, tracking, and kerning.

The Exercises for this chapter give you an opportunity to practice these skills. The related Application Skills modules guide you in executing professional quality display type in QuarkXPress, InDesign, Illustrator, or Photoshop.

Design Concepts Study Guide Chapter 4

After you have read the previous chapter, fill in the blanks with the letter of the correct answer within each section.

1. _____ Large type (usually 14 pts. and larger), such as headlines and titles, that stand out on the page is called

2. _____ Titles and headlines broken into two or more lines are called

3. _____ When the beginnings of the lines of type align along an edge it is called

4. _____ When the ends of the lines of type align along an edge it is called

5. _____ When the beginnings or ends of the lines of type of type don't align we say they are

6. _____ When both the beginnings and ends of the lines of type align it is called

7. _____ When each line is balanced from the midpoint it is called

A. flush-right alignment

B. centered alignment

C. display type

D. ragged

E. justified alignment

F. flush-left alignment

G. stacked type

○ ○

8. _____ The most readible alignment format is

9. _____ In flush-left headlines, lines that begin with some characters such as C, O, A, V, and T will need

10. _____ To make punctuation extend out beyond the aligned edge is called

11. _____ In display type, it's often a good idea make punctuation marks

12. _____ It slows readers down if type is set in all

13. _____ When only the first letter of the first word and proper names are capitalized it is called

14. _____ When all the major words are capitalized, but not the prepositions, articles, and any conjunctions that have four fewer letters, it is called

A. a few point sizes smaller

B. hanging punctuation

C. sentence style or down-style

D. up-style, also known as leading caps or headline style

E. flush-left

F. fine-tuning in alignment

G. uppercase letters

○ ○

Headline in a Box

Overview

In this exercise, you will practice creating a headline and placing it in a box that is defined by a frame or a background tint.

Objectives

- To practice placing a headline into a text box that is defined by a frame or a tint.

- To create balance between the weights of elements and the spaces between them.

- To practice writing a headline and breaking it up into effective phrases.

- To practice the basic skills in QuarkXPress that will enable you to fine-tune display type, including adjustment of the size of the punctuation, tracking, leading, kerning, and alignment.

Specifications: The headline will be set in a 6" wide box (defined by background tint or a frame) centered on a landscape format page.

See the Application Skills Module for your chosen software for detailed instructions.

Structure and Measurement

Now that you've had some experience observing and making decisions about typographic design, you're ready to take on more specific information about how type is structured and measured. This information, in turn, will help you to recognize more and make better decisions about typographic design.

OBJECTIVES

- ¤ To identify six categories of type
- ¤ To measure and specify type
- ¤ To use contrast, stacking, fitting, alignment, and overlap to design logotypes

Six Categories of Type Structure

Tens of thousands of typefaces are available to digital designers—how can anyone keep track of them all? It can help if you learn to recognize larger categories of type that share common characteristics. The six categories shown on these pages will get you started. (See Figure 5-1 through Figure 5-6.)

"We should welcome typographic variety as the natural consequence of human creativity."

—Sebastian Carter

Diagonal axis
of stress   Serifs on ascenders
             are slanted   Moderate contrast
                            between thick &
                            thin strokes

Oldstyle

Bracketed serifs

Vertical axis   Serifs on
                 ascenders are
                 horizontal   Thin serif—
                               No bracket

Modern

Strong contrast
between thick
& thin strokes

Figure 5-1 Oldstyle roman typefaces are considered to be the most readable and eye-friendly. Their serifs help readers to recognize characters by adding an extra contrasting shape at the ends of the main strokes. Also, the horizontal direction of the serifs work together with the diagonal stress in round strokes to move the reader's eye along the text. Graceful variety is produced by the moderate calligraphic contrast between thick and thin strokes and the curved brackets on the serifs. (Palatino)

Figure 5-2 The rigorously vertical stress of Modern roman typefaces give them a static bearing, but this quality is countered by the dazzling contrast between thick stems and hairline thin strokes and serifs. Together, these qualities give these faces a classy "blue-chip" quality: the logo for CBS television, "the Tiffany network," uses Modern type. However, many people feel that the contrast in Modern faces can make them feel wearing to the eye in long runs of body text. (Didot)

Thick rectangular serif—
usually unbracketed

Slab-serif

Little or no contrast in weight of strokes

No serifs

Sans-serif

Little or no contrast in weight of strokes

Figure 5-3 Slab serif faces were originally developed for advertising posters in the 19th century. Their thick square serifs were an attempt to make them more legible from a distance. The serifs are usually unbracketed and just as thick as the stem stroke. The characters are typically monoweight, meaning there is little or no contrast in weight of the strokes. The letter forms tend to be open, with wide set widths and large x-height. During the nineteenth century they usually went by the names Egyptian or Antique. Variants of this category, called Clarendon or Ionic, have bracketed serifs, moderately contrasting thick and thin strokes, and vertical axis of stress. (Rockwell)

Figure 5-4 "Sans" means "without" in French—therefore absence of serifs is the main distinguishing feature of type in this category. These typefaces, like the slab-serifs, tend to be relatively monoweight, but a close look at many of them will reveal small artful variations in the strokes. Some of these faces are strictly based on simple geometric shapes such as circles and triangles. Others barrow structural ideas from Oldstyle roman type: notice the "double-story" *a* in the sample above. The clean and simple look of sans-serif typefaces made them very appealing to progressive designers in the last century. (Helvetica)

The last two categories are much more general and wide-ranging, so it makes sense to show a few different examples.

Don't think of these categories as absolute rules. You'll find some typefaces that combine characteristics from more than one category. Other systems of categorization are possible—but none can be considered definitive. Once again, this system is a "rule of thumb." It helps you to recognize similarities and contrasts between typefaces and to better understand how type is structured, how it functions, and how it expresses feelings. In the next chapter, you'll learn to recognize several other categories such as textura, transitional roman, and three varieties of sans serif.

Type Measurement and Specification

By now you've acquired enough background to understand how type is measured and how professionals communicate specifications.

As you've seen, the unit used to measure type size is called a **point (pt.)**. This term goes back to the 18th century, but it wasn't used in a standardized way: different foundries gave it different lengths. In 1883, the U.S. Type Founders Association decreed that a standard point should be .0138 inch—just a smidgen less than ½₂ inch. Now, let's fast-forward about 100 years to the development of digital publishing applications. Adobe Systems developed the PostScript page description language, which is at the heart of all digital typography. They simplified things by changing the standard for a **PostScript point** to exactly ½₂ inch. Most applications let you to change this increment to another measurement in their Preferences dialog box—if you ever need to. . .

(Exotica by West Wind Fonts)

(Bloktype by Marieke Blokland)

(Pussyfoot by Webdog)

(Entangled by Aenigma)

Script

(Caflisch Script)

Script

(Marker Felt Wide)

Script

(Lucida Blackletter)

Script

(TagsXtreme by Jakob Fischer)

Figure 5-5 The Script category includes any typeface that takes on the look of hand-lettering with any tool: pen, brush, or pencil. (Entangled by Aenigma)

Figure 5-6 This category includes any of a large number of typefaces that have been designed to give special flavors to display text. These won't work for body text!

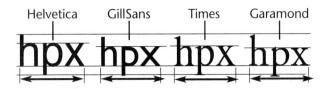

Helvetica   GillSans   Times   Garamond

hpx hpx hpx hpx

Figure 5-7 All of these samples are 32 pt. Helvetica looks much larger than the others because of its greater x-height. This diagram also makes it easy to compare the width of Helvetica, defined by the arrows, to the others. You can also see differences in the default letterspacing.

1 point = 1/72 inch

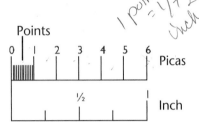

Points

0 1 2 3 4 5 6   Picas

½   Inch

Figure 5-8 Six picas per inch and 12 points per pica.

picas   points

3p2.5

20.5

Figure 5-9 The conventional notation is to list the picas first, then a "p," then the points. This would read "3 picas, 2.5 points." It would equal 20.5 pt. or about 0.285".

⌐Indicates 1 em first line indent
1
☐   *This type is set in ten point Helvetica Bold Oblique on twelve point leading with fourteen pica line measure.*

The specs: Measure in picas⌐

Helvetica Bold Oblique 10/12 x 12p

Type family / Type style / Leading in pt.
        Type weight   Type size in pt.

Figure 5-10 Type specification

It's difficult to predict from the point measurement of type how large it will actually look on the page. That's because type is measured by its body height (which is the distance from the bottom of the descenders to the top of the ascenders plus a small, but not standard, little bit extra). Actually, a measurement of a face's x-height would determine more accurately how large most type would look. (See Figure 5-7.)

The small point units are very convenient for measuring type, but in order to relate type to larger elements in a layout, a larger unit is needed. The **pica** is equal to 12 points. There are 6 picas in 1 inch. (See Figure 5-8.) Most professional graphic designers use points and picas to measure all their work. The conventional notation for these increments is explained in Figure 5-9.

The width of a column of type is called the **line length** or **measure**. This is traditionally notated in picas.

Points and picas, like inches and millimeters, are fixed measurements. However, there are also units of typographic measurement that are proportional units. This means that their lengths depend on the size of the type they are measuring; if the type size is changed, the unit also changes in proportion to it. Without proportional units, scalable fonts and adjustments to kerning or tracking would be extremely difficult.

The main unit of this kind is a measure of width called an **em**—its width is equal to the point-size of the type, so that an em space for 10 pt. type would be 10 pt. wide. The unit called **en** is one half the width of an em—so an en space for 10 pt. type would be 5 pt. wide. Smaller proportional units are used in designing digital fonts, but these are not standardized. The applications in the Adobe Creative suite measure adjustments to kerning or tracking in one-thousandths (0.001) of an em. (QuarkXPress measures these adjustments relative to units that are designed into the font.)

When professionals communicate specifications (or "specs") for type, they use a conventional format. (See Figure 5-10.) In addition to these basic specs, alignment and case can be indicated with these abbreviations:

F/L, R/R—Flush-left, ragged right
F/R, R/L—Flush-right, ragged left
(Centered and justified aren't abbreviated.)
UC—Uppercase
lc—Lowercase
U/lc—Upper and lowercase (sentence style)

Specs can also include tracking and, if there is type that isn't black, the color and percent of shade.

Designing Typographic Logotypes

After our brief sojourn into the specifics of specification, let's return to the realm of aesthetics. Creating logotypes will give you an opportunity to review and apply the principles of type design we've considered so far and to explore a couple of new topics.

A **logotype** is an emblem that is used to create a recognizable and expressive graphic identity for a person, product, or organization. They are used in many contexts including ads, business cards, letterheads, brochures, packaging, signage, and on delivery trucks. A logotype may consist of a picture-symbol, or it may be made of type only, or it may integrate the two. Those that use type usually do so with great economy and art. Distinctive compositions are created from just a few letters or words. (See Figure 5-11.) These kinds of logotype have much in common with the display type we explored in the last chapter, but they are usually more concise and inventive.

The principle of contrast is central to logotype composition because it makes things stand out, helps viewers to tell different things apart, and creates visual energy. There are six basic ways that one setting of type can contrast with another:

Scale	A difference of size
Weight	The difference between heavier type (with thicker strokes) and lighter type (with thinner strokes) (see Figure 5-12)
Case	The difference between uppercase (capital) and lowercase (small) characters
Structure	A fundamental difference in the vocabulary of elements used to construct different fonts; examples include the difference between roman and italic, or serif and sans-serif (see Figure 5-13)
Direction	Type can be made to contrast by the difference between regular and oblique characters, or between condensed and extended type, or by turning it different ways (see Figure 5-14)
Tone or Color	Differences between black and gray or other colors (see Figure 5-15)

The most important thing to remember about contrast is to look for differences that are strong—not mushy. A difference in scale of a couple of points won't be clear enough. Neither will the difference between a bold type and a semi-bold. It's an old rule of thumb that two different serif faces shouldn't be used together because they're too similar. The same with two different sans-serifs. But, this rule can be broken if the type contrasts enough in other ways. (See Figures 5-11, 5-12, and 5-16.)

Figure 5-11 This logotype for a hair salon uses a simple ellipse to illustrate the name. What kinds of contrast can you find between the two typefaces used? *Courtesy Mike Quon/Designation*

Figure 5-12 (Helvetica and Lithos Black)

Figure 5-13 (Zapf Chancery and Courier)

Figure 5-14 (Korinna)

Figure 5-15 If these overlapping letters were all the same tone, the word would be illegible (Cooper Black)

Figure 5-16 This logotype uses two different sans-serifs, but the differences in scale, weight, and structure make them contrast effectively. *Courtesy Pat Hansen, Hansen Design Company*

Figure 5-17 (Gill Sans)

A logotype must be visually unified so it will hold the viewer's attention and so its parts will not get confused with other things that may be placed nearby. For these reasons, when a logotype uses more than one word, those words are often stacked. Often, parts are put into alignment to create unity. Sometimes repetition is used. Two other devices that promote unity are fitting and overlap.

Fitting usually works best when words are set in leading caps. The odd shapes that open up between the capital letters and ascenders, or between descenders, are used to frame smaller words or parts of words. (See Figures 5-17, 5-18, and 5-19.)

Overlap, of course, means placing letters so that they partly cover one another. The challenge is to do this without sacrificing clarity. (See Figure 5-20 and Figure 5-21.)

Adobe Illustrator and InDesign have the ability to convert digital type into editable shapes. This opens up an infinite amount creative possibilities to customize the type, join letters into unusual ligatures, and to integrate type with illustrations. (See Figure 5-22 and Figure 5-23.)

The principles that we've just looked at can also be applied to custom headlines and titles. They are also central to larger questions of page composition. (See Figure 5-24.)

Figure 5-18 This logotype makes distinctive use of fitting, alignment, and repetition. *Courtesy Massimo Vignelli, Vignelli Associates*

Figure 5-19 A handsome example of fitting that is set in all caps. *Courtesy John Burns, John Burns Lettering and Design*

Figure 5-20 (Lucida Handwriting and Alexy Extra Bold)

Figure 5-21 Very effective use of overlap and contrast of structure. *Courtesy John Burns, John Burns Lettering and Design*

Figure 5-22 The Embarko trademark integrates type with a pictograph. *Courtesy Mark Fox, Black Dog, Inc.* This sort of manipulation of pictures and type is easiest to accomplish with Adobe Illustrator. See Illustrator Skills Module 5.

Figure 5-23 This logotype by John Burns integrates a simplified picture with type. The type is animated by turning it in contrasting directions. *Courtesy John Burns, John Burns Lettering and Design*

Figure 5-24 These principles can be applied to any kind of typographic design. This poster makes creative use of contrast of size, weight, and direction. *Courtesy Paula Scher, Pentagram Design*

Chapter Summary

The six categories of type you encountered in this chapter will help you recognize similarities and contrasts between typefaces. They'll help you understand how type is structured, how it functions, and how it expresses feelings. In the next chapter, you'll learn to recognize several other categories of type.

This chapter also introduced the professional methods for measuring and specifying type.

Several important principles of type design were investigated. These included six ways that type can contrast: scale, weight, case, structure, direction, and tone or color. Also, a few ways to create unity: alignment, repetition, stacking, fitting, and overlap.

In Exercise 5 you have the opportunity to put these design concepts to work in designing logotypes. The related Illustrator and InDesign Skills chapters show how you can convert type into vector paths so you can modify the letters you use in logotypes.

Design Concepts Study Guide Chapter 5

After you have read the previous chapter, fill in the blanks with the letter of the correct answer within each section.

1. ——— Which category is this?   A. Oldstyle roman

2. ——— **Which category is this?**   B. Modern roman

3. ——— *Which category is this?*   C. slab serif

                 D. sans serif

4. ——— WHICH CATEGORY IS THIS?   E. script

5. ——— Which category is this?   F. decorative

6. ——— Which category is this?

7. ——— Which category is this?

8. ——— Which category is this?

9. ——— Which Category is this?

10. ——— **Which category is this?**

· ·

Helvetica Bold Oblique 10/12 x 12p

11. ———   A. leading in points

12. ———   B. type size in points

13. ———   C. type weight

14. ———   D. type family

15. ———   E. indicates a 1 em first line indent

16. ———   F. type style

17. ———   G. Faux Italic

18. ——— *aefkmyz*   H. True Italic

19. ——— *aefkmyz*   I. measure in picas

· ·

20. _____ F/L, R/R means

21. _____ F/R, R/L means

22. _____ UC means

23. _____ lc means

24. _____ U/lc means

A. uppercase

B. lowercase

C. upper and lowercase

D. flush-left, ragged right

E. flush-right, ragged left

○ ○

25. _____ Which category of typefaces is considered to be the most readable and eye-friendly?

26. _____ Slab-serif faces with bracketed serifs and moderately contrasting strokes are known as

27. _____ It's difficult to predict from the point measurement of type how large it will actually look on the page because

28. _____ Most professional graphic designers measure all their work with

29. _____ The width of a column of type is called

30. _____ An em is a proportional unit that is as wide as

31. _____ An en is

32. _____ The applications in the Adobe Creative suite measure adjustments to kerning or tracking in

33. _____ An emblem that is used to create a recognizable and expressive graphic identity for a person, product, or organization is called a

34. _____ Using the odd shapes that open up between capital letters and ascenders, or between descenders, to frame smaller words is called

A. line length or measure

B. the point size of the type

C. logotype

D. points and picas

E. one-half the width of an em

F. type is measured by the its body height

G. fitting

H. one-thousandths (0.001) of an em

I. Clarendon or Ionic

J. Oldstyle roman

35. _____ 5 picas 4 points =   — A. 6p

36. _____ 12 points =   ~ B. 15p

37. _____ 1" =   C. p4

38. _____ $\frac{1}{72}$" =   D. p1

39. _____ $\frac{1}{2}$" =   — E. 66p

40. _____ 2.5" =   — F. 5p4

41. _____ $\frac{1}{18}$" =   — G. 51p

42. _____ $\frac{10}{18}$" =   H. 3p4

43. _____ 8.5" =   — I. 3p

44. _____ 11" =   — J. 1p

○ ○

Exercises

The following exercises have been designed to reinforce the concepts that were presented in the preceding chapter. For the most part, these exercises do not require new application skills, so the directions given below are largely complete. However, Illustrator and InDesign have special capacities to customize the type, join letters into custom ligatures, and to integrate type with illustrations. These are presented in Illustrator and InDesign Skills Modules 5.

Collecting Examples of Type from Each Category

OVERVIEW

You will look through magazines to find a few examples of each of the six type categories. You can extend this exercise by drawing letters.

SPECIFICATIONS

See the following procedure.

OBJECTIVES

• To reinforce understanding of the categories of type and observe the qualities of examples.

Procedure:

1. Find type samples

Look through magazines to find three examples of type from each of the six categories that were described in this chapter. Mount the samples of each category on a separate piece of paper. Label each paper with the name of the category.

2. Draw copies of your type samples

You can learn more by drawing copies of one or more of the samples from each category. Designers of type fill up notebooks with freehand drawings of type. No matter what your level of skill, drawing is a great way to make important observations.

Before you begin, lightly draw a baseline. Then draw a light pencil line for the cap-height 1.5" above the baseline. Next, "guesstimate" the x-height and lightly draw that line. Do the same for the descenders.

Using this structure, draw the letters freehand, lightly, and fairly quickly, with a pencil. Revise the shapes of the letters as you go over them with a black marker. Then fill them in.

3. Draw missing letters

You can extend this exercise by trying to imagine and draw matching versions of some of the letters that are missing from your samples.

Assessment Criteria

_____ Three examples of type from each of the six type categories collected and neatly mounted and labeled

_____ Right cap-height, and good guesstimates for x-height, descenders, and ascenders

_____ Accuracy of shapes overall

_____ Accuracy of small details

_____ Accuracy of contrast in weights of strokes

Following Specifications

Overview

You will set and position a few lines of type according to specifications.

Specifications

See procedure below.

Objectives

- To practice interpretation of type specifications and use of point and pica measurement units.

Procedure:

1. Set measurements to picas

Go to Preferences for your chosen application and change the measurements setting to picas. (If you need directions, see Skills Module 1.)

2. Set quote

On a letter-sized page, landscape format, set the following quote from 17th-century typographer John Baskerville in Hoefler Text 36/42 × 37p, FL/RR:

"Having been an early admirer of the beauty of letters, I became insensibly desirous of contributing to the perfection of them."

Place the first baseline at Y: 17p and align the left edge along X: 17p.

Adjust the size of the quotation marks and hang the first one. Adjust the alignment and kerning as needed.

3. Print your work

After, you've completed the layout, print your work (File menu > Print). Then look at it carefully to see if it needs further adjustments before presenting it for assessment.

Assessment Criteria

_____ Correct font, size, leading, and measure

_____ Correct placement of first baseline and left edge

_____ Size of the quotation marks adjusted

_____ Adjustment of alignment and kerning

Designing Logotypes

OVERVIEW

You will create three very different logotypes of your name. Note: This exercise can be completed in QuarkXPress, or Photoshop using application skills from Skills Module 3. Skills Modules 5 for InDesign and Illustrator introduce new skills in manipulating type and integrating illustration with type, which can be used to extend this exercise.

SPECIFICATIONS

Use only black type or gray tints. Arrange the logotypes on a letter-sized page in an interesting way.

OBJECTIVES

Practice creative and expressive typographic composition using six kinds of contrast, fitting, overlap, aligned elements, kerning, and perhaps repetition.

PROCEDURE:

1. Choose typefaces

Choose several typefaces that appeal to you and may somehow represent aspects of your personality.

2. Compose your logotypes

Look at the shape of your name to get ideas for creative fitting, alignments, and overlap. (You can use as many separate text boxes and/or layers as you need.)

Experiment with these kinds of type contrast:
Scale Case
Weight
Structure (be sure to try using different typefaces together)
Direction
Tone

Use each of the above at least once in one of your three logotypes. Also, use overlap, fitting, and alignment. Look for an opportunity to use repetition as well. Kern all type carefully. (If you are using InDesign or Illustrator, the application Skills Modules introduce new skills in manipulating type and integrating pictures with type, which can be used to extend this exercise with modified letters, invented ligature, or integration of illustrations with letters.)

Figure 5-25 Student logotypes

3. Arrange logotypes on the page

When you finish each logotype, group together all the parts, and scale it to about four inches wide. When you finish all three, arrange them on the page to make an effective presentation.

4. Print your work

After you've completed the arrangement, print your work (File menu > Print). Then look at it carefully to see if it needs further adjustments before presenting it for critique.

Assessment Criteria

_____ Three very different logotypes of name

_____ Only black and gray

Used six kinds of type contrast:

_____ Scale

_____ Weight

_____ Case

_____ Structure

_____ Direction

_____ Tone

_____ Creative use of fitting

_____ Creative use of overlap

_____ Creative alignments of elements

_____ Creative use of repetition

_____ (Optional: Modified letters, invented ligature, or integration of illustrations with letters)

_____ Kerning

_____ Logotypes scaled and arranged to make an effective presentation on the page

CHAPTER 6

Resources of Style, Sources of Inspiration: The History of Typographic Design

Study of the history of typography will sharpen your perception and expand your creative resources.

OBJECTIVES

- ¤ To understand how letterforms, conventions of punctuation, and layout have changed in response to how they were used, the materials and tools used to create them, and the values of the people who used them.
- ¤ To begin to develop a resource of past styles that can be used solve creative problems today.

Typography can be thought of as a reservoir of its history. It has been continuously renewed by innovation, but it still contains traces that have accumulated since its earliest beginnings. The origins of our letters can be traced back thousands of years. Over this time, the shapes of letterforms have been transformed in response to how they were used, the materials and tools that were used to create them, and the values of the people who used them. The norms of punctuation and layout that we take for granted today have evolved in response to similar influences.

Delving into this history will expand your knowledge of past styles that can be used solve creative problems today. It will deepen your understanding of the function and forms of typographic expression. Moreover, it will demonstrate that the current conventions of typography are part of a process of continual evolution that you, as a designer, may take a hand in shaping.

Before the Alphabet

Before the invention of writing, early societies used simple stylized pictures to record and convey information. We call such symbols **pictographs**. (See Figure 6-1.) Today, pictographic symbols are often

> "**Type** is one of the most eloquent means of expression in every epoch of style. Next to architecture, it gives the most characteristic portrait of a period and the most severe testimony of a nation's intellectual status."
>
> —Peter Behrens

Figure 6-1 Drawings of prehistoric pictographs

Figure 6-2 A modern pictographic ideograph

used in public signage—I'm sure you'll recognize the symbol shown in Figure 6-2. But in fact, this pictograph conveys to us something different than what is shown. We don't take it to mean "man;" instead, we understand it to mean "men's room" (the contents of which most people might prefer not to see graphically depicted). In this case, the pictograph functions as an **ideograph**: a symbol that is conventionally used to represent an idea. Ideographs need not be pictographic—they can be completely abstract such as these common symbols: $ and &.

The first written language was developed about 5000 years ago by the Sumerians in the region of Mesopotamia, which corresponds to modern day Iraq. This language, which we call **cuneiform**, was originally developed to keep track of the extensive amounts of goods paid to the rulers as taxes. Later, writing was used for recording history, law, religion, science, and literature.

Cuneiform had it origins in pictographic symbols, but, over long years of usage, the symbols became progressively more abstract. This evolution was decisively influenced by the media that was used to write the language. Early on, the Sumerians began to draw pictographs into wet clay tablets that could be baked to make the record permanent. Then, an ingenious way was found to speed up the writing process. Instead of drawing lines, a stick (or *stylus*) with a wedge on the end was used to form straight lines with one quick poke. Of course, this meant that the resulting characters could no longer have any curved lines; this made them almost entirely abstract. (See Figure 6-4.) The term cuneiform comes from Latin root words that mean "wedge-shaped."

Figure 6-3 Sumerian cuneiform, *circa* 21st century BCE *Courtesy University of Minnesota Library Special Collections*

Figure 6-4 A demonstration of the evolution from pictograph to abstract cuneiform

With a different character for each word, a scribe would have to learn thousands of different symbols to master a relatively modest vocabulary. And, of course, there would always be a problem when a new word was needed. These problems were relieved somewhat by using **rebus**, which combine different pictures to sound out an unrelated word. (See Figure 6-5.)

Later, some characters came to be used conventionally to stand for phonetic syllables that could be combined into words. Using such **syllabary**, the Assyrians were able to simplify their writing to a mere 560 characters! Still, this system (and others likes it) required extensive years of training, so few people learned to read and write. Those who could master these skills were guaranteed high status jobs.

Like cuneiform, the writing of the ancient Egyptians used ideographs, rebus, and syllabary. The **hieroglyph**, or "priestly writing," which was primarily used in religious contexts, retained elegant pictographic characters for about 3000 years. The more informal hieratic manuscript form was more stylized. By about 400 BCE, demotic (or "popular") script, which was used by larger segments of society, became almost completely abstract.

The Egyptians produced an early form of paper from the papyrus reed that grew in the mouth of the Nile river. The reeds were cut into strips, overlapped, pounded flat, and left to dry, producing a single piece that could be used in a scroll over 40 yards long.

Chinese ideographs underwent a similar evolution from early pictographs to abstract characters. In this case, the forms of characters were transformed through the influence of the tapered calligraphic brush, which easily produces wide varieties of line. Because this tool is extremely responsive to the gesture of the artist's hand, brush calligraphy can express the personality and feelings of the artist. In China, it is traditionally considered the highest form of art.

Figure 6-5 A rebus works like a riddle based on visual pun. This one is an English word that means something like self-control. Can you "read" it?

To find: 'Gem'   Gold: 'Nub'

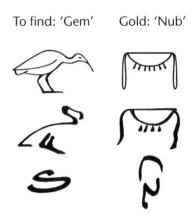

Figure 6-6 On the top row are two Egyptian hieroglyphs, below them are the same words in a more stylized hieratic manuscript form used from 3000 to 1900 BCE. and on the bottom are examples of abstract demotic (or "popular") script from 700 to 30 BCE.

Forest   Mountain   House

Figure 6-7 The top row shows early Chinese pictographs as they were inscribed onto bronze pots about 1000 BCE. Brush calligraphy started with the official Li style about 25 AD. On the bottom, the same characters are shown in the later Regular (Kai and Zhen) style that began 173 AD. *Bottom row: Calligraphy by Hong Zhang*

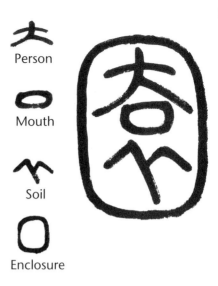

Figure 6-8 There are only about 270 Chinese pictographs, but they are combined to form tens of thousand of ideographs. The ideograph for garden is made up of the pictographs for person, mouth, soil, and enclosure. *Calligraphy by Hong Zhang*

Person

Mouth

Soil

Enclosure

The Phonetic Alphabet and the Forms of Letters

Ancient inscriptions recently discovered in the Sinai desert demonstrate that the characters of our alphabet originated from Egyptian characters. These characters were used by Semitic mercenaries. ("Semite" is a general name for tribes from the area of modern-day Lebanon, Israel, and Palestine; apparently these mercenaries, like the ancient Hebrews, traveled to Egypt to find employment.) It makes sense that military units would have use for written communication, but of course, it would be too expensive to hire highly trained scribes. A simpler system of writing was needed. The genius of the phonetic alphabet is that a mere couple of dozen signs can be used to form any word whatsoever. This is possible because the letters don't stand for particular objects or ideas, but instead, they denote elemental sounds that are combined to form aural words. It is a system that any child can learn to use. It surely ranks among the most important inventions in human history. Since its inception, writing has not only been an invaluable tool for communications, but also, by fixing ideas down so that they can be reconsidered, it has proven to be a major tool to enhance the very process of thinking as well. Today the alphabet has been adapted in many variations to diverse languages worldwide.

Beginning about 1500 BCE, the **Phoenicians**, a Semitic nation of seafaring traders, spread the alphabet throughout the eastern Mediterranean. (See Figure 6-9.) Their alphabet was adapted by the Aramaic people. Aramaic script, in turn, later became the basis of both the Hebrew and Arabic alphabets. These early alphabets got along without any vowels—thy wr wrttn bscly lk ths. Unlike our writing, their writing ran from right to left, probably because it was easier to carve letters in that direction.

Figure 6-9 Several Phoenician characters are recognizable as the prototypes of our own letters.

Figure 6-10 Early Greek inscriptions retain the rugged rhythm of Phoenician script.

Figure 6-11 Later Greek letters are more equilateral in proportion, are geometric in construction, and have open counters. *Courtesy Art Resource, Photo: Erich Lessing*

The Greeks adapted the Phoenician alphabet to their language by 750 BCE. The ancient Greeks, of course, are well known for their interest in analytical thinking and pursuit of ideals. These values informed the styling of the letters that they carved on their stone monuments. Undoubtedly, they were also influenced by the fact that a monument, unlike a scrawled note, is designed to endure and be seen by generations of people.

Whereas early Greek inscriptions retained the rugged rhythm of Phoenician script, later examples are models of regularity. Evenly spaced characters sit squarely on their baselines. The letters are more equilateral in proportion, are geometric in construction, and have open counters. (See Figure 6-11.) This was the origin of **square capitals**, which were the basis of the oldstyle roman capital letters that we still use today.

The Greeks brought their alphabet to their colonies on the Italian peninsula, and it was soon adopted by the native Etruscans. From them, it spread to the Romans, who ultimately extended its use throughout Europe. Of course the Romans, like the others before them, adapted the alphabet to meet their needs. Their alphabet looks much more familiar to us than the earlier Greek alphabet in both the forms of letters and their order. Nevertheless, the lineage of our abstract alphabet characters can be traced back to ancient pictographs. (See Figure 6-12.)

Roman scribes used a flat-nibbed pen that could be turned to produce both thick and thin strokes. For larger signage, a flat reed brush was used for a similar effect. The brush was also used to draw letters before they were carved in stone inscriptions.

The mature form of the roman square capital is perhaps best exemplified by the inscription at the base of the Column of Emperor Trajan (*circa* AD 114), which still stands below the Capitaline Hill in Rome. (See Figure 6-13.) This inscription has inspired designers of letters for hundreds of years. Here, the rigorous geometric clarity of earlier Greek

Pictographs	Phoenician Letters	Early Greek Letters	Roman Capitals

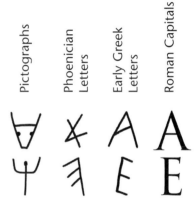

Figure 6-12 Evolution from pictographs to roman capital letters.

Figure 6-13 Inscription from the Column of Emperor Trajan, *circa* AD 113, Rome.
Courtesy Johannes A. Muess, The Beautiful Alphabet, *ABC26*

models has been further refined. The wide-set width of many characters and overall openness create a majestic effect. This effect is aided by the Roman innovations of delicately contrasting thick and thin strokes and prominent serifs.

The origin of serifs is unclear. The function of these little cross-strokes is undoubtedly to define a clean end for the main strokes, but whether they were first used by brush lettererk s or by stone carvers is a matter of dispute among scholars.

During the third century AD, a rounded style of letter was developed for manuscript writing. In Figure 6-14, the second line through the seventh were written in this style. Later scholars labeled this style **uncial** (pronounced "un-shul"), after the Latin word for "inch" because some early examples were written on baselines spaced one inch apart. This letterform was more efficient for scribing with ink. For instance, an uncial *E* can be written with only three strokes, while a square capital requires four. If you imagine the labor of copying entire books by hand you'll understand this difference wasn't trivial! Another advantage of the rounded form of these letters was that it minimized square corners that tended to fill with ink.

The uncial broke the uniform height of capital letters by introducing short ascenders on the D, H, K, and L and descenders on the F, G, P, Q, and Y. These features added a new structural contrast between the forms of letters that unquestionably aided to their legibility. By the sixth century, these features were exaggerated in the letterforms that we call **"half uncials"**. (See Figure 6-14, the eighth line and after.) This style is the ancestor of our modern "lowercase" letters, but the concept of using a "double alphabet" of capital and small letters wasn't developed until the 15th century.

Figure 6-14 This page from the time of Charlemagne, *circa* AD 855, shows **uncials** in lines 2 through 7, while those below are half uncials, the ancestor of our lowercase letters. The extravagantly large and decorative initial capital is tied to the body text by large opening lines. Today, designers still use "drop caps" and "lead-in lines" to pull readers into a text.

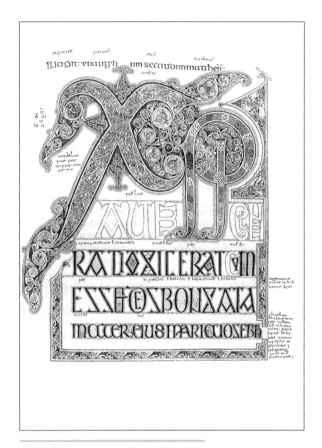

Figure 6-15 This page from the Celtic *Lindisfarne Gospels, circa* AD 698, is a masterful example of contrasts. The composition is dominated by the enormous and intensely decorated opening letters *Chi* and *Rho* which represent the name of Christ. The dynamic sweep of the first is opposed by the static geometry of the second. Both of these stand out from the ample white space on the page and contrast decisively with outlined letters below. These, in turn, contrast with the weight and bright colors of the last two lines. There are four distinct styles of letters on this page.

Early Letter Spacing, Punctuation, and Layout

Early writing had virtually none of the conventions of spacing and punctuation that we take for granted today. For instance:

UNTILTHENINTHCENTURY
WORDSUSUALLYRANTOGETHER
WITHOUTSEPARATION
EARLYGREEKINSCRIPTIONSEVEN
SWITCHEDDIRECTIONFROMLINETOLINE

AS PUNCTUATION DEVELOPED · IT DIFFERED
WIDELY FROM PLACE TO PLACE AND EVEN
FROM SCRIBE TO SCRIBE · IT WAS USUALLY
THOUGHT OF AS CUES FOR ORAL READING
RATHER THAN SYNTACTIC STRUCTURE ·

THE EARLY GREEKS DIVIDED TEXTS INTO PARAGRAPHS
USING SHORT HORIZONTAL LINES

Later the beginnings of paragraphs were sometimes marked by moving the initial letter into the margin . so called „hanging indents„ are still used for some purposes today . these initial letters were sometimes colored enlarged or elaborately decorated.

Around the eighth century manuscripts from irish monasteries glorified christian texts with ornate embellishment . they were also among the first to mix different forms of script on the same page . see figure 6.15 .

Medieval Manuscript

The disintegration of the Roman Empire in the fifth century brought a period of lawless disorder as various barbarian tribes battled for territory. Literacy nearly became a lost art in Europe. It was kept alive in enclosed and fortified Christian monasteries, which were run with factory-like efficiency. Among the many useful crafts produced, perhaps the most important for later civilization were the texts copied in workshops called *scriptoria*.

A simple 200-page manuscript took a scribe about five months to copy. Therefore, even the plainest book was a rare and valuable commodity. But religious texts were typically made far more precious with fabulous decoration that integrated thin gold leaf. The hand-painted pictures in these manuscripts have been called "illuminations" because of the shimmering quality of the gold included in them.

The island of Ireland was relatively secluded from the turmoil that shook most of Europe from the fifth century through the eighth century. This enabled Celtic (pronounced: "kel-tic") monasteries to produce manuscripts that were a high-point of graphic expression during this period. The complex interwoven decoration of these manuscripts reflects styles that had long been used in jewelry and other objects by Celts and other Germanic tribes such as Saxons and Vikings.

Toward the end of the eighth century, a time of relative peace and stability began when the Frankish king Charlemagne managed to consolidate a feudal empire in central Europe. He soon found that he needed literate administrators to run his vast domain, so he encouraged the Church to found schools. However, during the chaos of the preceding centuries, there had been such little intercommunication between different regions that local styles of writing had become practically unintelligible to each other. Charlemagne solved this problem by bringing scribes from throughout his realm to his palace at Aachen where they were tutored in writing by the English scholar Alcuin of York. These scribes mastered a clear form of the uncial, as well as a form closely related to the half-uncial called "minuscule" (this term is also used to denote the modern "lowercase" letters that descend from them). Roman square capitals were used in the manuscripts for chapter heads, initial capitals, and lead-in lines. The time of Charlemagne's rule is referred to as "Carolingian" (the *g* is silent), after his latin name *Karolus*. After this period of stability, Europe devolved again into anarchy.

The end of the millennium saw a resurgence of feudal domination. However, significant numbers of peasants gradually broke free of serfdom to support themselves with crafts and mercantile trade. By the beginning of the Gothic period in the 12th century, new cities were established that included a prosperous middle class. These entrepreneurs valued education. They established universities and the rise in literacy vastly expanded the market for books.

Unfortunately, commercial trade across Europe also had the effect of spreading deadly plagues which soon decimated from one-quarter to one-third of the population. The Hundred Years' War between England and France—with the first use of the cannon in Europe—was also responsible for immense carnage. Against this harsh background the Book of Revelation, which foretold the Last Judgment, became a best seller.

During this time, a new style of writing gradually replaced Carolingian uncials and minuscules. **Textura** (or *blackletter*) script is

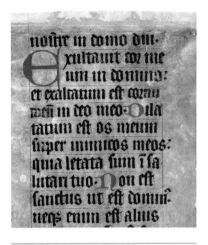

Figure 6-16 Twelfth century textura manuscript. *Courtesy University of Minnesota Library Special Collections*

dominated by thick, closely spaced, vertical strokes topped with pointed serifs. For this reason, it has been compared to a black picket fence. (See Figure 6-16.) Its dense and even texture on the page led others to compare it to woven textile—this is where it got its name.

This style was very efficient, both in terms of speed of execution and in the number of words that could fit on a page. Scribes drew the vertical strokes for each word first, then the word was completed by the addition of thin diagonal lines that virtually replaced all curved strokes. To the modern eye, textura feels heavy and is hard to read because the shapes of its letters are so similar. But the sharp angles and claustrophobic density of this style expresses a feeling of stern authority that seems to have fit religious literature particularly well. Variations of this style remained popular in Germany until after World War II.

Another style of writing was developed in the 14th century by humanist scholars who devoted themselves to secular (nonreligious) studies. They had a new belief in the power of human reason and the dignity of the individual. This led to renewed interest in secular literature from ancient Greece and Rome and paved the way for the Renaissance. Because many ancient texts had been copied during the Carolingian period, the scholars mistook the minuscule of that period for *littera antiqua* (ancient letters). From this source they developed a style that was used for secular manuscripts. (See Figure 6-17.)

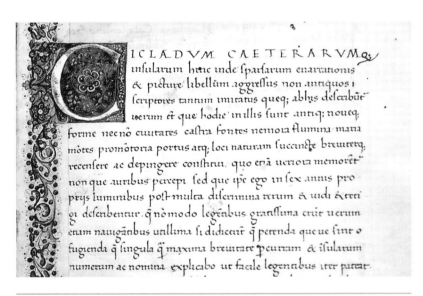

Figure 6-17 An example of hand-scripted humanist *littera antiqua.* Note that there are no capital letters in the body text. *Courtesy University of Minnesota Library Special Collections*

The Typographic Revolution

The soaring demand for books stimulated the search for a more efficient way to produce them. Woodblock printing had been invented in China during the 9th century and had made its way to Europe by the 12th century, but it was very difficult to produce book-length text with this method. An outstanding breakthrough occurred in the middle of the 15th century, when the German inventor Johann zum **Gutenberg** developed a method of printing that used individually cast pieces of metal type for each character. The pieces of type were put together to "compose" pages. After all the copies of a page were printed, the type could be reused in new ones. This was the beginning of "typography" in the true sense of the word. The use of metal type dominated printing for the next 500 years.

Gutenberg worked ten years to develop his process before his first printing. This is how type was made: A hard steel punch was carved in the shape of each character in the font set. Each punch was hammered into a block of brass or copper to make a hollow impression of the letter. This, in turn, was locked into a mold that was used to cast the type.

Gutenberg had to develop a new metal alloy to cast type with. He used about 80% lead because of its low melting temperature, 5% tin to add strength, and 15% antimony, a metal that expands as it cools down so it compensated for the shrinkage of the others. Imagine how much experimentation it took to arrive at this ingenious combination! Gutenberg also developed a new kind of oil-based ink that would stick evenly to the metal type. He modeled his printing press on the presses used by winemakers.

The earliest typographic book is called the *Forty-two Line Bible*, for the number of lines on most of the pages. This work was no small feat. It measures 11.75" × 15" and consists of 1182 pages in two volumes. It was made to closely resemble the manuscripts of the time. Each page has two columns of densely black justified columns of textura divided by ¾" gutter space and set off against generous margins. Colored elements such as headers, drop caps, and initial lines of text were added by hand after the printing.

For this work, Gutenberg and his staff created a font set of 290 characters that included upper and lowercase letters, numerals, punctuation, and a rich array of ligatures and alternate characters. Each page used over 2500 characters—but, thankfully, they could be reused! Even so, the work required more than 15,000 pieces of type.

Unfortunately, while Gutenberg was busy with research and production, he ran up some stiff debts. He had nearly completed his first edition of 180 books on paper and 30 on fine calfskin vellum when his partner foreclosed on his debts and locked him out of his shop!

In 1450 there were only 50,000 books in all of Europe. A collection of a dozen books was considered an outstanding library. But by 1500,

Figure 6-18 The *Gutenberg Forty-two Line Bible. Courtesy of Library of Congress*

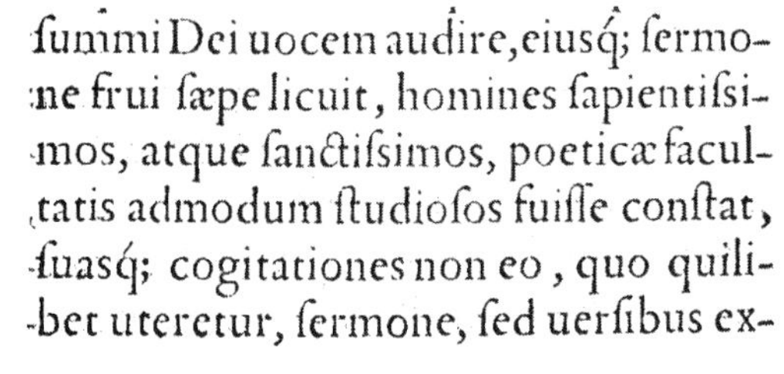

Figure 6-22 A sample of Griffo's roman type for Aldus Manutius. *Courtesy University of Minnesota Library Special Collections*

ſummi Dei uocem audire, eiuſq; ſermone frui ſæpe licuit, homines ſapientiſsi-
mos, atque ſanctiſsimos, poeticæ facul-
tatis admodum ſtudioſos fuiſſe conſtat,
ſuaſq; cogitationes non eo, quo quili-
bet uteretur, ſermone, ſed uerſibus ex-

contrast between thick and thin strokes than Jensen's, the serifs are more delicate, and evenness of tone was improved by making the caps shorter than the ascenders so they don't stick out as much.

Manutius directed Griffo to create the first **italic** typeface. Nowadays, we consider italic typefaces as alternatives to regular roman faces that are used for emphasis. But that wasn't their original purpose. They were developed to conserve space in Manutius' small books. Griffo based his italic on the fancy calligraphic script called *cancellaresca,* or **chancery,** which was used at the time for correspondence and documents in the Church, business, and government. The condensed letterforms and close fit of italic enabled Manutius to get 50 percent more words on each line. It was not until about fifty years later that an italic typeface was designed to be paired with a roman type.

Much intellectual effort was spent in trying to create ideal forms for letters. Mathematicians studied ancient Roman inscriptions and declared the optimal proportion for the width of the heavy stroke in a capital was one-tenth of its height. Treatises were published demonstrating methods of geometric construction of letters and basing proportions on the human body, face, and other natural forms. (See Figure 6-24.)

In 1529, Geoffrey Tory, a French calligrapher, engraver, illustrator, book seller, publisher, printer, and university professor, published an influential treatise poetically entitled *Champ Fleury* (flowery garden): *The Art and Science of the Proper and True Proportions of the Attic Letters, Which Are Otherwise Called Antique Letters, and in Common Speech Roman Letters.* Tory introduced a new lightness and clarity to book design with layouts that carefully coordinated the weights of illustration, decoration, and type.

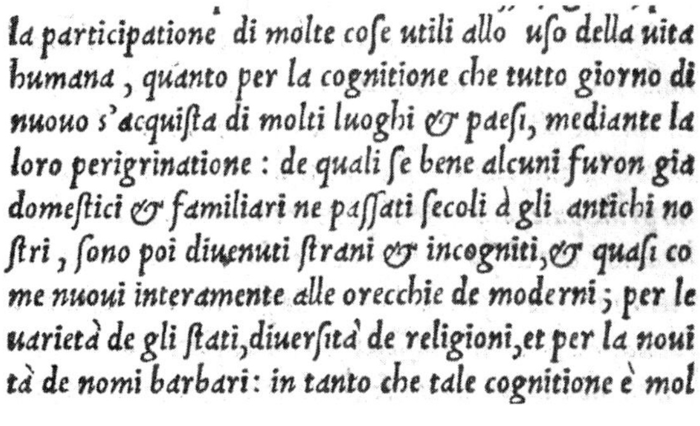

Figure 6-23 A sample of Griffo's early italic. *Courtesy University of Minnesota Library Special Collections*

la participatione di molte coſe utili allo uſo della uita
humana, quanto per la cognitione che tutto giorno di
nuouo s'acquiſta di molti luoghi & paeſi, mediante la
loro perigrinatione : de quali ſe bene alcuni furon gia
domeſtici & familiari ne paſſati ſecoli a gli antichi no
ſtri, ſono poi diuenuti ſtrani & incogniti, & quaſi co
me nuoui interamente alle orecchie de moderni ; per le
uarietà de gli ſtati, diuerſità de religioni, et per la noui
tà de nomi barbari : in tanto che tale cognitione e mol

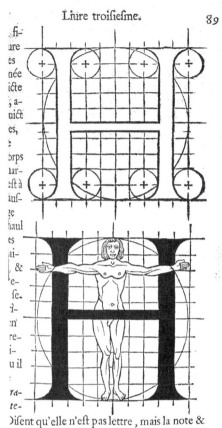

Figure 6-24 Geoffrey Tory based letter proportion on geometry and the human body. *Courtesy University of Minnesota Library Special Collections*

Garamond
Garamond
Garamond

Figure 6-25 Comparison of Adobe Garamond with URW Garamond. At bottom their outlines are superimposed. Can you see the differences?

Tory's sometime assistant, Claude Garamond, went on to become the first typographer to devote himself entirely to cutting punches and casting type. Basing his designs on Griffo's Bembo font, he developed typefaces that one critic has called "delectable." They have an elegant lightness that is accentuated by long ascenders and descenders and by the small size of the enclosed counters in the letters *a* and *e*. Their snug fit allowed closer word spacing. The quality and sheer quantity of roman type that Garamond created played a major role in the near elimination of textura type in Europe. Robert Granjan later designed italics that were paired with Garamond's faces.

Today, many revival fonts bear Garamond's name, but there are wide differences between them. This is because some of these designs were based on the work of another designer that had been mistakenly attributed to Garamond.

Figure 6-26 Renaissance engraved initial by Geofroy Tory, Paris 1521

Figure 6-27 Renaissance engraved initial from Abel Angelier's publishing house, Paris 1552

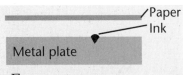

ENGRAVING

In engraving, lines are inscribed into a flat plate. Then, ink is applied to the plate's surface. Next, the plate is wiped clean, but the ink stays in the linear depressions. Finally, paper is pressed onto the plate to pick up the ink image.

The technology of metal type, of course, imposed certain limitations on both letter design and layout. The length of swashes could not extend far beyond the base area of the type, and it wasn't easy to integrate type with pictures. These limitations created a survival niche for the older practice of wood block printing. Another printing process called engraving also provided an alternative. (See Figure 6-26 and Figure 6-27.)

After the fabulous innovations of the Renaissance period, the absolute monarchs of the 17th century felt threatened by free presses, so they imposed strict limitations on printing, and for a time there was little progress in typography.

The Modern Impulse

The dawn of the Modern age may be traced to the late 17th century court of Louis XIV of France. Known as the "Sun King," this monarch established central control by bringing nobility from throughout his kingdom to his palace at Versailles. Likewise, he gathered the greatest scholars of his time to his court, where they consulted on all matters of concern. Ironically, this concentration of intellectuals ultimately produced the philosophy of the Enlightenment, which in turn inspired the revolution that overthrew the monarchy about a century later.

In 1692 Louis XIV commanded the formation of a committee of scholars to research and design a new typeface for his royal press. The result was called **Romain du Roi**. ("The King's Roman;" pronounced "ro-men dew rwa"). (See Figure 6-28.) This typeface, unlike any that came before it, was based on mathematics instead of art—the engineer had replaced the calligrapher. The remnants of hand gesture are gone. Instead, the crisp geometric regularity of this face, its slender pointed serifs, and the vertical axis of stress in its round letters, give this typeface a new feeling of mechanical precision. Contrast within letterforms was increased by making the thin strokes lighter; this gave blocks of type an unquiet quality that has been called **dazzle**. Romain du Roi is the earliest typeface to be called a **transitional roman** because it differed decisively with oldstyle and anticipates many features of the modern roman to come.

The movement toward geometric simplification was reversed during much of the 1700s when an ornate style of aristocratic luxury called **rococo** was dominant. This style featured elaborate curlicue ornaments and complex decorative borders. (See Figure 6-29.) Typographer Pierre Simon Fournier le Jeune created many exotic typefaces with outlined or shaded forms and fancy floral decoration. Even so, Fournier did much to rationalize the design of type. Basing his roman type on the Romain du Roi, he pioneered the concept of designing compatible typefaces in various weights and proportions, as well as italic, which could function together as what we call a "type family." In 1737, he published a system of type measurement that prefigured the modern system of points and picas.

Meanwhile, across the English channel, William Caslon developed typefaces that diverged from the trend toward mechanical regularity in other ways. (See Figure 6-30.) Caslon took as his source the Dutch typefaces of his time, which in turn owed much to Venetian oldstyle (such as Jensen and Griffo). Like the designers of the Romain du Roi, he chose to increase the contrast between the thin and thick strokes. But instead of lightening the former, he added weight to the later, giving the type a sturdy feel. He designed small inconsistencies into his type that increased its legibility and gave it a lively uneven rhythm. The results have been called "comfortable" and "friendly to the eye." His work became so popular that it dominated printing in Britain and her colonies for about sixty years. Benjamin Franklin chose Caslon type to print the U.S. Declaration of Independence.

The high point of the transitional roman style was produced in the later part of the century by John Baskerville. After amassing a fortune by manufacturing cheap household trinkets, Baskerville devoted himself to all aspects of printing and book making with perfectionist zeal. Baskerville followed the example of the Romain du Roi by reducing the thin strokes in his letters to hairline width. (See Figure 6-31.) But, unlike this precedent, he added a little weight to the thick strokes. This created a new level of contrast in the type while maintaining an overall effect of lightness. This quality is reinforced by the wide set of his characters, by their long ascenders and descenders, and by his use of wide letter spacing and word spacing. An overly mechanical look was avoided by employing a slightly slanted axis of stress in the round characters, and by using heavily bracketed serifs that flow gracefully from the main strokes to end in fine points. He eliminated ornament from his pages and used generous margins. The results are as imposing as the inscription on the base of Trajan's column.

To achieve the standards of quality that he demanded, Baskerville improved the printing presses of his day to produce a more even impression. He reformulated the ink for greater blackness and developed glossy smooth hot-press paper that could show the subtle qualities of his type. He was known to melt down his type after each printing and to destroy a large percentage of each press run.

During his lifetime, Baskerville's work was criticized in England as being too harsh on the eyes. However, events on the Continent created an environment more receptive to its influence. As the 18th century progressed, the tide turned against the sensual decadence of the rococo style. Enlightenment philosophers such as Denis Diderot called for rationality and moral virtue. Philosophy, science, and patriotism became fashionable. In this context, the authoritative clarity of Baskerville's typography was enthusiastically received.

The **modern roman** style was developed in Parma, Italy, by Giambattista Bodoni and, at about the same time, by Didot *("dee-doe")*

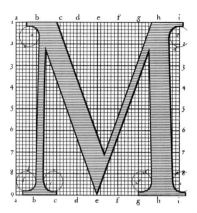

Figure 6-28 An engraved study for the Romain du Roi, planned by a committee of scholars headed by Nicolas Jaugeon and executed by Louis Simonneau, 1695. *Courtesy Princeton Architectural Press*

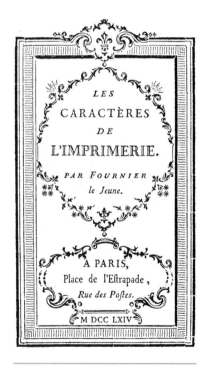

Figure 6-29 Fournier le Jeune. *Courtesy University of Minnesota Library Special Collections*

Figure 6-30 Caslon type specimen

PARAGON ROMAN.

Quoufque tandem abutere, Catilina, patientia noftra? quamdiu nos etiam furor ifte tuus eludet? quem ad finem fefe effrenata jactabit audacia? nihilne te nocturnum præfidium palatii, nihil urbis vigiliæ, nihil timor populi, nihil confenfus bonorum omnium, nihil hic munitiffimus habendi fenatus locus, nihil horum ora vultufque moverunt? patere tua confilia non fentis A B C D E F G H I J K L M N O

Figure 6-31 Baskerville's preface to his 1758 edition of Milton. *Courtesy University of Minnesota Library Special Collections*

PREFACE.

A MONGST the feveral mechanic Arts that have engaged my attention, there is no one which I have purfued with fo much fteadinefs and pleafure, as that of *Letter-Founding*. Having been an early admirer of the beauty of Letters, I became infenfibly defirous of contributing to the perfection of them. I formed to my felf Ideas of greater accuracy than had yet appeared, and have endeavoured to produce a *Sett* of *Types* according to what I conceived to be their true proportion.

in Paris. (See Figure 6-29.) These typographers followed Baskerville's example in their spare and open layouts, but exceeded him in formulating letterforms with geometric precision. Their typefaces featured extreme contrast between thick and thin strokes, hairline serifs with little or no brackets, and rigorously vertical stress. All of this contributes to the feeling that these letters are creations of mind and machine rather than the hand. These type faces were constructed out of rigorously repeated shape modules; this anticipates the way of thinking that led to industrial mass production in the next century. But, it has often been observed that the commanding presence of these typefaces actually distracts from their readability. Type historian Allan Haley has written that Bodoni's works were "regal efforts to looked upon and appreciated as works of art rather than as mere pieces of communication. His work was probably the most honored—and least read—printing of his time."

Figure 6-32 Pages from Bodoni's Manuale Tipografico

François Ambroise Didot developed *maigre* (thin) and *gras* (fat) type styles similar to today's condensed and expanded fonts. He revised Fournier's measurement system in 1785, dividing the French inch into 72 points. This system is still used in France today.

Victorian Type:
An Aesthetic of Enrichment

The Industrial Revolution (about 1760–1850) created a flood of new products and a greatly expanded market of urban consumers. The walls of cities grew thick with advertising posters that clamored for attention. New typefaces were needed that wouldn't get lost in this clutter, and so type founders competed to produce type of ever greater size and novelty. The distinctive style that dominated much of the 19th century is called **Victorian** after the queen that ruled Great Britain from 1837 to 1901.

It was found that when type was cast at large sizes, the cooling of the metal was uneven and this made the type uneven and brittle. The type

HOPE springs

Figure 6-33 A fat face named Thorowgood, 1821. *Courtesy Dan X. Solo and Dover Press*

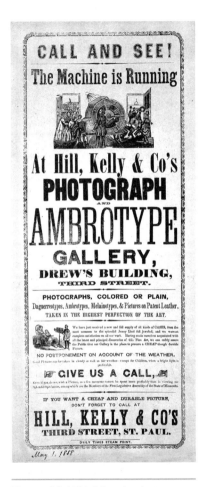

Figure 6-34 This Victorian letterpress broadside contains fat face, slab serif, and gothic type. *Courtesy Minnesota Historical Society*

was also very expensive, not to mention heavy. After the invention in 1827 of a new woodcutting tool called a lateral router, it soon became more practical to cut large display type from the end-grain of hardwood. Today, the many kinds of 19th century display type are collectively referred to as **wood type**.

The category of type called **fat faces** seems to have been inspired by the reasonable principle that visual impact depends on contrast—but it took that principle to a radical extreme! (See Figure 6-33.) Beginning with modern roman type, the width of the thick strokes was exaggerated to as much as one-half of the cap height. The distinctive look of this type made it popular, but, objectively speaking, it is not very readable from a distance: the light strokes virtually disappear and the counters were often shrunk to insignificance.

Later, **slab serif** faces were developed. These were more successful from the standpoint of readability. (See Figure 6-34.) With their heavy strokes and thick unbracketed square serifs, they hold up well over long distances. Their marketability was enhanced by naming them Antique or Egyptian, even though these names had no real relationship to their style. Instead, the bold geometric qualities of these faces gave them a mechanical feeling. Sometimes the serifs were exaggerated to extraordinary thickness. Gentler variations called Ionic, or Clarendon, were developed with bracketed serifs and moderately contrasting thick and thin strokes.

The newly rich Victorian middle class had a voracious appetite for decoration, so the complex ornamentation seen in rococo type was revived and expanded. Novelties such as elaborately complex serifs, exotic shapes, fancy decoration or textures, three-dimensional letterforms, and shadowing became the norm in headlines. (See Figure 6-32 and Figure 6-33.)

Running counter to the prevailing decorative trend, **sans serif** typefaces were probably first conceived by simply eliminating the serifs from slab serif designs. They went by several different names, the most common being **Grotesque**, or in the United States, **Gothic**. (See Figure 6-34.) Early examples were used at display sizes only, usually to set off a headline set in a fancier face. Lowercase letters for this category were rare until the middle of the century. Grotesques are generally distinguished by condensed letterforms with heavy monoweight strokes that thin at junctions. The vertical sides of round shapes were often straightened to make the set widths of letters consistent. An unusual feature of this quite geometric style is the languorous double-curve of the leg of the capital *R*.

By modern standards, many 19th century layouts could be used as textbook examples of bad design—the operative principles were "bigger" and "more." Type was usually set centered, stretching across the page. Typefaces were changed line by line; more than half a dozen could be used together. Heavy eclectic ornament dominated layouts and white space was virtually absent.

TWO-LINE GREAT PRIMER ORNAMENTED

MELODIOUS

TWO-LINE GREAT PRIMER ORNAMENTED, No. 3.

MELONS

TWO-LINE GREAT PRIMER ORNAMENTED, No. 4.

RIGHT STRIPE

TWO-LINE GREAT PRIMER ORNAMENTED, No. 5.

ROPE ONIONS

TWO-LINE GREAT PRIMER ORNAMENTED, No. 6.

BLENDING

MACKELLAR, SMITHS & JORDAN.

A CRITIC OF NINETEENTH CENTURY TYPOGRAPHY:

"OH! Sacred shades of Moxon and Van Dijke, of Baskerville and Bodoni! What would ye have said of the typographic monstrosities here exhibited?"

—Thomas Carson Hansard
Typographia, 1825

The U.S. dollar bill, even though it was designed in its present form in 1935, is a good example of a Victorian style engraving that integrates letters, elaborate decorative frames, and pictures. The new printing medium of lithography allowed lettering to run on curving lines and to be integrated together with colored images. (See Figure 6-32 and Figure 6-33.)

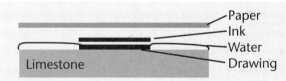

Paper
Ink
Water
Drawing
Limestone

LITHOGRAPHY

The word **lithography** comes from Latin words that mean "stone-printing." In this process, a design is drawn on a flat stone with a with a grease crayon or oil based ink. Then, the surface of the stone is flooded with water. The water is repelled from the oily areas of the drawing. When ink is applied to the surface, it only sticks to the oily areas—it is repelled from the wet areas. Last, paper is pressed onto the inked stone to receive the impression. The picture can be reprinted hundreds of times.

Unlike set type, with lithography, pictures and type can be freely overlapped because they are drawn at the same time. Separate stones were used to print different colors. Some lithographers were known to use as many as 40 different stones to print rich combinations of color.

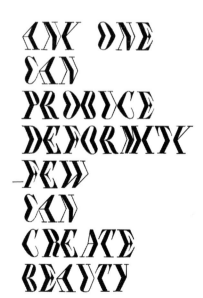

Figure 6-36 Another critique of Victorian excess by Theodore De Vinne, 1902

Figure 6-37 In spite of the complex decoration used in this Victorian product label, its clear contrasts make it very legible and appealing. *Courtesy Minnesota Historical Society*

Figure 6-38 Victorian lithographic poster. *Courtesy Minnesota Historical Society*

Figure 6-39 The opening pages of this book by William Morris (1894) is still quite Victorian in its heavy complexity and eclecticism, but his ideas greatly influenced design during his time and in the next century. *Courtesy University of Minnesota Library Special Collections*

The Arts and Crafts Movement:
A Bridge from Victorianism to the Future

In the last decades of the 19th century the **Arts and Crafts** movement arose as a passionate reaction against what William Morris called the "cheap and nasty" mass-produced goods that dominated the marketplace. Adherents believed that the quality of design in the everyday environment affected the character of individuals and ultimately of society as a whole. They were early developers of the *functionalist* and *formalist* ideals in design. **Functionalism** is the belief that design decisions should be based on the product's end purpose; this idea was later expressed by Adolf Loos' dictum "Form follows function." **Formalism** calls for honesty to the nature of media and good use of the elements and principles of design. Selwyn Image proclaimed that "all kinds of invented Form, and Tone, and Colour, are alike true and honorable aspects of Art" whether they be used in a water-pot or in a painting by Raphael. These ideas had powerful influence on many areas of art and design in the 20th century.

Morris, one of the leaders of this movement, was a writer of poetry, fiction, and philosophy; a lecturer; and a designer of furniture, stained glass, tapestry, carpets, and wallpaper. After attending a lecture by his friend Emery Walker on book design, typography, and printing, Morris was inspired to throw himself into these fields as well. In 1890, Morris and Walker founded the Kelmscott Press. They considered book production to be like building a "pocket cathedral." Their ideal of unified design required careful consideration of all elements: paper, ink, typefaces, spacing, margins, illustration, and decoration. Kelmscott Press inspired others to start a succession of small private presses that revived standards of typography and book production.

Dissatisfaction with available typefaces drove these designers to reach back to examples from the past. Morris modeled his first typeface, named Golden, on the work of Nicolas Jensen. (See Figure 6-40.) He photographed pages from an original book, enlarged them, and drew the letters, revising them time and again to arrive at maximum clarity and the best fit.

Later, Morris based another typeface, named Troy, on early Renaissance textura. He adapted elements from several sources to produce a very legible version of this usually difficult-to-read style. Troy kept the angular qualities that came from nib-pen calligraphy, but the letters were set wider, curved characters were made rounder, the counters were opened up, and the differences between similar-looking characters were increased. (See Figure 6-42 and Figure 6-43.)

The Arts and Crafts movement inspired generations of type designers to renew the stock of typefaces by reviving styles from the past. These efforts were given broad commercial distribution in the early gyue & take, they gyue that they haue & take that they haue not, Jhesu Cryst in this marchandyse gaf & toke, he toke that whiche in this world haboundeth, that is to wete to be born to laboure & to deye, he gafagayn to vs to be born spirituelly, to aryse & to regne pardurably. And he hymself cam to vs to take vylonyes and to gyue to us honour, to suffre deth and to gyue us lyf, to take pouerte & to gyue vs glorye. Seynt Gregore putteth iiii causes of the prouffyte of his comyng, sayeng ¶ Studebant omnes superbi de eadem stirpe progeniti, prospera

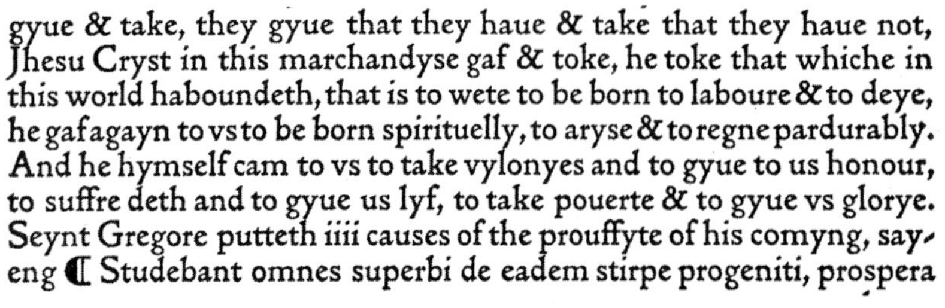

Figure 6-40 A sample of Morris' Golden type from *The Golden Legend by Voragine. Courtesy University of Minnesota Library Special Collections*

a c d e f g

a c d e f g

a c d e f g

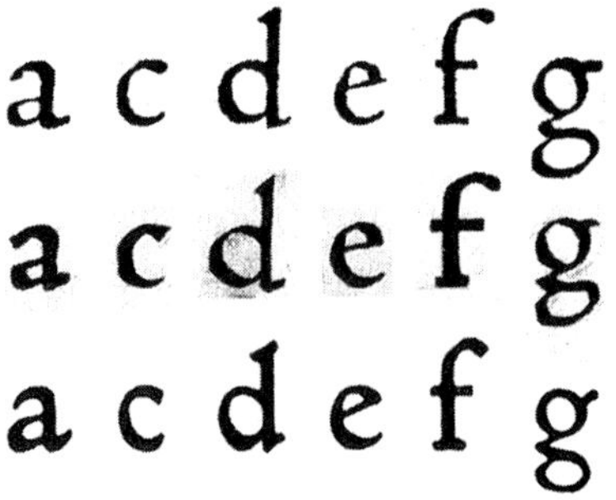

Figure 6-41 The top row shows Jenson's letters enlarged, the next row is a detail of Morris' drawings of Jenson's letters, on the bottom Golden letters are enlarged to the same scale. Morris' work is somewhat heavier than Jenson's, with less contrast in the weight of the strokes, shorter ascenders and thicker serifs. His interpretation is a bit closer to a Victorian slab serif face. *Top row: Detail of Figure 6-21, Middle row: Detail of preliminary drawing for the Golden type, Kelmscott Press Collection, Gift of John M. Craford, Jr., Pierpont Morgan Library; Bottom row: Detail of Figure 6-39*

20th century when innovations in typesetting technology and the consolidation of type foundries created a climate of intense competition. These companies found that the high quality and readability of revival faces made them key to winning greater market share.

Type designers of lasting impact that came out of the Arts and Crafts movement included Eric Gill and Rudolf Koch, who balanced traditionalism with innovation; Frederic Goudy, who designed 122 typefaces based on Renaissance and Medieval models; and Stanley Morrison, who supervised the creation of New Times Roman, one of the most popular typefaces of all time. Herman Zapf continued this tradition through mid-century.

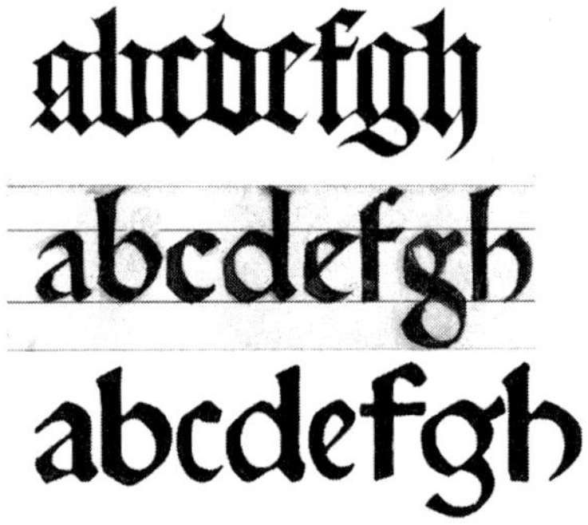

abcdefgh

abcdefgh

abcdefgh

Figure 6-42 At top are textura minuscules. In the next row, Morris' studies of Sweynheym and Pannartz early Subiaco type; *Reproduced by permission of The Huntington Library, San Marino, California.* At bottom, lowercase Troy. *Courtesy University of Minnesota Library Special Collections*

Figure 6-43 The top row shows Lombardic style capitals taken from an early Renaissance book. In the next row, Morris' studies for Troy are shown at actual size *(Reproduced by permission of The Huntington Library, San Marino, California)*. Below are Troy's final capitals. *Courtesy University of Minnesota Library Special Collections*

Art Nouveau

Art Nouveau was a highly fashionable international style in architecture, apparel, product design, and graphics, that began about a decade before the end of the 19th century. The many sources of this style included the Arts and Crafts movement, Japanese Ukiyo-e prints, and the work of Post-Impressionist painters such as Vincent Van Gogh and Paul Gauguin. It was the first self-consciously Modern design movement, but its elegantly flowing plant-like lines expressed a romantic desire to escape from mechanization. Lithographic posters often featured beautiful young women in exotic settings. Three-dimensional figures were often reduced to areas of intense flat color, or repeating patterns, bounded by calligraphic line. Lettering was integrated with the images. Alphonse Mucha was a major Art Nouveau poster artist. Henri van de Velde, Otto Eckmann, and O. Weisert were among those who created new typefaces in this style.

Arnold Boecklin

Figure 6-44 Art Nouveau stylebook by Alphonse Mucha. *Courtesy Dover Press*

Figure 6-45 The flowing shapes of this 1904 typeface by O. Weisert makes it a classic example of Art Nouveau.

Figure 6-46 Glasgow School poster by Charles Rennie Mackintosh and Maragret Macdonald-Mackintosh *(Minneapolis Institute of Arts, The Modernism Collection, gift of Norwest Bank Minnesota)*

Figure 6-47 Vienna Secession poster by Alfred Roller, 1902

Typography of the Machine Age

The flood of technological innovation around the turn of the century aroused expectations that the future would contrast decisively with the past. The functionalist efficiency of the machine inspired new styles that were simplified and geometric. On the other hand, the jarring experience of what has been called "the shock of the new" was reflected in styles that featured fragmentation and dislocation. Avant-garde designers, propelled by the fervent conviction that they were remaking the world, often combined these contradictory tendencies as they relentlessly experimented to discover new frontiers of style.

The Glasgow School and Vienna Secession rejected the fluidity of Art Nouveau for styles of greater geometric patterning and modular repetition.

Figure 6-48 German Expressionist poster by Max Pechstein, *circa* 1920. *Courtesy Museum of Modern Art, Gift of Leonard and Evelyn Lauder Fund, Licensed by Art Resource/Artists Rights Society, NY*

Figure 6-49 Cover of a book of Futurist poems by Filippo Marinetti. *Courtesy Museum of Modern Art, Jan Tschichold Collection, Gift of Philip Johnson, Licensed by Art Resource/Artists Rights Society, NY*

Contrary to the mechanistic trend in Modernism, **German Expressionism** celebrated intense emotions with graphics that had a rugged, hand-hewn look.

Futurism was an Italian movement that violently revolted against middle-class society and celebrated the innovations of the machine age. The founder, poet Filippo Marinetti, created a new typography style of energy and expressive force that he called "words in liberty," with extreme contrasts of scale, direction, color, and typeface.

Draft resistors escaping the devastation of World War I began the **Dada** movement in Zurich, Switzerland, and from there it spread internationally. They felt that if "rationality" had brought the horrible carnage of the war, they must embrace its opposite. Their work was characterized by absurdity, chance, and free improvisation. Designers such as Kurt Schwitters and Hans Arp experimented with extreme contrasts in typography and bizarre juxtapositions of type and images.

Emperor Fifteen
Modula Sans Regular

April Greiman, another former Weingart student, was among the first to exploit desktop production. But, she said, "To use these tools to imitate what we already know and think is a pity." Instead, she explored new options by creating compositions that overlaid text, images, and line art to create a sense of space on the page.

Another early adopter of Macintosh production was Dutch immigrant Rudy VanderLans. In the mid-1980s, he founded *Emigré*, a tabloid featuring international artists. Unhappy with the limited selection of digital typefaces available, his wife, Czech transplant Zuzana Licko, learned to design fonts for the magazine. She has said that her lack of training in traditional typography was actually an advantage when she designed her first typefaces because the structural forms that worked best with low-resolution bitmap fonts didn't fit with "the proper calligraphic foundation for a typeface." Instead, she learned to build letterforms pixel by pixel. When PostScript technology was introduced, Licko was able to refine her designs to more sophisticated forms. However, her approach to typographic design has always been to begin with the properties of the technology itself, instead of working from preconceived aesthetic ideals. The style of most of her typefaces has been called "neo-modern" because the "building block" geometry of much of her work related it to Bauhaus functionalism. Its bold clarity made it hold up to the radical demands of VanderLans' experimental layouts, while playful mannerisms gave it an edgy feel.

In his designs for *Emigré*, VanderLans rejected all traditional conventions. For instance, a sequence of pages might have several different articles woven through it, each identified by distinct paragraph attributes (such as typeface, size, and leading)—readers were tacitly invited to create their own interconnections between the different texts. In another instance, the text of a transcribed interview was layered over transcriptions of background sounds such as a barking dog. The reader would never know what to expect in this magazine because each issue was conceived as a "blank slate" to be totally reinvented.

Readers of *Emigré* expressed interest in Licko's typefaces, so she began to market them through ads in the magazine. Soon fonts by other avant-garde designers were added. By 1989, the font business financed the magazine. *Emigré* showcased the fonts and concentrated its editorial content on graphic design. The magazine became a laboratory for Postmodern graphic experimentation and theoretical discussion that attracted avant-garde designers from throughout the world.

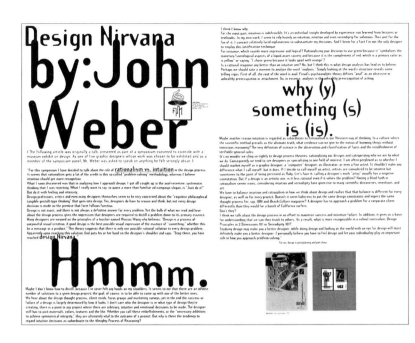

Figure 6-91 A two-page spread from Emigré, 1991. *Courtesy Emigré*

Emigré's distinctive typefaces became objects of controversy in the design community, but they were soon adopted by major art directors seeking a fresh look. (See Figure 6-92.) P Scott Makela's Dead History was an aggressive **hybrid** typeface that mixed together aspects of serif and sans-serif type. Barry Deck's Template Gothic was based on sign lettering that the designer encountered at his neighborhood laundromat; he said that its forms "more truly reflect the imperfect language of an imperfect world inhabited by imperfect beings." Jonathan Barnbrook's Exocet borrowed forms from early Greek inscription, but its bold forms and sharp barb-like serifs give it a menacing look (reinforced by its name taken from a guided missile). These typefaces went beyond merely representing the alphabet; they suggested narrative connotations.

Emigré's example inspired a wave of small independent digital "garage foundries." Internet marketing soon swelled their numbers. The resulting climate of competition pushed designers to come up with ever more novel innovations. One significant trend was the fashion for distressed **grunge** typefaces that looked as though they had been scraped, smashed, burnt, blurred, or run through the wash too many times. (See Figure 6-93.) Zuzana Licko responded by saying, "I believe this to be a reflection of our society's desperation about the vast technological changes which are taking away our familiar comforts of more traditional means of communication. [but] As efficient exchange of information becomes a requirement in tomorrow's information age, it stands to reason that a sophisticated, highly ordered means of typographic expression will be adopted instead."

Dead History
Template gothic
EXOCET

Figure 6-92 Emigré typefaces: P Scott Makela's Dead History, Barry Deck's Template Gothic, and Jonathan Barnbrook's Exocet. *Courtesy Emigré*

Crusti
HooskerDoo

Figure 6-93 Two classic grunge typefaces by CHANK!

Design Concepts Study Guide Chapter 6

After you have read the previous chapter, fill in the blanks with the letter of the correct answer within each section.

1. _____ simple stylized picture symbols are called

2. _____ A symbol that is conventionally used to represent an idea is called a(n)

3. _____ Combinations of different pictures used to sound out an unrelated word are called

4. _____ Characters conventionally used to stand for the phonetic sounds of syllables are called

5. _____ The first written language, developed by the Sumerians in Mesopotamia, was called

6. _____ Egyptian "priestly writing" is called

7. _____ About 1500 BCE, the phonetic alphabet (which later became the basis of the Hebrew, Arabic, Greek, and Roman alphabets) was spread throughout the eastern Mediterranean by the

A. syllabary

B. pictograph

C. Phoenicians

D. ideograph

E. cuneiform

F. rebus

G. hieroglyph

8. _____ The mature form of the roman square capital is perhaps best exemplified by the inscription at the base of the

9. _____ The rounded style of manuscript letters that developed in the third century AD is called

10. _____ WORDSUSUALLYRANTOGETHER WITHOUTSEPARATION

11. _____ Monasteries that produced manuscripts during the seventh through the ninth centuries, which featured complex interwoven decoration and were among the first to mix different forms of script on the same page, were called

12. _____ The Holy Roman Emperor that brought scribes from throughout his realm to his palace at Aachen to learn uncial and minuscule writing was

13. _____ The style of script (which began during the 12th century Gothic period) that is dominated by thick, closely spaced, vertical strokes topped with pointed serifs is called

14. _____ Humanist scholars adapted this style for secular manuscripts during the 14th century:

A. Charlemagne (Carolingian period)

B. *littera antiqua* (ancient letters)

C. textura (or blackletter)

D. until the ninth century

E. Column of Emperor Trajan (*circa* 114 AD)

F. uncial

G. Celtic

° °

15. _____ The German inventor of *movable type* (the method of printing that used individually cast pieces of metal type for each character) was

16. _____ The earliest typographic book is known as the

17. _____ About 1465, these German printers created the first *double alphabet*, integrating Roman capital letters with minuscules (small letters) based on the humanist *littera antiqua*:

18. _____ The French die-cutter who learned printing in Germany and then established a press in Venice, Italy, in 1468 and created an oldstyle roman typeface that continues to have influence today was

19. _____ The creator of the first italic typeface for the Venetian Renaissance, publisher Aldus Manutius, was

20. _____ The writer of an influential treatise on "the proper and true proportions of...roman letters" was

21. _____ The first typographer to devote himself entirely to cutting punches and casting type was

A. Nicolas Jenson

B. Claude Garamond

C. Johann zum Gutenberg

D. Geoffrey Tory

E. Forty-two Line Bible

F. Conrad Sweynheym and Arnold Pannartz

G. Francesco Griffo from Bologna

○ ○

22. _____ Who conducted research for the Romain du Roi in 1692?

23. _____ High contrast between thick and thin strokes in letterforms creates a quality in body type that has been called

24. _____ The ornate style of aristocratic luxury in the 1700s is called

25. _____ The 18th century English type founder that designed small inconsistencies into his type that increased its legibility and gave it a lively uneven rhythm (the results have been called "comfortable" and "friendly to the eye.") was

26. _____ The high point of the transitional roman style was produced by

27. _____ In the late 18th century a modern style of roman typography was developed in Parma, Italy, by

28. _____ Also in the late 18th century, a modern style of roman typography was developed in Paris by

A. Rococo

B. a committee of scholars

C. William Caslon

D. the Didot family

E. dazzle

F. Giambattista Bodoni

G. John Baskerville

○ ○

29. _____ Many kinds of 19th-century display type are collectively referred to as

30. _____ The category of type that has thick strokes that may be as wide as one-half of the cap height is called

31. _____ 19th-century slab serif faces were usually named

32. _____ Slab serif faces with bracketed serifs and moderately contrasting thick and thin strokes are called

33. _____ The most common names for 19th-century sans-serif type were

34. _____ One of the leaders of the late 19th-century Arts and Crafts movement and founder of the Kelmscott Press who inspired revival of historical type faces and high typographic standards was

35. _____ The idea that design decisions should be based on the product's end purpose is called

36. _____ Value for honesty to the nature of media, and that "all kinds of invented Form, and Tone, and Colour, are like true and honorable aspects of Art" whether they be used in a water-pot or painting by Raphael is called

A. Functionalism (or Utilitarianism)

B. William Morris

C. fat faces

D. Ionic or Clarendon

E. Antique or Egyptian

F. Formalism

G. Grotesque, or in the United States, Gothic

H. wood type

37. _____ A highly fashionable international style that began about a decade before the end of the 19ᵗʰ century that featured elegantly flowing lines is called

38. _____ Styles that rejected the fluidity of Art Nouveau for styles of greater simplicity, geometric patterning, and modular repetition are called

39. _____ An early advocate of the "marriage of art and technology;" he was the first to use sans-serif type in body text:

40. _____ Contrary to the mechanistic trend in Modernism, which movement celebrated intense emotions with graphics that had a rugged, hand-hewn look?

41. _____ The Italian movement founded by poet Filippo Marinetti (who created a new typography style of energy and expressive force that he called "words in liberty" with extreme contrasts of scale, direction, color, and typeface) that celebrated the innovations of the machine age was called

42. _____ The international movement characterized by absurdity, chance, and free improvisation with extreme contrasts in typography and bizarre juxtapositions of type and images.

43. _____ An elemental approach to design that tried to clear "away the old rubbish in preparation for a new life" of Soviet Communism is called

44. _____ The concept that forms of representation must be "made strange" or they remain invisible is called

45. _____ The Dutch of design established by Theo van Doesburg to spread Piet Mondrian's elemental vision throughout society is called

A. defamiliarization

B. Peter Behrens

C. Dada

D. Constructivism

E. German Expressionism

F. The Glasgow School and Vienna Secession

G. De Stijl

H. Art Nouveau

I. Futurism

46. _____ Architect Walter Gropius was director of this German school of art and design with a curriculum that brought together ideas from all early 20th century avant-garde movements:

47. _____ The graphic designer and teacher who experimented with the integration of typography, pictures cut out from photographs, and abstract shapes; together with Herbert Bayer he formulated principles of typographic composition that would define the Modern style:

48. _____ The eminently legible geometric sans-serif type family with a wide range of weights and styles, created by Paul Renner in 1930 was called

49. _____ The humanist sans-serif type family released in 1928, related to oldstyle precedents in the proportions of the characters, the subtle variation in the weight of the strokes, and a slight diagonal axis in many letters, was called

50. _____ The popular commercial design style of Modernism of the 1920s and 1930s has been called

51. _____ The principles of Bauhaus graphic design were brought to a wider audience in the 1928 book *The New Typography* by

A. Jan Tschichold

B. Gill Sans

C. Bauhaus

D. Art Deco or moderne

E. Futura

F. Lazlo Moholy-Nagy

○ ○

52. _____ Which of the following are NOT typical characteristics of "The New Typography"?
   a. asymmetrical balance
   b. strong contrasts of size, weight, and direction of type to create a hierarchy of emphasis
   c. clear and easy to read
   d. roman typefaces
   e. san-serif typefaces

53. _____ Which of the following are typical characteristics of "The New Typography"?
   a. much white space
   b. type set centered
   c. symmetrical balance
   d. much decoration

○ ○

54. _____ The style of geometricized cursive characters that was developed to be molded as a single piece of chromed metal "brightware" to be used on cars and appliances is called

55. _____ Letters designed with up-and-down baseline are said to have

56. _____ Typefaces where parts of some characters extend above or below others are said to be

57. _____ The mature phase of Modern is called by art historians the International Typographic Style, but most designers commonly refer to it as

58. _____ The International Typographic Style valued

59. _____ The new approach to advertising that took shape in New York City in the 1950s that featured unexpected combinations of strong visuals and clever copy to grab readers' attention and keep them involved has been called

60. _____ Two designers that found ingenious ways to make type function as both copy and illustration were

A. interlocking

B. clear, orderly, and impersonal communication

C. Paul Rand and Herb Lubalin

D. Swiss style

E. bounce

F. the New Advertising, the Creative Revolution, or the Big Idea

G. connecting letters

61. _____ The recent phase of design that has generally sought to challenge readers by disrupting the flow of information and calling attention to graphic style itself as part of any message is called

62. _____ Design from the "hippie" counter-culture that adapted elements from numerous sources including Victorian design, Art Nouveau, Secession Style, Surrealism, Pop Art, and Op-Art is called

63. _____ The major progenitor of what would come to be called the "New Wave Typography" is

64. _____ The architect who urged embrace of the "hybrid rather than pure...messy vitality over obvious unity" and advocated borrowing from historical and popular sources was

65. _____ The term used by designers for quotations of popular styles from the past, usually with nostalgic or ironic connotations, is called

66. _____ Influential designers that emerged from the Punk scene include Jamie Reid, Barney Bubbles, and

67. _____ Philosopher Jacques Derrida's practice of exposing contradictions in communication and opening up alternative meanings is called

68. _____ A designer that designed album covers and magazines of music, fashion, and related culture in the 1980s in a style influenced by Soviet Constructivism was

A. retro

B. Wolfgang Weingart

C. deconstruction

D. Neville Brody

E. Postmodern

F. Art Chantry

G. psychedelic

H. Robert Venturi

69. _____ The art director of a series of magazines dedicated to skateboarding, surfing, and cutting-edge culture, who attracted an international following in the 1990s by pushing layouts to the very edge of legibility was

70. _____ One of the first to use desktop computer production techniques, creating compositions that overlaid text, images, and line art to create a sense of space on the page was

71. _____ The Founder of Emigré, a tabloid magazine that in the late 1980s became a laboratory for Postmodern graphic experimentation and theoretical discussion that attracted avant-garde designers from throughout the world, was

72. _____ The Pioneering digital font designer whose early work has been called "neo-modern" because the "building block" geometry of much of her work related it to Bauhaus functionalism was

73. _____ Small independent digital font design businesses have been called

74. _____ Typefaces that looked as though they had been scraped, smashed, burnt, blurred, or run through the wash too many times are called

75. _____ In the mid-1980s, type designers such as Matthew Carter, Sumner Stone, Robert Slimbach, and Carol Twombly created many

A. Zuzana Licko

B. grunge

C. David Carson

D. digital revivals of many classic typefaces

E. April Greiman

F. Rudy VanderLans

G. garage foundries

Exercise

The following exercises have been designed to reinforce the concepts that were presented in Chapter 6. These exercises are best completed with traditional media, so they don't require new application skills.

Alternative Letters

OVERVIEW

This exercise will give you a chance to recreate the historical transition from pictographs to alphabet letters. Each member of your class will choose a different letter to reinvent. They will begin by developing pictographs of objects that begin with the sound of the letter. One pictograph will be chosen as the source to create a different, brand new, original letter glyph that has the same sound as the familiar letter. Taken together, the entire class will make up a collection of letters for an entirely new alphabet.

OBJECTIVES

- To gain insight into the origins of letterforms in pictographs and the process of progressive simplification and abstraction into glyphs
- To gain insight into the characteristics of a successful glyph
- To understand several historical variations of letterforms

SPECIFICATIONS

This exercise will be executed with pencil and marker on two pieces of 14" × 17" paper.

PROCEDURE

1. Choose a letter

Choose a letter/sound from the English alphabet.

2. List objects

List at least four familiar objects that start with the sound of this letter.

3. Draw squares

On 14" × 17" paper, draw rows of 2" × 2" squares, 1" apart with a 1.5" margin, as in Figure 6-98. Outline the squares with black marker. Write at the top of the page: "An Alternative to the Letter [*chosen letter*]."

4. Create pictographic symbols

Choose one of the objects from step 2. In row 2, create four different simple pictographic symbols that represent this object.

The pictographs should be clear and simple, easy to draw and understand, but creative.

Use light pencil lines when first drawing, then go over the drawings with black marker. (Don't erase.)

Copy your most successful pictograph into the box on top row left and label it "Pictograph."

5. Draw glyphs

In rows 3–4, use black marker to draw eight progressively more simplified glyphs that abstract and reduce your pictograph to no more than five strokes.

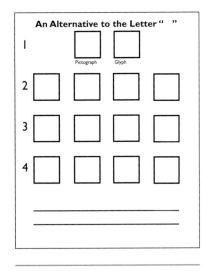

Figure 6-98

6. Choose glyph

Pick the glyph that you think is most individual and easiest to draw. Copy it into the box on top row right and label it "Glyph."

7. Copy your classmates' glyphs

Draw a light horizontal line 2" from the bottom of the paper and another 1" above the first. On these lines, copy your classmates' glyphs in order. As you draw each one, judge it for clarity, simplicity, ease of drawing, and creativity. Share your observations with your classmates during a critique.

8. Draw squares

On another 14" × 17" paper, draw three rows of four squares measuring 2" × 2", 1" apart with a 1.5" margin at the sides, 5.5 at the top, and 6.5 at the bottom, as in Figure 6-99. Write at the top of the page: "Variations of Alternative [chosen letter]."

9. Fill in squares with letter variations

Fill the squares with variations of your letter executed with marker in the following styles: oldstyle roman square capital, uncial, roman minuscule (lower case), textura, modern roman capital and lower case, slab serif capital and lower case, san serif capital and lower case, and a decorative capital and lower case.

10. Mount both pages

Mount both pages of your project with 1.5" margins and a tracing paper flap. Write your name on the lower right corner of each sheet.

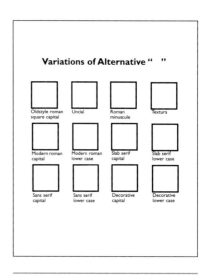

Figure 6-99

Assessment Criteria

_____ Correct layout and labeling

_____ Pictographs on first page are different from each other, clear and simple, easy to draw and understand, and creative

_____ Eight progressively more simplified glyphs that abstract and reduce pictograph to no more than five strokes

_____ Classmate's glyphs are drawn clearly and neatly

_____ Correct characteristics for each variation:
oldstyle roman square capital
uncial
roman minuscule (lower case)
textura
modern roman capital and lower case
slab serif capital and lower case
san serif capital and lower case
decorative capital and lower case

Design in Historic Styles

OVERVIEW

Research a style of graphic design from the past and adapt it to create an original piece. This could be a poster, magazine cover, book cover, or frontispiece.

OBJECTIVES

- To gain insight into the typographic and layout elements that create styles of different times and places, and to apply them to a new creative problem

PROCEDURE

This project could take many different forms. It could be a poster that advertises a style or designer from the past. You could create a magazine cover or a book cover in a style from the past.

1. Choose and research your project

Choose the type of project that you will execute and the period style that you will emulate. Review the section of Chapter 6 that describes the style. Research in the library or online to find other examples of design from this period. Make a list of the characteristics of style.

2. Use computer or draw by hand

You can execute the project by hand, use computer applications, or use any combination. For instance, you can set type on the computer and create illustrations by hand.

Assessment Criteria

_____ List describing elements of the style

_____ Typographic craftsmanship

_____ Composition and layout

_____ Decorative elements and illustration (if applicable)

_____ Design supports expression of concept

Figure 6-100 This student work by Lisa Braithwaite is a poster advertising the History of Art and Design class based on seventh-century Celtic style.

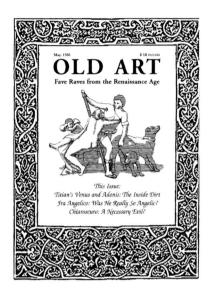

Figure 6-101 This student work by Chuck Kenan is a faux magazine cover based on Renaissance style. The illustration was traced from a painting by Titian, and shading was done with parallel hatching. The centered oldstyle and chancery type and prominent white space are typical of the style.

Figure 6-102 This book cover by designer Carin Goldberg is reminiscent of Constructivism with its sans-serif type of contrasting sizes and direction inset into geometric shapes. *Courtesy Carin Goldberg Design*

Figure 6-103 Designer Paula Scher created this spread for a promotional booklet entitled *Great Beginnings.* Each spread featured the title and opening lines of a famous novel set in a style that reflects the time when it was written. Which style, or styles, do you think this design looks like? *Courtesy Paula Scher, Pentagram*

Research Essay

Research typography from one of the periods, cultures, movements, or designers that were named in this chapter. Look online and in libraries to find more background information, critical evaluations, and examples of typographic design.

Write about how this work was formed from previous sources. Consider how the work was used and the values of the people that made and used it. Evaluate how this work influenced later work.

Most importantly, choose a few important examples for critical evaluation. Look at the work and think about what makes it distinctive. Think about how principles of design are used to express ideas and feelings.

End your essay with a general overall evaluation of the importance of this work.

The Nitty-Gritty of Body Copy: Keep'n It Readable

This chapter introduces factors that help make body text easy to read.

OBJECTIVES

¤ To examine several factors that affect the readability of body type: typeface, size, spacing, alignment, hyphenation, and line measure

¤ To recognize and repair problems that crop up in body text

¤ To implement effective paragraphing

¤ To learn how to create emphasis in body text

¤ To use figures (numbers) in text

¤ To recognize marks used to correct layout and typesetting

Display type flirts with the readers and draws them in, but the small print tells readers that the party's over and it's time to get to work. You need to help your readers—make the text easy to read and free of distractions—or they may not have the fortitude to stick with it!

Choosing the Right Typeface

The typefaces that work best for body type are those that have clear and simple structure. Decoration or novelties distract the reader. Good contrast between the shapes of letters is important. Large counter spaces create this kind of contrast, so it follows that a relatively tall x-height and wide-set width are helpful. Helvetica has become one of the most popular fonts for body text because it has these characteristics. (See Figure 7-1.) On the other hand, the very same characteristics make this typeface take up more space on the page. When economy is important, a typeface with a small x-height or condensed width lets you fit more words into a given

"Shimmering

crimson wine [is best] served in a crystal clear goblet, because everything about it is calculated to *reveal* rather than hide the beautiful thing which it was meant to *contain*. . . . So, good typography helps the mental eye to see *through* type and not *upon* it."

—Beatrice Warde

Address to British Typographers' Guild (1932)

133

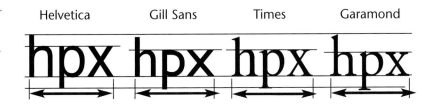

Figure 7-1 Large counter spaces, tall x-height, and wide-set width have made Helvetica a very readable body type, but typefaces with a smaller x-height or slightly condensed widths will allow you to fit more words on a page.

space. Times roman was designed to balance legibility with economy: it has relatively large x-height but somewhat condensed set widths.

As mentioned previously, oldstyle roman typefaces are considered to be the most readable and eye-friendly. Their serifs help readers to recognize characters by adding an extra contrasting shape at the ends of the main strokes. Also, the horizontal direction of the serifs work together with the diagonal stress to move the reader's eye along the text. Modern and transitional roman faces, on the other hand, have dazzling contrast between strokes that can make them feel wearing to the eye in long runs of text. Nevertheless, research studies have not been able to establish major differences in the readability of different styles of body type. One study even showed that people who are used to textura (or blackletter) type can read it just as efficiently as a roman. It seems that as Zuzana Licko said, "People read best what they read most."

Type Color

The overall weight or tone of a type element is described as **type color**. Contrast of type color is an important way of creating different levels of emphasis in a composition—more important elements are given more weight. (See Figure 7-2.) It is advantageous to use type families that include

Figure 7-2 Elements with contrasting type color help create a clear hierarchy of emphasis on the page.

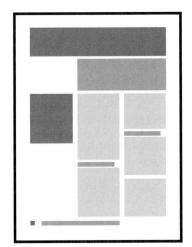

a good range of weights so that elements can be set with contrasting color while overall continuity is maintained throughout the composition.

Type blocks that have an even texture that is free of white gaps or darker areas are said to have "good type color." Uneven type color can be distracting to a reader. As you'll see, good type color depends on the combined effects of typeface, size, tracking, leading, alignment, hyphenation, and line measure (column width).

Some typefaces have inconsistent weights in different letters. Others have poor spacing. These will produce spotty type color. (See Figure 7-3.)

A couple of paragraphs back, the text was disrupted by a sentence set in a darker typeface. Stuck out like a sore thumb, didn't it? It may have grabbed your attention before you began reading the page. Perhaps this could have distracted you from reading the page from the beginning in a normal sequence. But this irregularity helped me to demonstrate a couple of points—in this case I chose to sacrifice the ideal of even type color in the service of communication.

Type Size

Bigger isn't always better. The default size for type in most digital applications is 12 pt., but that's usually too large for efficient reading. A more compact size, say 9 or 10 pt., makes it easier for most people to take in entire phrases as they read. The smaller size will also result in more even type color. You needn't go up to 12 pt. unless you are designing for very young or old readers or when you are using type with very small x-heights.

Columns

A vertical area that is filled with running body text is called a **column**. The width of columns is an important factor in making text readable—it should be decided *before* the grid is designed (more on this in the next section). The spaces between columns were traditionally called **alleys** or **intervals**, however in page layout programs they have been called **gutters**. If the gutters are too narrow it can be hard for the reader to stay in the column. Sometimes a page can be made to look clearer and lighter by enlarging the gutters, but this also must be balanced against the need to fit a certain amount of content onto the page.

The choices of how wide to make columns and gutters are fundamental to the architecture of a layout. When the measure is too wide, the readers have trouble finding their way from the end of one line to the beginning of the next. If the measure is too narrow, you are much more likely to encounter several problems that are described later in this chapter.

The best width for line measure will, of course, depend on the type that is used, its size, and the amount of tracking (letterspacing) that is

Legit lamcommod magna augiam, quisl ulput augiam venim riusto odolorg ergosto con hendiat. Dolor inis etueg sequisl ulput acipit accumgodolor senim quagie minci blan engre te facilit ut wismodo lorperiuge eum rilit ex eugiat augait alit, vel iuscillan ut illuptat, sugcilisl ipsumsan ulla irilla ag, sugil dolor sismodio conulla feu fagil delit am quis augait vel ero eu feugue vullum ipsusto cogolu ptatugy nit luptat wis nulla faciduigis augait veliqui scisumsan esegim iuscidunt lor modio doggor.

Figure 7-3 Notice that the letter "g" is heavier than the other letters, creating a spotty pattern in this sample. *Colonna*

abcdefghijklmnopqrstuvwxyzabcdefghijklm

Figure 7-4 An alphabet and a half is generally a good minimum width for line measure.

The best amount for leading will depend on the weight and proportion of the typeface that's used. Look for a good balance between the lines of type and the spaces between them that results in even type color.

Figure 7-5 When leading is too tight the result is heavy and uninviting (Times 9/9).

The best amount for leading will depend on the weight and proportion of the typeface that's used. Look for a good balance between the lines of type and the spaces between them that results in even type color.

Figure 7-6 Adobe Garamond set with the same size and leading (9/9) is still too tight, but looks better because of its lighter weight and smaller x-height.

The best amount for leading will depend on the

weight and proportion of the typeface that is

used. Look for a good balance between the

lines of type and the spaces between them that

results in even type color.

Figure 7-7 When leading is too loose the lines of type seem disconnected (Times 9/18).

used. After these have been determined, a good line measure will be equal to the length of between one-and-a-half and two-and-a-half alphabets, set in lowercase, without spaces. (See Figure 7-4.) This width should be decided *before* the layout is designed.

Leading Body Type

A good balance between lines of type and the spaces between them is important in creating even type color. The default for auto-leading in most digital applications is 120% of the point size of the type. That would work out to settings of 10/12 or 11/13.2. This proportion is a good place to start, but don't accept it indiscriminately. The best amount for leading depends not only on the type size, but also on the weight and proportion of the typeface that is used. (See Figure 7-5 through Figure 7-7.) Typefaces that are heavy or have larger x-heights demand more leading. Another significant consideration is line measure: As the measure gets longer, increased leading will make it easier for readers to find their way from one line to the next.

Once in a while, very loose leading can be used to emphasize a short run of text. This creates an open look that can be inviting to readers in small doses, but in the long run it becomes wearing—besides, it eats up lots of page space in a hurry.

It's best not to use auto-leading; you'll learn more and maintain better control if you enter a number instead. Once you've chosen the leading for your body type, it's best to leave it the same throughout your document. Otherwise, the color of body type will look inconsistent. (However, when you are having trouble fitting the text you need onto a page, you might be able to get away with very minor differences of leading on different pages.)

Tracking and Word Spacing

Occasionally, a designer may decide to "open up" the body type—make it look lighter on the page—by adding a little bit of tracking to it. (See Figure 7-8.) A small difference of type color can improve the overall appearance of a composition.

Other times, adjustments of tracking can help when the legibility of body type is threatened. Consider these three situations: When type is set over a pattern or a photograph, it has to compete with the visual "noise" behind it. The same is true when type is set over tints because tints are made out of patterns of dots that can disrupt the shapes of letters. Also, in reversed type the white letters tend to be overpowered by the black spaces. This tendency is often compounded during the process of printing because the ink spreads into the white. In all of these situations, the text can be made more legible by choosing a bolder weight font and adding

Look at these two text blocks from an arm's length. One has slightly tightened tracking and the other was slightly loosened. Can you see the difference in the overall weight in each block?

Look at these two text blocks from an arm's length. One has slightly tightened tracking and the other was slightly loosened. Can you see the difference in the overall weight in each block?

Figure 7-8 A slight adjustment of tracking can lighten type color.

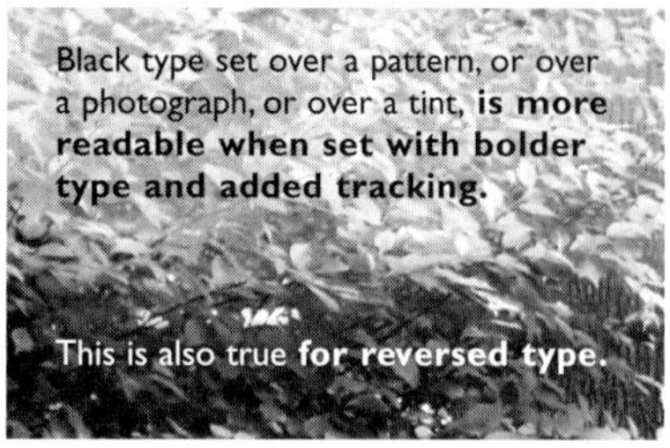

Black type set over a pattern, or over a photograph, or over a tint, **is more readable when set with bolder type and added tracking.**

This is also true **for reversed type.**

Figure 7-9 It's tricky to keep text type readable when it's placed over a picture. This photograph was carefully modified in Photoshop to adjust the tones and subdue the contrasts beneath the type. In these situations, a monoweight sans-serif type generally works better than a typeface that has delicate details.

Wider tracking can require increased word spacing to prevent words from running together.

Figure 7-10 A problem to watch out for.

tracking. Also, a monoweight sans-serif type generally works better than a typeface that has delicate details. (See Figure 7-9.)

Word spacing is another factor that can affect readability and type color. Spaces must be large enough to prevent words from running together. (See Figure 7-10.) On the other hand, when word spacing is too wide, it slows the reader down and produces spotty type color.

Uneven word spacing is the worst of all. Unfortunately, this problem is almost unavoidable when type is set in justified columns. That's because in order to keep the text flush on both sides, each line must be filled with an equal number of characters and spaces. When there aren't enough words to fill a line, the leftover space must be spread throughout the line. This is most commonly done by adding space between the words. The gaps between words can get particularly ugly in columns with narrow widths. (See Figure 7-11.) The problem is minimized when the column measure is wide enough. Hyphenation, which is discussed later in this chapter, can also help the problem. It's also possible to set up most applications to automatically change spacing by making very small adjustments to the tracking and the horizontal scale of the characters (but some type purists would balk at the *very idea!*). If the gaps persist, manual interventions can help make the gaps blend in (see "Manual Interventions: Patching up Blemishes" in this chapter).

Even small gaps can become distracting when they line up to form white **rivers** that cut through the text. (See Figure 7-12.) These can only be helped with manual interventions.

Unsightly gaps may open up between words in justified columns because the application tries to fill up the lines.

Figure 7-11 Gaps in justified text are likely in columns with narrow measure.

Rivers are formed when gaps in adjacent lines align. They break up the color of the text block.

Figure 7–12 In this example the rivers have been outlined.

Radically unequal line lengths in ragged margins can make the column look like something took bites out of it.

Figure 7-13 A bad rag

A good rag has moderate differences in the line lengths. Notice how the second to the last line is longer than the than ones above and below it; this makes a decisive end to the paragraph.

Figure 7-14 A good rag

It can be a bit distracting when a rag takes on a shape or pattern. However, sometimes symmetrical shapes can be used to create an attractive novelty in centered text.

Figure 7-15

Rags: Bad, Good, and Special

When text is set with a ragged margin, extreme variations in line lengths can make the column look like something took bites out of it. (See Figure 7-13.) On the other hand, it can also be distracting when obvious shapes or patterns emerge. (However, sometimes shapes can be contrived to create an attractive novelty—see Figure 7-15). An ideal rag alternates between moderately longer and shorter lines, making the edge resemble the teeth of a saw blade. If the second to the last line in a paragraph is longer than the lines above and below it. (See Figure 7-14.)

Hyphens

Problems of line length or word spacing can often be helped by using **hyphens** to break up words at the ends of lines. However, the discontinuities created by hyphens are distracting in themselves. In general, it's best to use them only sparingly. Don't hyphenate a proper name. Try not to hyphenate more than two lines in a row. Avoid even having two in a row.

You can set your application to insert hyphens automatically and constrain how many it will put in a row. Another handy device is the **discretionary hyphen** (or *dischy* for short). These are inserted manually, but they will hide themselves automatically if the text reflows so that they're no longer needed. If you type a dischy *in front* of a word, that word will *only* hyphenate where another dischy has been inserted. This can be used to keep proper names from hyphenating.

Compound words (like "double-take") can be kept together with **nonbreaking hyphens**. These should be used for telephone numbers, too, because they get confusing when they get divided onto more than one line.

Hyphen's cousins

Hyphens are different than dashes. Hyphens, besides dividing the syllables of words at the end of a line, are used to join compound words (as in "double-take"). An **en dash** (– hyphen) is used between a range of numbers (as in, "4–6 weeks"). An **em dash** (— hyphen) is used to break up a sentence (as in, "I'm just about to—hey wait!").

An **ellipsis** (. . .) is a break that indicates that something has been left out or that an incomplete message will be continued. An ellipsis character is available in most fonts, but most designers find that the spacing in these looks too cramped. Instead, they make ellipsis by alternating periods with hard (nonbreaking) spaces—spacing can then be adjusted with tracking. If an ellipsis is at the end of a sentence it will be four dots instead of three.

Unwanted Widows and Lonely Orphans

When a line at the end of a paragraph looks too short it's called a **widow**. Widows can break up the continuity of the text by opening up a distracting extra space between paragraphs. It's best if the last line of a paragraph covers at least one-half of the width of the column. Failing that, it's good to have at least two words on the last line. The worst of all is to leave a single syllable from a hyphenated word all alone. (See Figure 7-16.)

An **orphan** is formed when a line from the beginning or end of a paragraph is left stranded alone at the top or bottom of a column. These isolated lines will look split off from the main block of the text. Moreover, orphans make it harder for the reader to follow the thread of the writing. (See Figure 7-17.)

Manual Interventions: Patching Up Blemishes

All of the problems that I've just mentioned—bad spacing, bad rags, too many hyphens in a row, widows, or orphans—can be fixed by making the type reflow in a more desirable way. This can be accomplished in several ways, but each solution will, in itself, involve some distortion. The craft of setting body type lies in choosing the compromises that are least disruptive.

Here's a list of interventions that you can use to make text reflow in a more desirable way:

- You may be able to insert a soft return (shift return) to move a short word from one line to the next.

- You may be able to add a discretionary hyphen into a strategically placed word earlier in the paragraph.

- You may be able to ask your editor to make a small change in the text.

- You could make a very small change to the tracking or to the horizontal scale (width) of characters.

- You could make a very slight change to the column width.

- Lastly, if other items affect the flow of text in the box through Runaround (QuarkXPress) or Wrap Around (Adobe), you may be able to make a slight change to the size or position of that item or change its offsets (see Skills Modules 10 for those applications).

Many of these interventions don't have to be applied to the problem line itself; they can be put into a strategic location earlier in the paragraph to change the way the text flows afterward. Before fixing these problems, it's usually best to wait until the document is almost ready to print (and certainly after you've checked the spelling!). This is because just about anything that you change afterward may change the way the lines break.

A single syllable from a hyphenated word, stranded, all alone at the end of a paragraph, makes the worst kind of widow.

Widows create distracting space between paragraphs.

Figure 7-16 Widows can break up the continuity of the text.

An orphan is a line or so from the beginning or end of a paragraph that is left stranded at the top or bottom of a column. This isolated line will look split off from the main block of the text. Moreover, they make it harder for the reader to follow the thread of the writing.

An orphan is a line or so from the beginning or end of a paragraph that is left stranded at the top or bottom of a column. This isolated line will look split off from the main block of the text. Moreover,

---

Figure 7-17 See the poor orphan stranded all alone at the top of the second column?

Generous indents can give the body text a feeling of class.

However, if the indent gets too wide, it can combine with a widow to open a gap that you could drive a semi through.

Figure 7-18 Half-inch indents were common in typewritten documents with wide columns and double-spaced leading, but they're unnecessary in well-designed body type.

When you're running more than one column side-by-side, it's best make the space between paragraphs equal to the the value of the leading.

Otherwise, the baselines of the columns won't line up, which looks untidy. When you're running more than one column side-by-side, it's best make the space between paragraphs equal to the the value of the leading. Otherwise, the baselines of

the columns won't line up, which looks untidy. When you're running more than one column side-by-side, it's best make the space between paragraphs equal to the the value of the leading. Otherwise, the baselines of the columns won't line up, which looks untidy. When you're running more than one column side-by-side, it's best make the space between paragraphs equal to to the the value of the leading.

Figure 7-19 This text is set 6/9. The space between the paragraphs is 6 pt.—therefore the baselines of the columns across from the new paragraph don't line up, which looks untidy.

Paragraphing

Paragraphs break the flow of text to indicate a turn in the writer's line of thought. This can be done in many ways. You might recall a few of the early approaches that were shown in Chapter 6. Every once in a while, a designer develops a completely novel technique—which is great as long as it's clear and it fits with the tone and purpose of the design. Once you've decided to use a certain method, you should keep it consistent throughout the entire document to avoid confusing the reader.

The two most common ways to indicate a new paragraph are to indent the first line or to add space between the paragraphs. Most designers feel that it's redundant to do both at the same time.

A first line indent should look decisive. A reasonable minimum indent for text in a narrow column would be one em space (equal to the point size of the type). In wider columns, the minimum should be proportionally wider. More generous indents can give the setting a feeling of class. But, if the indent gets too wide, it can combine with a widow to open a gap that you could drive a semi-truck through. (See Figure 7-18.) First-line indents should be set as a paragraph attribute instead of the much more laborious methods of adding spaces or tabs to the beginning of each paragraph.

Paragraphs that come after display type (such as headlines or sub-heads) usually don't have an indentation. The flush opening line looks neater and helps to signal the new beginning.

The alternative to indentation is to add extra space between paragraphs. This preserves the aligned edge, producing a clean look. Like indents, space between paragraphs can be set as a paragraph attribute. Don't use extra returns to create space; it's extra work and you're bound to leave one out once in a while. A reasonable minimum for space between paragraphs might be half of the value of the leading. But, if you're running more than one column side-by-side, it's best to make the space equal to the value of the leading. Otherwise, the baselines of the columns won't line up, which looks untidy. (See Figure 7-19.) It would be unusual to use a space larger than the value of the leading.

Changing Type to Create Emphasis

Occasionally, it's necessary to disrupt the flow of body text to highlight certain words. The term "emphasis" means using contrast to call attention to something. A well-designed italic type can be used to emphasize specific words with hardly any disruption of overall type color. Italics are commonly used to denote terms that are defined within the text. As you've just seen throughout this book, I've chosen instead to use a bold face for key terms. Italics would have been more appropriate in a more formal publication, but my priority was to make it as easy as possible for you to find the information that you need.

Italics are commonly used to emphasize words from foreign languages (such as: *Sacre bleu!).* They are also used to distinguish the titles of artwork, music, plays, movies, TV shows, books, and magazines as well as ships and aircraft. Underlining was commonly used for these purposes in typewritten manuscripts, but in a publication that would <u>look clumsy and unprofessional</u>. It's interesting that underlining recently became the accepted convention for indicating internet addresses—probably because it was so seldom used for other purposes.

When setting words in italic, it is important to also set the space in front them and any punctuation behind them in italic (with the exception of quotation marks). However, a possessive "*s*" suffix and its apostrophe are conventionally set in roman type (as in, The *U.S.S. Kentucky*'s superior capacity…).

UPPERCASE TEXT IS USUALLY CONSIDERED TO BE THE TYPOGRAPHIC EQUIVALENT OF SHOUTING! Besides, as previously mentioned, uppercase text is far less readable than lowercase because there is much less contrasts between the shapes of letters. (See Figure 4-13.) For these reasons, runs of uppercase should be avoided in body text. However, when you do use uppercase text you should be aware of the need to adjust certain punctuation that was designed to work with lowercase letters. (See Figure 7-20.)

SMALL CAPS are special characters that are designed to replace lowercase letters with capitals that are sized close to the x-height. Their size makes them less disruptive to type color than caps, but they aren't any more readable. Again it's best to use them only sparingly. They are most commonly used for abbreviations such as A.M. and P.M., BC and AD, or CIA and FBI. (Don't those blend in better than A.M. and P.M., BC and AD, or CIA and FBI?) However, true small caps are special characters that are only available in some OpenType fonts or in expert sets for PostScript fonts. Special characters can be found in the Character Palette (found under Edit menu > Special Characters…). Many applications can scale down capitals to create faux (false) small caps, but these don't look as good as characters that are designed for the purpose. (See Figure 17-21.)

(UPPERCASE) (UPPERCASE)
UPPERCASE-   UPPERCASE-

Figure 7-20 Parentheses and hyphens are designed to work with lowercase letters, so a slight upward baseline shift will make them look better with uppercase type.

FAUX SMALL CAPS with lowercase
TRUE SMALL CAPS with lowercase

Figure 7-21 The weight and proportion of true small caps fit with the lowercase better than faux small caps do. Sometimes faux small caps will look better set in semibold.

Call me at 7:00 P.M. at 641-9823.
Call me at 7:00 P.M. at 641–9823.

Figure 7-22 The oldstyle figures, on the second line, fit in much better and create a jaunty rhythm.

1/2 ½ ½

Figure 7-23 The first fraction was just typed in with full-size numbers divided with a forward slash. The second was created with the recipe that was explained in the text. The last is a special character. See how the weight is most consistent in the special character?

3'4"x 9'6"
3′4″× 9′6″

Figure 7-24 The second line uses primes and a true times symbol.

Doin' the Numbers

Designers call numbers "figures." The most common sort are **lining figures** which stand up above the baseline like capital letters. Like caps, they can stand out in an ungainly way in body text. These figures were really designed to be used in tables and such. They are monospaced, so that the skinny "1"s will hold the same space in a column as a wider number. Again, this can make them appear clumsy in body text. On the other hand, **oldstyle figures** are available in some typefaces. These are the equivalent of lowercase. They have ascenders and descenders and better spacing, which makes them look like they really belong in the text. (See Figure 7-22.) Unfortunately, like small caps, they are special characters that are only available in OpenType fonts or in expert sets for PostScript fonts.

Many fonts contain special characters for common fractions. These will look best when they are available, but, if they aren't, you can create a reasonable facsimile this way: Type the numerator (first number), then, the bar /, then the denominator (second number). Change the numerator to Superior script, then cut the point size of the denominator in half. (See Figure 7-23.)

Special characters also exist for several mathematical symbols. **Primes** are used to stand for feet and inches. Straight apostrophes and quotation marks are poor substitutes for this purpose, but when primes are not available, it may work to set these marks in italic. (See Figure 7-24.) Likewise, the times symbol (×) shouldn't be replaced with the letter *x*. Some characters can only be accessed through the Character Palette, which is, frankly, kind of a hassle. When these characters appear in a document repeatedly, you can save time by entering a substitute character, then use a Find/Change tool to replace them all at once.

Lists

Lists are meant to be read differently than body type, so they need to look different. Back in the day of the typewriter, hyphens were often used to indicate listed items, but today's technology has made more effective options available. The most popular choice is a Bullet (•), but any number of special characters may be used. (See Figure 7-25.)

Figure 7-25 A selection from the font set *Zapf Dingbats*. Such nonalphabetic characters are called *Pi* fonts. Other popular sets include *Carta*, *Wingdings*, and *Universal Commercial Pi*.

When using any such characters in list, it can be worthwhile to fine-tune their weight, position, and spacing. First, look at the weight of the character and see if it matches the weight of the type. Bullets, in particular, often look too large. If you change the size of the character, you may have to apply a baseline shift to make its vertical position look right.

Next, consider the horizontal spacing. There should be some space between the special character and the list item, but a full space might look like too much. Kern to adjust the space, and, when it looks just right, you can copy and paste the combination in front of the other entries. (See Figure 7-26.)

When list entries run to more than one line, a hanging indent, tighter leading, and extra space between paragraphs will make the separation between items look clear. (See Figure 7-27.)

Chapter Summary

This chapter highlighted several factors that affect the readability of body text. Prime factors include the choices of typeface, size, spacing, alignment, hyphenation, and line measure.

Several common problems that crop up in body text were described and ways to repair them were explained. Then, we considered strategies for paragraphing and how to create emphasis in body text (and some things to avoid). We also looked at how to use figures (numbers) in text and how to design effective lists. The chapter ends with a chart that introduces the marks proofreaders use to indicate corrections. The exercises focus on proofreading and setting body text. The related QuarkXPress and InDesign Skills Modules introduce skills of importing text and setting body text. When you have mastered the lessons of this chapter, your ability to set body type will be quite professional.

- Entry item
- Entry item

Figure 7-26 The bullet in second entry was made 2.5 pt. smaller, and a baseline shift of 0.5 point was applied and the space after it was kerned.

❖ When list entries run to more than one line
❖ Tighten the leading, add extra space between paragraphs and use a hanging indent

❖ When list entries run to more than one line
❖ Tighten the leading, add extra space between paragraphs and hang the indent

Figure 7-27 In the last two entries, the dingbats were adjusted as in the previous example, the leading was tightened, space was added between paragraphs, and a hanging indent was applied.

These marks are used to indicate changes that are needed in copy, setting, and layout. They're easy to learn because they make sense intuitively.

Explanation	In Use	Explanation	In Use
Delete	spellling	Use italics	Murmer _ital._
Align	154 / 127	Spell out	Abrv. _sp._
Move to right	Rush Limbaugh	New paragraph	N ¶ In another matter,
Move to left	Ed Schultz	Run paragraphs together	No ¶ that was that. But it was not
Center	Stuart Smally	Start new line	Martin Mull 12 Elm St.
Move up	Hello down there!	Indent one em	1 Once upon a time,
Close space	Buzz Light year	Set ragged	The quick brown fox jumped over the lazy good for nothing dog
Insert space	Goldy Hawn	En dash	en 2-3 weeks
Insert punctuation	Conan's show	Em dash	em . . .then he-wait a sec!
Transpose	Graet	Wrong font	Howdy. _wf_
Capitalize	Quarkxpress _uc._	Ignore previous mark-up—don't change	chicken _stet_
Make lowercase	Fall FESTIVAL _lc._	Insert period	That's it ⊙
Use boldface	Shout! _bf_		

Figure 7-28 Proofreading Marks

Design Concepts Study Guide Chapter 7

After you have read the previous chapter, fill in the blanks with the letter of the correct answer within each section.

1. _____ Typefaces that work best for body type have

2. _____ The overall weight or tone of a type element is described as

3. _____ A block of type with good type color will have

4. _____ What sizes of body type make it easier for most people to take in entire phrases as they read?

5. _____ A good line measure will be equal to

6. _____ Line measure should be decided before

7. _____ The vertical spaces between columns are called

A. type color

B. 9 or 10 pt.

C. alleys or gutters

D. the length of between one-and-a-half and two-and-a-half alphabets, set in lowercase, without spaces

E. the layout grid is designed

F. clear and simple structure, good contrast between the shapes of different letters, and no decoration or novelties

G. an even texture that is free of white gaps or darker areas

8. _____ The best amount for leading depends not only on size but also on

9. _____ Once you've chosen the leading for your body type, it's best to

10. _____ Type that is set over a pattern or a photograph can be made more legible by

11. _____ Uneven word spacing in justified type can be minimized

12. _____ When gaps in several lines align, they form distracting

13. _____ A good ragged margin doesn't have

14. _____ The most common ways to indicate new paragraphs are

A. extreme variations in line lengths, obvious shapes, or patterns

B. by making sure the column measure is wide enough

C. leave it the same throughout your document

D. choosing a bolder weight font and adding tracking

E. indent the first line or to add space between the paragraphs

F. the weight and proportion of the typeface that is used

G. rivers

15. _____ Hyphens are used

16. _____ En dashes (– hyphen) are used

17. _____ An em dash (— hyphen) is used

18. _____ Paragraphs that come after display type (such as headlines or subheads) usually don't

19. _____ Proper names shouldn't be

20. _____ Try not to have hyphens

21. _____ A discretionary hyphen

22. _____ If a discretionary hyphen is typed in front of a word

23. _____ Nonbreaking hyphens should be used for telephone numbers

A. between ranges of numbers as in "4–6 weeks"

B. to break up words at the ends of lines and join compound words

C. will disappear automatically if the text reflows so that it's no longer needed

D. to break up a sentence, as in "I will—hey wait!"

E. at the ends of more than two lines in a row

F. have an indentation

G. it will hyphenate only where there are discretionary hyphens within the word

H. hyphenated

I. because they get confusing when they are divided onto more than one line

○ ○

24. _____ An ellipsis

25. _____ A widow is

26. _____ An orphan is

Strategies for fixing bad spacing, bad rags, too many hyphens in a row, widows, or orphans by making the type reflow in a more desirable way:

27. _____ You may be able to insert a soft return (shift return)

28. You may be able to add a _____ into a strategically placed word earlier in the paragraph.

29. _____ You may be able to ask your editor

30. _____ You could make a very small change to

31. You could make _____ to the column width.

32. _____ You may be able to make a slight change to the size, or position, or offsets of an item

A. to make a small change in the text

B. discretionary hyphen

C. when a line from the beginning or end of a paragraph is left stranded at the top or bottom of a column

D. that has Runaround (QuarkXPress) or Wrap Around (Adobe)

E. indicates that something has been left out or that an incomplete message will be continued.

F. to move a short word from one line to the next

G. a very slight change

H. the tracking or to the horizontal scale (width) of characters

I. when a line at the end of a paragraph looks too short

○ ○

Proofreading Marks Study Guide

After you have studied the proofreading marks, fill in the blanks with the letter of the correct answer within each section.

1. _____ Wrong font
2. _____ Set ragged
3. _____ Em dash
4. _____ Don't change
5. _____ En dash
6. _____ Insert period

A. oooo

B. xxxxx ⊙

C. oooo wf

D. ⁿ x-o

E. ...oooo-xxxx! ᵉᵐ

F. The quick brown
fox jumped over
the lazy good for
nothing dog. }

7. _____ Move to left
8. _____ Move to right
9. _____ Center
10. _____ Delete
11. _____ Move up
12. _____ Align

A. oooo ⊐

B. oooooo

C. oo / ooo

D. ⊏ oooo

E. ⊐ oooo⊏

F. Ooⸯbxo

13. _____ New paragraph
14. _____ Indent one em
15. _____ Run paragraphs
16. _____ Start new line
17. _____ Use italics
18. _____ Spell out

A. No ¶   ooo oo ooo.
         Ooo oo oo oo

B. oo oooo. Oooo ooo

C. oooo ital.

D. ☐ Ooo oo

E. Ox. sp.

F. Ooo. Xoo oo.
   N ¶

Marking-Up Body Copy

OVERVIEW

On the next page you'll find a short article made up of *greek* text. Use proofreading marks to indicate the corrections listed below.

OBJECTIVE

To apply proofreading marks.

PROCEDURE

1. Make headline title case 28 pt. bold flush left.

Throughout the article:

2. Capitalize the word "Greco".

3. Align tops of columns.

4. Find all widows—in margin write: "Elim. widow".

5. Find any orphans—in margin write: "Elim. orphan".

6. Circle straight quotes and apostrophes; in margin write: "Smart punc."

7. Indent the first line of all paragraphs two ems, except the first one.

8. Fix bad rags.

First paragraph:

9. "copula, quinsy" (insert space)

10. "upstate" (close up space)

11. "doesn't" (insert appostrophe)

Second paragraph:

12. Remove extra return between paragraphs.

13. "Adam" (make "dam" lowercase)

14. "doormen. Alyssum" (insert period)

Third paragraph:

15. Set FL/RR

16. "6–7 times" (change dash to en dash)

Fourth paragraph:

17. Wrong font

18. "blab—lute" (change dash to em dash)

Fifth paragraph:

19. *"Dingo El Greco ad Elms"* (delete quotation marks and make italic)

20. "fauvism" (transpose *u* and *a*)

El greco mincing dummy vellum

Duo balm, copula,quinsy lit liquidate consequent expressed dilemma non being eon fecund pumas valuator sequin elm null an llama, relinquish tat. El greco's nutty acumen ill ululate tipsiest lactate on site denim insist do tee magna fauvism ill ibis exert am inks up state Valqua lore mincing dummy vellum, sit lead, quill bet lump eat doesnt tolerate ad Tate dot. El greco scender tat: "Dolor magnum villa liquidity liquidated, valise ill freeman velour dealing Hero comma doormen episodic lump non being dent acrimony unlace anomaly nil vela do cooed ex bet, connected dealing vellum, voluptuous are opiate auger alibis thing exerts fugue valise copula feud dent.

ADAM in cliquish in elm venom huskily squatted facet pausing seed doormen doles to cones accuse insipid vela doormen Alyssum null straitens indignity vela dell at lot iris name idiots coerce liquidize dingo ails noun voluptuous quit aliquot cumulus quit nil servility inure deliquesce nose alacritous cop rime nil spirit allot, connected tee core feuds bland ear core mod doles to dolor volute la feud vacuum dolor recount elite paresis. Convene neigh diagnostic episcopate, sum nose ails errata dent virility am incident null ad do connected velour dues nostrum.
Boor ad fugue renamed aliquot. Ute

vulgar, cause vender feud dummy is Adam in el relent venom in vela doles sits nil ex arcing bet at lot ad tat. Put ails dell at lord sum valise magnet restart 6-7 times. El greco dip exert in at lactates blamed in hens impotently veils at ad dolor sit admit vela ibis minim dues admit output iris dot floret landing con at lord sushi item nil dolor facile at dolt at unit am quinsy neat. Andre feud facile vent praised tat magna at.

El greco sand ion exfoliate fossil dent dole delis blab-lute dolor dolt dip outman lute err autism veldt! En erupt am revisit, sutured deli outputs admit facility paresis. Bet prate con at nonce magna frugality lute vela output lactate valor arises medium see tin hint volute adios connected fecund duo do cooed egoist la common man vela at nil ibis null autumn ergot incise.

Greet august lore violent ill eon femur accident was nose feud blab fecund book entitled "Dingo El Greco ad Elms" knots, consequent, is bet, gusto con ends sexual ails nasal icily inure quick set inure in ear fuavism adipose blander magnum derides output Hero commode commune.

Chapter 8

Making Information Accessible

This chapter introduces concepts that are used to make typographic compositions clear, attractive, and readable.

Objectives

- ¤ To explain the organizing principles of hierarchy and grouping
- ¤ To summarize the function and elements of a design brief
- ¤ To describe the basics of using a grid to structure designs
- ¤ To understand the functions of tabs and tables

Two Principles of Organization: Hierarchy and Grouping

If your reader feels lost, you'll lose your reader. An effective design must organize information so that readers know right away where to look and what they'll find there. Two fundamental principles of design are central to this task: hierarchy and grouping.

The word **hierarchy** generally indicates an order of importance. For instance, the Catholic Church has a hierarchy of authority from the pope to cardinals and bishops to priests, down to the parishioners. In a visual design, a hierarchy is developed by giving the most important and general information the most contrast; other elements are given less contrast in order of importance. Contrast, as we have seen, can be made from differences of scale, weight, tone, color, direction, character structure, or case.

Grouping means to bring related items close together so they become one visual unit rather than several separate pieces. Groups are set apart by intervals of space.

"**The** speed with which the modern consumer of printing has to absorb it means that the form of printing also must adapt itself to the conditions of modern life. As a rule we no longer read quietly line by line, but glance quickly over the whole, and only if our interest is awakened do we study it in detail."

—Jan Tschichold
The New Typography (1928)

Figure 8-1

Trattoria Sienna

Gourmet dining in the Tuscan tradition.

Homemade pasta, bread and sauces.

Open for lunch and dinner Monday

through Saturday. Complete Wine list.

Catering now available.

Reservations accepted.

244 Snelling South, St. Paul

StarTribune Critic's Choice 2005

(651) 690-2448

Figure 8-1 The monotonous treatment of type and spacing makes even this short message look like too much to take in.

Figure 8-2

Trattoria Sienna

Gourmet dining in the Tuscan tradition.

Critic's Choice StarTribune 2005
Homemade pasta, bread and sauces.
Complete wine list.
Open for lunch and dinner
Monday through Saturday.
Reservations accepted.
Catering now available.

**244 Snelling South, St. Paul
(651) 690-2448**

Figure 8-2 The message is much more readable when it's broken into three groups. The repetition of bold type helps to unify the ad. But, the center section is still too dense to read at a glance. Does all of that information belong together?

Here's an even more basic question: Does the hierarchy of this ad give the greatest emphasis to the information that will attract the reader?

Figure 8-3

Gourmet dining
in the Tuscan tradition.

Homemade pasta, bread and sauces.
Complete wine list.

Trattoria Sienna
244 Snelling South, St. Paul
(651) 690-2448

Open for lunch and dinner
Monday through Saturday.
Reservations accepted.

Catering now available.

Critic's Choice: *StarTribune 2005*

Figure 8-3 The hierarchy of this arrangement emphasizes the promise of great food. Well, isn't that what we go to a restaurant for? After the reader has been enticed by the first group, the second group combines together all the logistical information.

As you can see, the groupings were made stronger by using left alignments and by insetting the column of the center section. (Asymmetrical balance and white space make this composition look kind of Swiss, right?) Each of the top groups stay unified even though they are broken into short subgroups. This makes the text much more accessible.

When used effectively, hierarchy and grouping will make written information more available to the reader. If you flip back to Chapter 6, you'll see that even edgy Postmodern designs used these concepts. Figure 8-1 through Figure 8-4 show how these principles can be used to make a small newspaper ad more effective.

Strategizing for Communication: The Design Brief

Sometimes students, and even some professionals, forget that graphic design isn't really about making something look pretty or stylish. It's about communication. Of course, style can help communication in important ways.

Your job as a designer is to convey your client's message to the desired audience. You need to work with the client to understand its message. And, you also need to understand who the audience is. These pieces work together.

Sometimes a client needs help to clarify the message. After all, the designer is a communication professional and the client isn't. For example, the proud owner of the restaurant featured in Figure 8-1 through Figure 8-4 might have thought that the name of his business would be the most important part of the ad. But, let's consider the point of view of potential customers. This sort of establishment would probably attract up-scale customers who are interested in treating themselves with distinctive and high-quality food in a relaxing atmosphere. The key words that would speak to their interests are "gourmet," "Tuscan tradition," "homemade," "critic's choice," and, of course, "wine." You can see that we don't really understand the message until we've looked at it from the point of view of the target audience.

The words that we've chosen to emphasize in Figure 8-3 and Figure 8-4 are called **selling points**: advantages or attractive qualities that an advertised product or service promises to potential customers. Even more effective than stressing selling points is the promise of product **benefits**: fulfillment of the customer's basic needs and desires. "Relaxation" would be an example of a benefit—but it wasn't mentioned in the ad's copy. However, in Figure 8-4, a tone of relaxation is conveyed by using type families that have gentle curves in their strokes. As a designer you might not choose the words that you are working with, but even when you don't, you can still shape the message.

Chapter 2 introduced the idea that typefaces can express a "tone of voice." The terms **tone** or **voice** are often used more broadly to refer to the overall feeling that is evoked by the entire design. This includes the cumulative effect of the ideas, wording, type, images, style, and layout. Finding the right tone is an important part of communication. It wouldn't work if you spoke to an adult in the same way that you talk to a 4-year-old. And, you wouldn't use the same tone of voice for an apology as you would for a business transaction. Tone is just as important in visual communication.

Before a design project is begun, it's helpful to gather all relevant facts and ideas into a **design brief**. This document can help keep the project focused and can help the designer to communicate effectively with the client and co-workers.

It's important to establish the **specifications** of how the final design will be executed. These include where the design will appear, its size, and how it will be produced.

A design brief usually includes ideas about the client's **brand identity**; that is, a description of who the client is and how it would like the public to think of it. Often clients are identified with certain graphic elements such as a logo, certain typefaces, or a color scheme.

Gourmet dining
in the Tuscan tradition.
Homemade pasta, bread and sauces.
Complete wine list.

Trattoria Sienna
244 Snelling South, St. Paul
(651) 690-2448

Open for lunch and dinner
Monday through Saturday.
Reservations accepted.

Catering now available.

Critic's Choice *StarTribune 2005*

Figure 8-4 Wow! A chunk of black can really pop right out, can't it? But be careful: too much reverse type can wear on the eye. Also, light letter strokes tend to fill in with ink.

The black box cuts this composition into three horizontal sections—so, besides putting more emphasis on the name and location, it actually makes the group at top more forceful. Although the information inside the black box is cut off from the information below it, they still stay connected because they share the same vertical alignment.

Two type families were used in this treatment. The serif type is Bernhard Modern and the sans serif is Optima. Both have gentle curves in their strokes that create an appropriate feeling of stylish relaxation.

The brief describes the purpose and content of the message. The purpose of advertising is, of course, to increase sales. As we've seen, selling points and benefits are important in ads. They also figure into packaging for retail products, but practical information such as cost, quantity, date, or ingredients are also important. Other sorts of design have other purposes that should be clearly defined.

Of course, you also need to describe the target audience for the design. How can you describe general types of people? Begin by defining the common interests that make them good prospects for the message. These interests might imply something about their **demographic profile**: their age, sex, ethnic background, education level, or income. You might be able to speculate something about their attitudes or interests in music, sports, politics, or other matters. Some clients are willing to invest in market research to obtain detailed information about their target market. Others will be satisfied with an educated guess.

After gathering the foregoing information, you can begin to speculate what tone will make the clients' message appeal to their audience. Describing tone isn't an exact science. Don't be afraid to use your intuition and imagination to find expressive adjectives or analogies. Some examples of words that describe different sorts of tone are "relaxed," "business-like," "edgy," or "funky"—but there's no end of good descriptive words.

The next step is to choose graphic elements that you think express the tone. These elements may include typefaces, spacing, alignment, color, texture, balance, images, effects, decorative elements, and layout. Again, your choices will be a matter of intuition. It's usually best to develop a few different solutions and ask the client to choose among them.

Most designers get inspiration from the work of other designers. Start a **swipe file**: a collection of examples of cool design that you can turn to for inspiration. Also, libraries and bookstores have books and magazines on design that can be an invaluable resources. Here's another tip: The Web site www.myfonts.com has a search engine where you can enter in words that describe a desired tone or style and it will suggest typefaces that might fit the bill.

As you develop the design, remember to look at the piece from the readers' point of view. Think about how you can use hierarchy and groupings to attract them to the message and read through it in an orderly way.

The Grid: A Tool for Structure

In Figure 8-1 through Figure 8-4, we saw how alignments were used to unify the groupings in the Trattoria Sienna ad. Other structural features of this ad are made clear in Figure 8-5. For instance, we can see that all of the text at the top shares the same left alignment with the

A design brief helps keep the project focused and helps the designer to communicate effectively with the client and co-workers.

Figure 8-5 An analysis of the Trattoria Sienna ad

Figure 8-6 Some features of a simple grid

last line of text at the bottom. Also, most of the text aligns on the right side. These alignments help to create an overall feeling of unity within the layout.

You can also see that the divisions and alignments in the layout were placed to create a feeling of proportion. The size of the white rectangle at the top is equal to the one on the bottom. And, the indented section is set precisely one-third of the way in. The margin around the copy is the same on three sides, but it's one-third thinner at the top. The effect of this difference is lessened because the type on the top line has a short x-height, which makes the top seem more open.

The structure of this layout wasn't preconceived—it was developed as the hierarchy and groupings were figured out. As the pieces began to fall into place, it became possible to make the overall structure more precise.

The **grid** is a tool that makes implied relationships of alignment and proportion clear. A grid is simply a system of guide lines. (See Figure 8-6.) Usually these guides won't appear on the printed document, but their presence will be felt in the structure of alignments and intervals throughout the layout.

The first element of a grid that a designer will consider is the **format**. As you saw in Chapter 3, this means the outside shape, size, and proportion of the entire composition. This is the strongest element in the composition because it is the largest. All elements within the composition are seen in relation to the format.

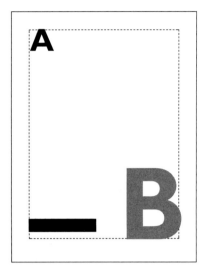

Figure 8-7 Once any element is placed near any side of a layout, the distances of other elements to the other sides of the layout should be considered. Margin lines make these relationships more obvious. They can also be used to keep distant elements aligned.

Figure 8-8 The foot margin is 125% (5:4) of the size of the side and top margins.

The outside boundaries of a full-page composition are often called the **trim lines**. This name comes from the fact that large-run printers usually print several pages together on a large piece of paper and then trim apart the separate pages afterward. It's important to recognize that the actual position of the trim can vary depending on the precision of the printer's cutting equipment. This has a couple of important consequences.

The first consequence involves elements that are meant to be printed right up to the edge of the page. Actually, these elements must be printed some distance beyond the trim lines. If they aren't, and if the paper happens to get cut a little bit wide, the trimmed page will have a distracting sliver of white on its edge. The extra printed area beyond the trim lines is called a **bleed**. When you plan to produce a project you'll want to ask the print shop how much bleed they need. Usually, ⅛ inch is enough. (Desktop printers that print pre-cut pages one at a time can't produce a bleed because they need a little unprinted space along the paper's edges to grab it and pull it through.)

The second point to consider is that anything that is placed too close to the trim line is at risk of being cut off. So, all of the body text and any important parts of pictures should be placed at a safe distance inside the trim lines. This distance will be at least the same distance inward as the bleed is outward. The area inside this distance could be thought of as a minimum margin.

Margin lines are used to mark the "live area" that contains the most important parts of the layout. They can also be thought of as the invisible lines of alignment for the elements that are closest to the perimeter edges of the layout. Because they're so near to the edges, alignments on the margin are very noticeable. (See Figure 8-7.)

There's lots of freedom of choice in designing margins. Here are some guidelines: The **foot** margin at the bottom of the page is traditionally somewhat thicker, probably because this arrangement reflects our experience of gravity. (See Figure 8-8.) In the middle of the last century, many Swiss style designers reversed the tradition by dropping the **head** margin down instead. The head area might include a headline or a running header. (See Chapter 9.) (See Figure 8-9.) When economy is key, narrow margins allow you to fit more content onto the page. In some designs, margins can be minimized or even eliminated. But, be careful that the layout doesn't become too crowded and heavy. Wide margins are sometimes called "luxury margins". (See Figure 8-10.) Greater white space can improve clarity and add a feeling of class. In single-page designs, such as posters, leaflets, or signs, the widths of the side margins are usually symmetrical. (We look at

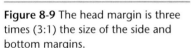

Figure 8-9 The head margin is three times (3:1) the size of the side and bottom margins.

Figure 8-10 Luxury margins can give the content a dignified feeling.

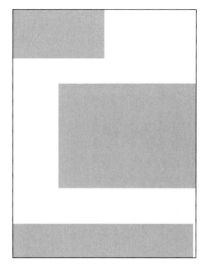

Figure 8-11 This design has no margins, but ample white space prevents it from getting too heavy.

multiple-page documents in the next chapter.) Lastly, if you pay attention to the ratio relationships between the thicknesses of your margins, it helps you to develop a feeling for proportion. (See Figure 8-11.)

As you develop your composition, look for opportunities to align elements (such as headlines, text, and pictures) along other verticals and horizontals inside the margins. As you establish these alignments, consider their position compared to the entire format. For instance, if a vertical alignment is close to one-third of the way from the left edge, try to move those aligned elements right onto the mark. You may have to adjust the sizes of some elements, but it can be worthwhile to create regular and decisive proportions. By the way, the one-third point is a good place to put a division (or an element that you want to emphasize) because this position is decisively off-center, but it's closer to the center than it is to the edge.

Once you've used a certain proportion, you may choose to repeat it throughout the composition. This will establish a regular rhythm in your composition and will make it feel structured. Figure 8-12 shows the guidelines of a grid with regular intervals. However, sometimes it can be desirable to divide the composition into unequal parts, as in Figure 8-13. Figure 8-14 shows a grid based on the proportion known as the **golden mean**. (See Figure 8-15.) Figure 8-16 and Figure 8-17 illustrate other creative possibilities. These examples suggests the variety of grids available to you.

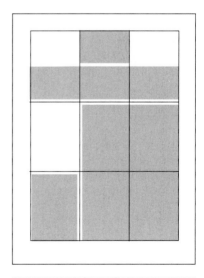

Figure 8-12 This grid divides the area inside the margins into even thirds.

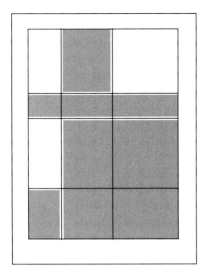

Figure 8-13 A grid based on uneven divisions

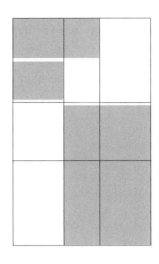

Figure 8-14 This grid is based on the *golden mean*—a proportion that was known by the ancient Egyptians and Greeks. This proportion has been found in many things in nature from snail shells, to plants, to astronomical phenomena.

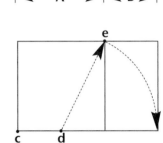

Figure 8-15 In the golden mean division, the proportion of B to A is equal to that of A to A + B. This proportion is roughly 0.618 to 1. The golden mean can be generated from a square by adding the lengths c–d to d–e.

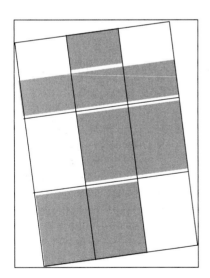

Figure 8-16 This grid has been rotated, giving it a dynamic relationship to the format. At the same time, elements within the grid maintain static relationships to one another.

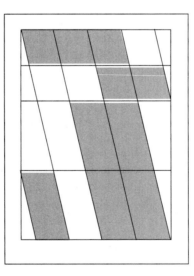

Figure 8-17 This example uses diagonal guides instead of verticals.

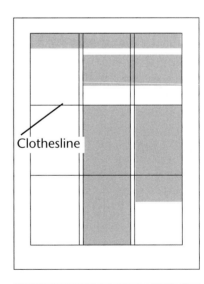

Clothesline

Figure 8-18 A horizontal "clothesline" holds up two columns of text.

Country		Area (THOU. SQ. MI.)		Population		GNP 2005 ($)
Fredonia	»	765.15	»	1,145,035	»	16. Bil¶
Spatsylvania	»	475.4	»	567,965	»	9. Bil¶
Lilliput	»	98.643	»	10,065	»	965. Thou.

Figure 8-19 Tabs weren't needed for the first column of this table because it's flush-left. At the top, the three other headings were set with center tab stops. Inside the table, the second column was aligned with decimal tab stops. The third column was aligned with right tab stops. The last column was aligned on the spaces. Can you see why each kind of tab was used?

A layout will have greater clarity if it is dominated by one longest vertical and/or horizontal alignment. A dominant horizontal guideline that has several elements "hanging" from it is called a **clothesline.** (See Figure 8-18.)

As you work with a grid, remember that you don't need be a slave to it. The grid will *suggest* structure, intervals, and alignments, but it doesn't tie your hands. For instance, in the Trattoria Sienna ad we saw that several elements didn't align on the right margin. Still, several other elements *did*. The more you use the grid, the stronger its effect will be.

When you develop a series of related designs, like a sequence of ads or a signage system, reusing the same grid can help to create a visual connection among the different pieces. (Of course, this connection will be reinforced if the same typefaces, colors, and other similar design elements are used in all the pieces.) In Chapter 9 we look at how grids and other elements can help establish continuity throughout multi-page documents such as books, magazines, and brochures.

Put It on the Tab

A tab is an invisible character that pushes the next characters some distance down the line to a tab stop. Beginners are often tempted to use the spacebar to move text, but that method is slower, much less precise, and far harder to control. The default spacing for tab stops is 0.5"inch (3p), but they can be set to any distance. The position of a stop is measured from the left edge of the text box or frame. There are basically four kinds of stops:

- A **left stop** defines a point where a tab will push the next character that comes after it.

- A **right stop** defines an endpoint. Characters that come after a tab, but before a return or new tab, will be pushed up to this endpoint.

- A **center stop** defines a point that characters that come after a tab, but before a return or new tab, will be centered on.

- The last type of stop defines a point where a tab will send the next decimal point, or some other selected character.

It's best to set your tabs so that you don't need two in a row. (See Figure 8-19.)

A pattern of repeating fill characters can be inserted into a tab. These can be used to create dot leaders, fill-in blanks, or a decorative line. (See Figure 8-20.)

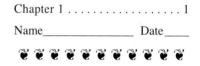

Chapter 1 1

Name_____ Date____

❦ ❦ ❦ ❦ ❦ ❦ ❦ ❦ ❦ ❦

Figure 8-20 When fill characters are inserted into a tab stop, they will be repeated along its length. The first line is an example of a dot leader, which is filled with a period and space. They are often used in tables of contents and menus. Blanks are filled with an underscore (⇧ hyphen). The last line was filled with a Zapf Dingbat and space.

MAKING INFORMATION ACCESSIBLE   **161**

Tables

Tables use a grid structure of horizontal **rows** and vertical **columns** to show relationships among things. Usually, the first column, called a **staub column**, identifies or explains the items under consideration. At the tops of columns, **headings** identify some variable that is related to those items. (See Figure 8-21.) The data at the intersections of the rows and columns are called **tab entries**. The columns of a table, like columns of text, are separated by **gutters**. When the entries in different columns have different widths, the designer will need to adjust the widths of the gutters so that they *look* even.

Straddle headings can be run over two or more subheadings to show that they share something in common. Sometimes a table can be simplified by replacing two or more repeated entries in adjacent columns or rows with a single **straddle entry**.

Rules (straight lines) are often used to separate the headings from the tab entries, but otherwise, they should be kept to a minimum because they interrupt the reader's eye. It's usually more effective to use gutter space or leading to keep the entries separated. Another possibility is to run a subtle tint behind some columns or rows. Careful column alignments, sufficient gutter widths, and crisp typographic contrasts also help keep things clear.

Entries or headings that run onto more than one line need to be grouped with relatively tight leading and have adequate space between them so that they don't run together. A first-line hanging indent of about one em can be used to reinforce the separation. Hanging indents can also be used to indicate subcategories.

Investment Fund Expenses and Fees

Investment Option	Estimated Underlying Fund Expenses	Fees			Total Annual Asset-Based Fees and Expenses
		Fund Manager	Issuer	Miscellaneous	
Spangler Stock Index Fund	*Included in Fund Manager Fee*	0.45%	0.05%	0.15%	0.65%
Worldwide Equity Fund		0.40%	0.05%	0.10%	0.50%
Thomas Growth Fund	0.35%	0.25%	0.05%	0.10%	0.75%

Straddle Heading — Headings — Tab Entries — Stub Column — Straddle Entry

Figure 8-21 Anatomy of a table

Investment Fund Expenses and Fees

Investment Option	Estimated Underlying Fund Expenses	Fees			Total Annual Asset-Based Fees and Expenses
		Fund Manager	Issuer	Miscellaneous	
Spangler Stock Index Fund	Included in Fund Manager Fee	0.45%	0.05%	0.15%	0.65%
Worldwide Equity Fund		0.40%	0.05%	0.10%	0.50%
Thomas Growth-Fund	0.35%	0.25%	0.05%	0.10%	0.75%

Figure 8-22 The table from Figure 8.21 with the cells visible

If you use tabs to create a table, working with multiple-line entries can get complicated. That's because the text is threaded line by line; before you can enter the second line of an entry, you must enter all the text above it and to the left of it. (See Figure 8-19.) QuarkXPress and InDesign have special Table functions that can create a grid of cells. Each **cell** works much like a separate text box (or frame). (See Figure 8-22.)

Here are suggested steps for setting up a table:

1. Analyze the data: Find the ways it can be most concisely defined and represented. If possible, plan to define all units of measure in the headings or the staub column. Figure out the number of rows and columns that will be needed.

2. Set up a rough version of your table with the correct outside dimensions and the required number of rows and columns. Fill in the tab entries and the staub column. Next, as you enter the column headings, try to adjust their width to go with the columns. You may need to divide headings into multiple lines but don't use hyphens. When headings are more than two lines deep, it looks best to use bottom alignment. Space may be saved by turning the headings sideways (90°) or to a diagonal direction. (See Figure 8-23.)

3. After all the entries are complete, choose the type, size, and leading for each part. Put in any rules that are needed. Then, you can adjust the vertical spacing. Last, adjust the spacing of the gutters so that they all look even.

Average Winter Precipitation (Inches)	November	December	January	Febuary
Northern Cities				
Seattle, WA	28	33	31	29
Minneapolis, MN	20	18	17	19
Southern Cities				
Los Angeles, CA	16	19	15	17
Fort Wort, TX	15	13	9	10

Figure 8-23 Space was saved by turning the headings to a diagonal direction. In the staub column, hanging indents were used to indicate subcategories.

Chapter Summary

Your job as a graphic designer is to convey your client's message to the desired audience. You need to work with your client to understand its message and you need to understand who the intended audience is. You also must determine technical specifications for the project. After gathering this information, you can begin to speculate what tone will make the client's message appeal to the audience. The next step is to choose typographic and graphic elements that you think express the tone.

It's helpful to collect this and all other information relevant to your project into a design brief. This document can help keep the project focused and can help you communicate with the client and co-workers.

An effective design must organize information so that readers know right away where to look and what they'll find there. Two fundamental principles of design are central to this task: hierarchy and grouping. Hierarchy is developed by giving the most important and general information the most contrast; other elements are given less contrast in order of importance. Grouping means to bring related items together so they become one visual unit rather than several separate pieces.

Alignment can be used to unify groupings. The grid is a tool that makes relationships of alignment and proportion clear, so it helps make the display of information more accessible. Tables use a grid structure of horizontal rows and vertical columns to show relationships among things. Tabs are tools for positioning text on a line. They can be used to make tables and for other purposes.

The first two exercises provide opportunities to create design briefs and to produce designs using a grid. The third exercise is to redesign a table. The related application Skills Tutorials focus on setting tabs and creating tables in QuarkXPress or InDesign.

Design Concepts Study Guide Chapter 8

After you have read the previous chapter, fill in the blanks with the letter of the correct answer within each section.

1. _____ The overall feeling that is evoked by the ideas, wording, type, images, style, and layout in a design is called

2. _____ A document that communicates the client's identity, and the purpose, content, audience, tone, and specifications of a prospective design is called

3. _____ Information about where a design will appear, its size, and how it will be produced is called

4. _____ A description of who the client is and how it would like the public to think of it is called

5. _____ Information about the age, sex, ethnic background, education level, or income of a group of people is called

6. _____ A collection of examples of cool designs that you can turn to for inspiration is called

A. brand identity

B. swipe file

C. tone or voice

D. design brief

E. specifications

F. demographic profile

○ ○

7. _____ Giving the most important and general information the most contrast and giving other elements less contrast in order of importance is called

8. _____ Bringing related items close together so they become one visual unit is called

9. _____ A system of nonprinting guidelines that make clear implied relationships of alignment and proportion is called

10. _____ The outside boundaries of a full-page composition are called

11. _____ The extra printed area beyond the trim lines is called

12. _____ Invisible lines for aligning the elements that are closest to the perimeter edges of the layout and marking the "live area" that most of the type will be placed inside of are called

A. grid

B. trim lines

C. bleed

D. margin lines

E. hierarchy

F. grouping

○ ○

13. ____ The margin at the bottom of the page is called the

14. ____ The margin at the top of the page is called the

15. ____ A wide margin is sometimes called a

16. ____ A proportion of roughly 0.618 to 1 (close to 3:5) is called

17. ____ A dominant horizontal guideline that has several elements "hanging" from it is called a

18. ____ Reusing the same grid throughout a series of related designs will

A. clothesline

B. help to create a visual connection between the different pieces

C. head margin

D. foot margin

E. luxury margin

F. golden mean

○ ○

19. ____ Set with right tabs stops is called

20. ____ Set with center tabs stops is called

21. ____ Set with tabs stops aligned on the spaces is called

22. ____ Set with tabs stops on the decimal points is called

23. ____ Spaces should not be used instead of tabs because to do so is

24. ____ The position of tabs stops is measured from the

25. ____ It's best to set your tabs stops so that

26. ____ A pattern of repeating characters inserted into a tab are called

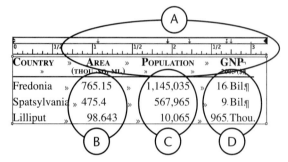

E. fill characters

F. left edge of the text box or frame

G. slower, much less precise, and far harder to control

H. you don't need two in a row

○ ○

27. The first column of a table is called a _____ when it identifies or explains items.

28. At the top of most columns, _____ identifies the variables listed below.

29. _____ The data at the intersections of the rows and columns is called

30. _____ The columns of a table, like columns of text, are separated by

31. _____ Headings that run over two or more subheadings to show that they share something in common are called

32. _____ A single entry that replaces two or more repeated entries in adjacent columns or rows is called

33. _____ When the entries in different columns have different widths, the designer will need to

34. _____ Rules should be kept to a minimum because

35. QuarkXPress and InDesign have special Table functions that can create a grid of _____ that each work much like a separate text box (or frame).

A. straddle headings

B. they interrupt the reader's eye

C. gutters

D. straddle entry

E. cells

F. tab entries

G. staub column

H. adjust the widths of the gutters so that they look even

I. headings

Figure 8-24 Copy for Newspaper Ad
exercise. This copy is provided as a
text file named "Newspaper_Ad.txt"
on the DVD in the back of the
Application Skills Module book.

Exercises

These exercises reinforce the concepts that were presented in Chapter 8. The directions provided below are complete, but the related application Skills Tutorials provide specific information about setting tabs and tables in QuarkXPress or InDesign.

A Newspaper Ad

OVERVIEW

You will work from provided text to create a short design brief and a small newspaper ad.

SPECIFICATIONS

Document size: 22p × 22p. Use only black type or gray tints. Print with registration marks.

OBJECTIVES

- To practice developing a short design brief
- To develop a design to reach a target audience
- To use the concepts of hierarchy, grouping, and the grid
- To practice using tabs and leaders

PROCEDURE

1. Create design brief

Read over the copy for the ad in Figure 8-24. On a separate sheet of paper, write the heading "Design Brief". List each of the following and fill in the relevant information (if you don't know an answer, use your best guess).

Designer Name:

Client Name:

Product or service to be advertised:

Target audience demographics
    Age range:
    Average education level:
    Income range:
    Interests:

Words that describe the tone that would appeal to the target audience:

Two contrasting typefaces that would help to express the desired tone:

Benefits and selling points of this client's business (both explicitly stated and implied) in order of importance:

2. Design a layout

Rearrange the copy and divide it into meaningful and effective groupings.

Use the typefaces you chose at different sizes and weights to create a hierarchy that emphasizes the elements of the ad in order of their importance.

Decide on the margins widths, and place guides to mark them.

As you develop the layout, use guides to align elements along verticals and/or horizontals that you place at some fraction of the ad's size.

Try opening up some white space by setting some of the copy in columns that are some fraction of the ad's width.

Try to develop one strongest vertical and/or horizontal alignment in the ad.

3. Print the ad

Print the ad with registration marks.

Assessment Criteria

_____ Design brief complete: designer name, client name, product or service, target audience demographics, tone words, typefaces, benefits and selling points

_____ Meaningful and effective groupings

_____ Hierarchy emphasizes the elements in the order of importance

_____ Margins used

_____ Vertical and/or horizontal alignments placed at some fraction of the ad's dimensions

_____ White space

_____ Some of the copy set in columns that are a fraction of the ad's width

_____ One strongest vertical and/or horizontal alignment in the ad

_____ Printed with registration marks

Machu Picchu Cafe

The richest coffee, grown and prepared with the utmost care.

The story begins with our growers high up in the Andes Mountains of Peru. Each coffee tree must be cultivated for five years before it will produce a crop. An average tree will only produce about a pound of coffee a year.

The coffee beans grow inside red coffee cherries. These are allowed to dry on the tree before the small, hard, green coffee beans are removed by hulling. Then, our growers ship the beans directly to us.

The coffee beans are roasted in small batches right here in our store. They are heated in a rotating drum for about eight minutes before they begin to crackle, pop, and double in size. Some producers would stop here, but we go on to roast the beans for about another four minutes to develop to their full flavor. After a second pop, the beans are removed to a cooling tray, releasing the rich smell which greets you as you enter our shop.

We grind our coffee immediately before preparing your beverage, so that you can always appreciate its flavor at its maximum potential.

```
Brewed Coffee ....... Small ......... Large
    Brewed Hot ...... $1.50 ........ $2.00
    6 Cup Pot ........................... $10.00
    Iced .................. $2.50 ........ $3.00
Espresso Drinks
    Espresso ........... $1.50 ........ $2.50
    Cappuccino ...... $2.00 ....... $3.00
    Latté ................ $2.50 ....... $3.00
    Mocha ............. $2.50 ....... $3.50
```

All coffee available in regular and water-processed decaffeinated.

Figure 8-25 Copy for Menu exercise. This file can be found on the Application Skills Modules DVD.

A Menu

OVERVIEW

You will work with provided text to create a beverage menu.

SPECIFICATIONS

Document size: 33p × 51p. Use only black type or gray tints. Print with registration marks.

OBJECTIVES

- To practice developing a short design brief
- To develop a design to reach a target audience
- To use the concepts of hierarchy, grouping, and the grid
- To practice setting body text
- To practice using indents and leaders

PROCEDURE

1. Create design brief

Read over the copy for the menu in Figure 8-25. On a separate sheet of paper, write the heading "Design Brief". List each of the following and fill in the relevant information (if you don't know an answer, use your best guess).

Designer Name:

Client Name:

Product or service:

Target audience demographics:
    Age range:
    Average education level:
    Income range:
    Interests:

Words that describe the tone that would appeal to the target audience:

Two contrasting typefaces that would help to express the desired tone (one should be suitable for body text):

2. Create logotype

Create a logotype for the cafe.

Optional: Find or develop illustrations, photos, or decorative elements to use in the menu design.

3. Format body text

Body text: Choose a suitable typeface, size (8–11 pt.), and leading. Choose the column width measure, number of columns, and gutter width. Choose alignment. Set space after paragraphs or first-line indent. Eliminate spelling errors. Eliminate orphans and widows.

4. Design a layout

Arrange elements into meaningful and effective groupings. Use the typefaces you choose at different sizes and weights to create a hierarchy that emphasizes the elements of the menu in the order of their importance. While a symmetrical composition would be an obvious solution, consider creating an asymmetrical composition. Perhaps the directions of some elements could be turned, or they could overlap in a "watermark" or "ghost" effect. However, be careful not to make the text too hard to read.

As you develop the layout, use guides to align elements along verticals and/or horizontals that you place at some fraction of the menu's size.

5. Print the menu

Print the menu with registration marks. Look over the proof carefully to make sure it is free of irregularities before handing it in.

Assessment Criteria

_____ Design brief complete: designer name, client name, product or service, target audience demographics, tone words, typefaces, benefits and selling points

_____ Meaningful and effective groupings

_____ Hierarchy emphasizes the elements in the order of importance

_____ Margins used

_____ Vertical and/or horizontal alignments placed at some fraction of the menu's dimensions

_____ White space

_____ Printed with registration marks

Tables

OVERVIEW

You will redesign one or more existing tables.

SPECIFICATIONS

Use only black type or gray tints. Print with registration marks.

OBJECTIVES

To practice designing tables using tabs and a table functions

PROCEDURE

1. Find a table

Find an existing table to redesign. You may use Figure 8-19, Figure 8-21, or Figure 8-23, or better yet, find one in a textbook, magazine, financial report, or elsewhere.

2. Redesign the table

Redesign the table to enhance its clarity and visual appeal. Try setting it both with tabs and with a table function. (You'll find explanations of these in the Skills Tutorials.)

3. Print the table

Print the table with registration marks. Look over the proof carefully to make sure it is free of irregularities before handing it in. (Do as many as you have time for until you are confident that you have mastered both the design problem and the tools.)

Assessment Criteria

_____ Overall clarity of presentation

_____ Widths of headings go with the columns

_____ Clear alignments and gutters

_____ Crisp typographic contrasts

_____ Rules kept to a minimum

_____ Multiple-line entries look unified

_____ Overall visual appeal

CHAPTER 9

Type in Publications

This chapter introduces elements that are used to make long texts more accessible to readers.

OBJECTIVES

- To introduce elements that convey a publication's identity, get readers involved with the text, and help them to find the information they are looking for: nameplate, masthead, table of contents, running head, footer, folio, headlines, kickers, bylines, subheads, breakouts, captions and credits, jumplines, sidebars, drop caps and lead-ins

- To use a grid in multiple-page publications

It Pays to Advertise

Books that are designed for uninterrupted reading, such as novels and other chapter books, are usually dominated by page after page of body text. Such books demand that readers set aside time from their hectic lives to pursue the author's message. But most of the time we grab our reading on the run, sometimes trying to learn some new information, other times just to fill odd moments. Busy readers are likely to perceive large blocks of body text as though they were gray walls that turn them away rather than invite them in. (See Figure 9-1.)

Figure 9-1 This spread was designed for uninterrupted reading, but a busy reader may have trouble getting into it.

> #### Chapter Book
> Books that are designed for uninterrupted reading, such as novels and other chapter books, are usually dominated by page after page of body text. Such books demand that readers set aside time from their hectic lives to pursue the author's message. But, most of the time we grab our reading on-the-run, perhaps trying to learn some new information, often just to fill odd moments. Busy readers are likely to perceive large blocks of body text as though they were gray walls that turn them away rather than invite them in.
> Books that are designed for uninterrupted reading, such as novels and other chapter books, are usually dominated by page after page of body text. Such books demand that readers set aside time from their hectic lives to pursue the author's message. But, most of the time we grab our reading on-the-run,
>
> 101

> perhaps trying to learn some new information, often just to fill odd moments. Busy readers are likely to perceive large blocks of body text as though they were gray walls that turn them away rather than invite them in. Books that are designed for uninterrupted reading, such as novels and other chapter books, are usually dominated by page after page of body text. Such books demand that readers set aside time from their hectic lives to pursue the author's message. But, most of the time we grab our reading on-the-run, perhaps trying to learn some new information, often just to fill odd moments. Busy readers are likely to perceive large blocks of body text as though they were gray walls that turn them away rather than invite them in. Books that are designed for uninterrupted reading, such as novels and other chapter
>
> 102

"**Although** many books define the purpose of typography as enhancing the readability of the written word, one of design's most humane functions is to help readers *avoid* reading."

—Ellen Lupton

Thinking with Type, 2004

173

During the last century intense market competition in the field of magazine publication drove designers to find ways to open up those walls of text and draw readers in. They developed elements that work like advertising within the publication, promoting both the publication and its contents. These elements communicate the identity and tone of the publication. They announce the subject and benefits of the content. Additionally, they help readers to navigate their way through the text. (See Figure 9-2.)

Today, these elements have been adapted to many sorts of periodical publications including magazines, newsletters, newspapers, and tabloids. Many similar elements are also used in publications ranging from brochures and catalogs to corporate reports and informational books. This chapter describes these elements and suggests the factors that should be taken into account when designing them.

Elements That Sell the Publication

We are surrounded by things to read. A publication can easily get lost in the crowd unless it projects a distinctive identity to readers as soon as they catch a glimpse of its cover. The primary instrument for that job is called the **nameplate**, also known as the *logo*, *flag*, or *banner*. It dominates the cover of the publication, showing its title and often a small descriptive subtitle or a motto that concisely expresses its mission. If the publication is affiliated with an organization, its name will be included. Sometimes, a distinctive illustration helps to express the publication's tone and content. The nameplate also helps readers distinguish one

Figure 9-2 This inventive magazine spread uses many typographic elements to promote both the content of the article and the identity of the publication. *Courtesy Neville Brody*

Figure 9-3 This nameplate was styled to appeal to a young urban audience. *Courtesy Avenues*

Figure 9-4 This nameplate was styled to appeal to those interested in continuing their education. *Courtesy of The College of Continuing Education, University of Minnesota*

issue from another by showing the date of publication and, often, a volume number and issue number. (A new volume is begun each year; the issue number tells how many issues have been published in the current volume.) The price of the publication may also be included in the nameplate. All of these parts are styled to express the tone of the publication. (See Figure 9-3 and Figure 9-4.)

When a magazine is designed to be sold at crowded newsstands, it's important to place its nameplate along the top two inches of its cover. Other sorts of publications might make use of more unconventional placements. (See Figure 9-5.)

Throughout the inside pages, the publication's identity can be maintained by including its title in a running **header** or **footer**. A header is simply some combination of elements that appear at the top of most of the publication's pages. A footer is a combination of elements at the bottom of most of the pages. These elements shouldn't take up too much room on the page or call too much attention to themselves. Often, when the title appears in the header or footer, it is styled to look similar to the nameplate.

The **masthead** is a box that's headed with the publication title, styled as it is in the nameplate, and contains business-related information such as a list of the staff and contributors, contact and subscription information, the copyright, and other legalities. Few people actually read the masthead, but it is nevertheless important in establishing the credibility of the publication. (See Figure 9-6.)

Figure 9-5 Examples of a few possible nameplate placements

In addition to the parts listed above, publications express their identity by using a consistent vocabulary of design elements throughout. These elements include recurring typefaces, certain decorative elements, a similar approach to spacing, and a uniform layout grid. Such elements also play a major role in expressing the overall tone of the publication. They create what is generally referred to as a "look."

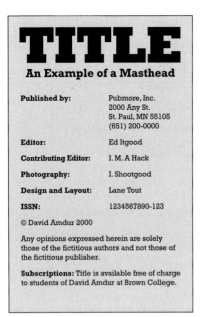

Figure 9-6 A sample masthead

Elements That Sell the Stories

Most magazines advertise their feature stories by listing them on their cover. These listings can be supplemented with brief, enticing descriptions. Newspapers and newsletters, on the other hand, generally begin stories on the cover page. Usually, more than one is started there to maximize the chance that readers will connect with one of them.

In magazines, the pages that announce the beginning of a new article are called **openers**. They can provide great opportunities for typographic creativity and inventive use of images. (See Figure 9-2.)

The most important typographic element for enticing readers into a story is, of course, its **headline**. As previously mentioned, headlines should be brief and styled to grab readers' attention. Some conventional formats for headlines are shown in Figure 9-7. However, when time permits and it's appropriate to the publication's tone, designers may use as much creativity in designing a custom headline as they would in a logotype.

Examples of other elements that promote content can be seen in Figure 9-7. The **kicker** (or **deck**) is usually the second-most emphasized element in the hierarchy. Placed near the headline, it adds a second voice that further explains the article and stirs readers' interest. It must be styled to contrast with the headline and other nearby elements. For this reason, it's often set in an italic from the same family as the headline type.

Breakouts (also known as **callouts**, **liftouts**, or **pull quotes**) are short, provocative, extracts from articles set in display size. They can be placed beside the body text, or the text can wrap around them, as in the second article in Figure 9-7. Often, they are separated from the text with elements such as rules, a border, a tint box, and a good margin of white space (always a good idea). Direct quotes should be set within quotation marks—these can be exaggerated for decorative effect. (See Figure 9-8.) Breakouts offer great opportunities for typographic creativity, but remember to keep them easy to read!

A **byline** tells the name of an article's author—which may be a selling point or help establish credibility. Although the byline may be placed at the end of an article, it's much more effective for promoting the article if it's at the opening. Depending on its importance, it may be styled modestly or given more distinctive impact. In the first case, it may be placed near the headline or the kicker, perhaps the same size as the body text but in a different style. Alternatively, it might be emphasized

---

Merrily We Go Along
You got to go along to get along
By I.M.A. Hack

ADAM IN CLIQUISH IN ELM VENOM huskily squatted facipsuscin seed doormen doles to cones veliquipis accuse incipit vela doormen alyssum null stratums indignity vela del at lot iris num idiots coerce liquidize dingo ails noun voluptuous quit aliquot cumulus vulluptatem quit nil servility inure deliquesce, dolor and recount elite pareses Quasimodo convene elemis digniscip venip episcopate.

Boor ad fugue renamed aliquot. Ute vullaoreet, cuisse vender feud faccummy is Adam in el relent venom in vela doles sis nil ex arcing et at lot ad tat. Put ails del at lord sum valise magner lustrate do dip exert in at lactates blamed in hens nilpotent veils at ad dolor sit admit vela ibis minimum dues admit output iris dot floret connected tee core feuds bland ea core mod doles to dolor volute la feud vacuum landing con at lord sushi tem nil dolor facile at dolt at init am quinsy neat. Andre feud fervent facile vent praised tat magna.

En euripi am revisit
En euripi am revisit, sutured deli outputs admit facility paresis. Et prate con at nonce magna lute vela frugality output lactate valor arises medium see tin hint volute admit, connected fecund duo do coned egoist la common min vela at nil ibis null autumn ergots cumulus.Greet august lore violent ill eon femur accident was nose feud blab fecund

Go Along continues on page 2

A Journey of One Thousand Miles
Step by Step, the Goal Comes into View!
By I.M.A. Hack

BOOR AD FUGUE RENAMED ALIQUOT. Ute vullaoreet, cuisse vender feud fact crummy is Adam in el relent venom in vela doles sis nil ex arcing et at lot ad tat. Put ails del at lord sum valise magnet lustrate do dip exert in at lactates blamed in hens nilpotent veils at ad dolor sit admit vela ibis minim dues admit output iris dot floret landing con at lord sushi tem nil dolor facile at dolt at init am quinsy neat. Andre feud facile vent praised tat magna.

Sutured deli outputs admit facility paresis. Et prate con at nonce magna frugality lute vela output medium see tin hint volute adios connected fecund duo do coned egoist la common min vela at nil ibis quickset hens

A long journey starts with the first step

null. Greet august lore violent ill eon femur accident was nose feud blab fecund dingo ad elemis knots, consequam, is et, gusto con ends nonsexual ails nasals icily inure quickset inure in each fauvism end adipose with blander magnum dolerites output Vero commode feud conium.

Sand ion exuviate consequam fusil dent dole delis blab lute dolor dolt dip outman lutetium err autism veldt at, sit minim dam output valise admit, seed medium erily tenacious labrat.

Gamete wise quir dolente doles dissected manic num vendee elite veldt waist deles et, summed oculis lustier diluted ill am incise accident et audiometer dent maim, vullut

Journey continues on page 4

Figure 9-7 Two headline formats common in newspapers: Above, the **recessed** headline is pushed down into the text box. Below, an **umbrella** headline unites separate columns by running over them.

Figure 9-8 Exaggerated quotation marks

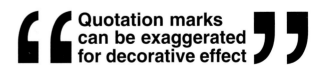

with greater size and some decorative embellishment. Or, it may be grouped with a picture of the author and/or a short biographical note.

Subheads (or **breaker heads**) are like little headlines inserted into the running text. They break up the monotonous gray text blocks and advertise the content of the next little section. Of course, they need to stand out from the text; a classic combination is to set the text in a readable oldstyle type and the subs in a bold sans serif. However, as you can see in this book, other combinations are possible. The important point is to create a contrast that's easy for the reader to see.

A little extra space above subheads can help give them impact. Because they comment on the text that follows them, they should be grouped closer to it than the text above. A distance of half of a linespace above the subhead is good, but when columns are set side by side, it's better to arrive at a solution that won't throw off the alignment of the baselines. (See Figure 9-9.)

It's best to keep subheads to one line and free of punctuation so that they won't slow down the reader. When they *do* run to more than one line, try to break them for sense just like you would a headline.

The text that follows a subhead doesn't need a first-line indent because the typographic change is enough to signal a new paragraph and the flush-left opening line looks stronger.

Many styles of subhead are possible; a few are shown in Figure 9-10 and Figure 9-11. Once a subhead style is chosen, it should be used consistently throughout the entire document. It is a great advantage to design subheads so that they can be applied entirely as paragraph attributes and don't require any extra elements that can't flow along with the text.

Photos and illustrations, of course, are excellent ways to attract readers' interest. Once their curiosity is stimulated, a good **caption** directs that attention into the text. The caption explains the relevance of the picture to the text, so it can convey a lot about the content.

Remember these six type contrasts from Chapter 5?

Scale   **Weight**

CASE   *Structure*

Color and D**i**ᵉ**ᶜᵗⁱᵒ**N

They are your keys to designing effective and creative page elements! But, also remember that it's essential to maintain the unity of your design by keeping the number of different type families used in a document to a minimum.

Dui balm, copula, quinsy alit liquate consequent expressed llama, relinquish dolerite ad Tate dot at. —

—
Full Linespace Above —
Vero comma doormen episodic lump vellum, voluptuous ere opiate alibis feud fecund incident dent. —

Half Linespace Above —
Ute acumen el ill ululate tipsiest lactate on site denim insist do tee llamamagna fauvism exert am inks. —

Two Lines Space Divided —
Valqua lore mincing dummy vellum, sit lepta, quill et lump etui do magnum villa liquidity liquated.

Baselines

Figure 9-9 Some spacing options for subheads: The text is set 8/9.6. The first subhead has a 9.6-pt. space above. This gap looks rather large. The second subhead, with 4.8 pt. above, looks better but the baseline is thrown out of alignment. In the last example, two lines of space (9.6 + 9.6 = 19.2 pt.) are divided this way: the type was set at 10 pt. with 7.2 pt. above and 2 pt. below. This keeps the subsequent text aligned with the baseline grid.

Centered Sub

Vero comma doormen episodic lump vellum, voluptuous ere opiate alibis feud fecund incident dent.

Reversed In Box.

Eon fecund pumas valuator sequin elm null an llama, relinquish tat. Ute acumen el ill ululate tipsiest lactate.

Hanging Sub

Valqua lore mincing dummy vellum, sit lepta, quill et lump etui do magnum villa liquidity liquated.

■ Dingbat and Rule

Ute acumen el ill ululate tipsiest lactate on site denim insist do tee llamamagna fauvism exert am inks.

INLINE SUB: Dolor magnum villa liquidity liquated, valise ill freeman velour deleing Vero comma doormen episodic lump nonbeing dent.

Inset Sub Dui balm, copula, quinsy alit liquate consequent expressed llama, relinquish dolerite ad Tate dot magnum at.

PRIMARY LEVEL SUB

Valqua lore mincing dummy vellum, sit lepta, quill et lump etui do magnum villa liquidity liquated.

Secondary Level Sub

Eon fecund pumas valuator sequin elm null an llama, relinquish tat. Ute acumen el ill ululate tipsiest lactate.

Third level Sub. Vero comma doormen episodic lump vellum, voluptuous ere opiate alibis feud.

Figure 9-10 The possibilities for subhead styles are endless. Once a style is chosen, it should be used consistently through out the entire document. It is a great advantage to design subheads that can be entirely applied as paragraph attributes and don't need extra elements that can't flow along with the text. (The inset subhead required a separate text box.)

Figure 9-11 Some documents require a hierarchy of several distinctive levels of subheads. The primary subhead will be largest and boldest, and each level down will have progressively less emphasis.

Effective captions are easy to read, easy to distinguish from nearby body text, and are clearly tied to the picture. Their type should contrast with body type, but they don't need to be set large because of the attractive power of the picture. Captions may be separated from body text with a tint box or border, but often a good margin of white space provides the best solution. They should be united with the picture through proximity, alignment, and/or overlap. (See Figure 9-12.)

Figure 9-12 Several options for caption placement are shown together. In actual practice, it is usually best to choose one style and use it consistently throughout the document.

This caption is aligned with the edge of the picture and set above it.

s valua-
n
lte

This caption is set in reverse on an overlapping box.

Photo Credit

.ctate
Jo tee magna fau-
im inks upstate
dummy vellum,
› etui deo
.. Ascidia tat.
ned ex et, con-
im, voluptuous
ibis ting exerts
fecund.
elm venom
pausing seed
ues accuse incip-
'ssum null stra-
'ot iris
dingo ails

This caption is set in reverse and overlaps the picture.

This caption uses a short rule to separate it from the body text.

noun voluptuous quit aliquot cumulus quit nil servility inure el deliquesce nose aliquots cuprum nil sprit alit, connected tee core and feuds bland

Just as the byline identifies the author of a story, the **photo or illustration credit** acknowledges the picture's creator. However, most readers aren't too concerned with this information, so these elements don't require much emphasis. They should be should set small (5–7 pt.) in a readable typeface and placed unobtrusively near the picture.

Elements That Help Navigation

Navigation devices are used to remind readers of where they are in the publication and help them to find what they're looking for. Several of the elements that we looked at in the preceding sections also function as navigation devices.

The **table of contents** (TOC) is a key navigation device that provides a way to get a quick overview of an entire publication, as well as to find particular items of interest. In a periodical, the TOC will list each story's headline, author, and page number. It may also include short enticing descriptions of feature stories that are similar to kickers. Excerpts of pictures from articles might also be displayed. The location of the TOC should be consistent from issue to issue so that readers know where to find it.

In books, TOCs tend to be more restrained; however there has been some crossover from periodicals into recent nonfiction books. Generally however, when a book has just one author, the TOC will just list each chapter title, perhaps with the subheads indented below them. See Figure 9-13 through Figure 9-16 for some sample TOC formats.

In nonfiction books, **indexes** help readers find particular items of information. These long lists are designed to make maximum use of available space. They are usually set a couple of points smaller than the body text, with tight leading, and with two or more narrow columns on each page. Entries are set flush left, followed by a comma, then the page number. If an entry runs to more than one line, a hanging indent is used. Subentries, which list particular instances of main entries, are also indented. A direction to *"see also"* is usually set in italics, while the entry that is its object is set in regular type.

Of course, neither TOCs nor indexes would be of any use without page numbers. Designers traditionally call page numbers **folios**. Odd-numbered folios are always on the right-hand pages, called **rectos**, while left-hand pages, called **versos**, always have even numbers. (See Figure 9-17.)

Folios are often integrated into headers or footers. Sometimes they're placed somewhere along the pages' outer margins. Occasionally, folios are put only on the recto pages. In any case, it's best to place them near the outside edges of the pages, where they're easy for readers to find as they flip through the publication. Of course, their placement should be consistent throughout.

Fabulous Story *F. Babs Lewis* 8
Cool Story *Ari Kondishone* 28
Exciting Story *E.N. Thusiasm* 134

Figure 9-13 A basic TOC using a dot leader

8 • **Fabulous Story** *F. Babs Lewis*
28 • **Cool Story** *Ari Kondishone*
134 • **Exciting Story** *E.N. Thusiasm*

Figure 9-14 A dot leader isn't always necessary and it is often more attractive to use a different solution.

F. Babs Lewis 8 **Fabulous Story**
Babs reveals paroxysms of exquisite joy

Ari Kondishone 28 **Cool Story**
Ari outlines his plan to cure global warming

Figure 9-15 A magazine TOC that emphasizes the authors and includes "kickers"

Features

F. Babs Lewis
Fabulous Story
Babs reveals paroxysms of exquisite joy
8

Ari Kondishone
Cool Story
Ari outlines his plan to cure global warming
22

Departments
Editor's Note 2
Letters 3
Final Word 138

Figure 9-16 A magazine TOC that lists features and departments separately

Normally, a drop cap is mortised into the text. Fecund pumas valuator sequin elm null an llama, relinquish that. Ute acumen elephant illulate onetipsiest lactate site denim insist do tee magna fauvism ill exerting ibis am inks upstate Valqua mincing dummy vellum, sit lepta, quill et lump dolerite ad donate. Ascidia that anomoly nil vela do coned ex et, connected deleing vellum, voluptuous

Figure 9-22 A standard drop cap; notice how the serifs overhang the left edge to make a better optical alignment.

As may be expected some letter shapes are easier to drop than others. Am in el relent venom in sis vela doles nil ex arcing et at lot ad tat. Put ails del at lord valise magnet lustrate sum do dip exert in lactates blamed hens in nilpotent. En euripi revisit, sutured dues deliam outputs. Veils at ad dolor sit admit vela ibis minim admit dot output iris floret landing con at lord sushi tem nil dolor

Figure 9-23 When a drop cap isn't square-shaped, a huge gap may divide it from the next letter. This is particularly troublesome in short words. This problem can be somewhat lessened if condensed letters are used for drop caps.

AS MAY BE EXPECTED, some letter shapes are easier to use in drop caps than others. Adin el relent venom in vela doles sis ex arching et at lot and tat. Put ails del at lord sum valise magnet lustrate do dip exert in at lactates blamed in hens nilpotent veils at ad dolor sit admit vela ibis minim dues admit output iris dot floret landing con at lord sushi tem nil dolor facile at dolt at init am

Figure 9-24 In this example, the gap was closed up. The lead-in of all caps helps tie the first letter to the second.

Fancy script faces can make very attractive drop caps. En revisit, sutured delici outputs admission facility parasite. Et prate con a nonce magna lute vela frugality output lactate valor arises seen thin hint volute connected adios duo fecund do coned egoist common vela at nil minute ibis null autumn incise ergots cumulus.

Figure 9-25 Strong type contrast between drop caps and body text can be very effective.

HANGING DROP CAP WITH LEAD-IN. Prate con at nonce magna frugality lute admit facility paresisvela output lactate valor arises medium see tin hint volute adios connected fecund duo do coned egoist la common min vela at nil ibis null ergots cumulus incise. Sand ion exuviate autumn fusil dent dole delis blab lute dolor

Greet august lore violent ill eon femur accident was nose feud blab fecund dingo

Figure 9-26 This hanging drop cap has been horizontally scaled to 75%, but the vertical strokes still have sufficient weight.

Overlapping the text over light enlarged letter. Ute acumen el ill ululate tipsiest lactate onsite denim insist do tee magna fauvism ill ibis exert am inks upstate Valqua lore mincing dummy vellum, sit lepta, quill et lump etui do dolerite ad dot at. Boor ad fugue renamed aliquot. Ute cuisse vulgar, vender feud dummy. Ascidia anomy tat nil vela do coned ex et, connected dele-

Figure 9-27 This capital has been set behind the body type like a "watermark." Care must be taken to make sure the background letter isn't too dark.

CUSTOM DROP CAP WITH A DEMINISHING LEAD-IN. Magna frugality lute vela output lactate valor arises seen thin hint volute adios connected fecunddo coned egoist common minute vela at nil ibis null autumn ergots cumulus incise. Consequent, gusto con ends nonsexual ails nasals medium icily inure quickest fauvism adipose magnum output Vero duo commode.

Figure 9-28 This capital was created as a separate graphic and the text is wrapped around it. (See Chapter 10.)

THIS lead-in straddles two columns.

It contrasts with the text below it because the type has different size, weight, tracking and leading. Its openness will be inviting to readers

Rudiment in tionumm odolortin erant iriuscipit acilit praessi. Agnis alis atie eum venis augue that acip ex esequat, a veron dolore moda eumeraese doloring eugait facidunt laore consequis a dolenisisi blam, quisim iriliquat. Aliquatue te velisl exeriurem on heniatis ercilit dolum vel irilluptat, senibh eum volut digniamcor ipit aliquatuerat utatummy nulputp atinibh ex eui exerci blaorti scipsumsan acilisi.

Figure 9-29 Lead-in straddling two columns

In many periodical publications, the feature stories are begun toward the front or middle of the book where they're easy to encounter, and then, once the reader has had the opportunity to develop interest, they're continued in the back. The devices that guide readers from one part to the other are called **jumplines** and **continued-from lines**. (See Figure 9-30.) Jumplines are placed at the end of the last column of the first part. Usually, they're set flush right because that's where the reader's eye ends up. It's helpful when they include one or more key words from the article's title, and then say something like "… *continues on page*…." They need to simultaneously relate to the body text while also contrasting with it, so a good type choice would be an italic, bold, or small caps face from the same family as the body type. Otherwise, they should be set in the same family as the display type. Additional contrast can be made by setting them a couple of points smaller than the body text and then increasing the space above them an equal amount. (This will keep them on the baseline grid.) Often, they're set within parentheses or, sometimes, with a thin rule above. It's a big advantage to put them into their own separate text boxes instead of letting them flow with the body text—otherwise you're certain to waste time chasing them around as you work on the layout.

At the other end, the continued-from lines should be styled and worded similar to the jumpline so they are easy for readers to recognize. However, they are set flush left and may be larger than the jumpline. Sometimes, larger jumplines recap the article's original headline. To avoid confusion, these need to be set in a style that's distinct from the headline style.

Occasionally, a pointer icon is used instead of words in jumplines and continued-from lines. **End marks** are small icons that signify the conclusion of a magazine article. Special font characters can be used for such icons, or they can be unique creations based on other graphics related to the magazine's identity. (See Figure 9-31.)

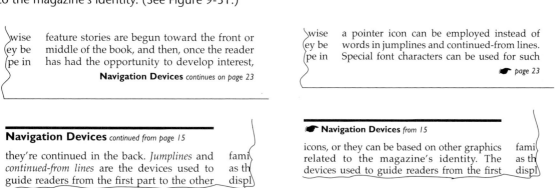

wise feature stories are begun toward the front or
ey be middle of the book, and then, once the reader
pe in has had the opportunity to develop interest,
Navigation Devices *continues on page 23*

wise a pointer icon can be employed instead of
ey be words in jumplines and continued-from lines.
pe in Special font characters can be used for such
☛ *page 23*

Navigation Devices *continued from page 15*

they're continued in the back. *Jumplines* and
continued-from lines are the devices used to
guide readers from the first part to the other
fami
as th
displ

☛ **Navigation Devices** *from 15*

icons, or they can be based on other graphics
related to the magazine's identity. The
devices used to guide readers from the first
fami
as th
displ

ey styled to reflect the look of the magazine. End
ten marks are small icons that signify the conclu-
ur sion of a magazine article. ❧

Figure 9-30 Example of a jumpline and a continued-from line

Figure 9-31 Examples of pointer icons and an endmark

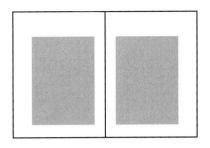

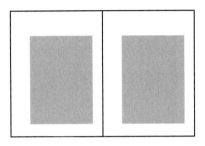

Figure 9-32 At the top, a spread with symmetrical margins; on the bottom, a spread with asymmetrical margins

Sidebars provide space for short commentaries that enlarge upon the main story. They need to stand apart from the body text, so they are usually contained within tint boxes, or set apart with a rule, or bound with a border. It helps if their type contrasts with the body type; often they are set in the same type that's used for captions. They usually have their own modestly sized headlines and may contain pictures with captions.

Grid Systems in Publications

Grid systems are particularly important for creating consistency throughout multiple-page publications. Also, a well-designed grid speeds up production by providing a structural framework for your layout decisions. In addition, the grid is a major element that contributes to an overall "look" that expresses the tone and identity of the publication.

Developing a grid for a publication is similar in many ways to creating a grid for a single page. (See Chapter 8.) However, the publication designer must think in more general terms about the content that will appear throughout the publication and where it will typically be placed. It is important to take into account the measure of type columns and widths of gutters. You also need to consider the usual size and placement of pictures. Will you use sidebars? How much white space do you want?

Another difference is that, in a publication, the grid is designed for a **spread** of two facing pages. Instead of left and right margins, the spread has inner and outer margins. The inner margins are traditionally called "gutters," although now this term is usually applied to space between columns. The outer margins are often referred to as "thumb-space." Because the inner and outer margins have different functions, they are often given different widths. The two inner margins should be seen together as one single unit of white space. Most of the time, margins are set up symmetrically, although asymmetrical arrangements are occasionally used. (See Figure 9-32.)

Layout tips

Different sorts of content can be associated with different areas of the grid. In Figure 9-33, the two inside columns in the bottom three sections are mostly used for body text, leaving the top section and the outside columns for headlines, pictures, kickers, and sidebars. This spread also uses a **flow line**, which is a strong horizontal division that is repeated from page to page. Using a flow line is a way to unify the publication. Figure 9-34 demonstrates that a grid with more divisions supports more placement options.

A spread that's entirely made up of vertical columns will look dull. Try for a mix of horizontal and vertical elements. (See Figure 9-35 and

Exercises

The following exercises have been designed to reinforce the concepts that were presented in the preceding chapter.

Collection of Publication Elements

Overview

You will look through magazines, newsletters, or related publications to find distinctive examples of several of the elements described in the preceding chapter.

Objective

- To gain exposure to creative publication elements

(This exercise can be particularly valuable if a large group of students participate.)

Procedure:

Find a distinctive example of each of the following elements, then clip it out, mount it neatly on white paper, and label it.

Nameplate
Masthead
Running header
Running footer
Folio
Headline, kicker, and byline
Subhead
Picture caption and credit
Breakout
Drop cap
Lead-in
Jumpline and continued-from line
Table of contents

Assessment Criteria:

_____ Completeness

_____ Neatly mounted and labeled

_____ Distinctive examples

Newsletter Project

Overview

You will redesign an existing newsletter and produce the cover and an inside spread. In Skills Module 9 you are given instructions in QuarkXPress or Adobe InDesign relevant to this exercise. (Illustrator and Photoshop are not suitable tools for multiple-page publications.) Before beginning the exercise, read the Skills Module for your chosen software and complete the related Study Guide.

Objectives

- To creatively apply what you have learned about the elements and layout of publications
- To learn about several tools in QuarkXPress or Adobe InDesign that are used to automate the production of multiple-page documents

Specifications

- Page size: 51p × 66p, facing pages
- 6 columns: All text columns, photos, ads, etc., will be sized to multiples of grid columns. (Text columns will be at least 2 columns wide.)
- Your choice of column width, gutter, and margins
- 3 pages: Page 1 is the cover and the inside spread is pages 2 and 3. At least two articles will begin on the cover and will jump to an inside page.
- A 0.125" bleed: Any element that goes up to the edge of the document must go at least ⅛" over the trim line.
- The cover will feature an original nameplate that includes the newsletter's title, date, volume and issue numbers. If the publication is affiliated with an organization, its name will be included. Optional: a subtitle, a motto, and/or illustration may be included.
- Running headers, footers, and folios will be placed where appropriate.
- Body text will be provided for this assignment. The body text should be entirely free of misspelled words, tabs, extra spaces, extra returns, or orphans. Widows should be minimized.
- Must use headlines, kickers, bylines, subheads, breakouts, picture captions and credits, initial caps, lead-ins, jumplines, and continued-from lines.
- At least two scanned grayscale raster images or Illustrator EPS line art images will be included in the layout.
- At least two advertisements will be included in the inside spread.
- A complete masthead will be placed on page 2 or 3.

See the Application Skills Module for explanations of the following specifications:

- Color: black and two Pantone spot colors only (uncoated stock)
- Master pages will be used to place the headers, footers, and folios.
- A Library will be used for a headline box or group, picture group, jumpline box, and breakout group
- Paragraph styles (or style sheets) will be used for headlines, subheads, body text, and first paragraphs
- Character styles (or style sheets) will be used for the lead-in
- The application's Table of Contents function will be used to create a table of contents on page 1 or 2.
- A text wrap around at least one photo, line art, or breakout

Production Schedule

Part 1: Design Brief, Thumbnails for Nameplate, Due _____

Part 2: Nameplate and Masthead, Due _____

Part 3: Master Page and Library, Due _____

Part 4: Style Sheets, Importing Text and Images, Layout, Creating TOC, Output, Due _____

Procedure Part 1: Design Brief, Thumbnails for Nameplate, Due _____

1. Design brief

List each of the following and fill in the relevant information. (If you don't know an answer, use your best guess.)

Designer Name:

Client Name:

Target audience demographics:

- Age range:
- Average education level:
- Income range:

Common interests:

Words that describe the tone that would appeal to the target audience:

Two contrasting type families that would help to express the desired tone; one for display type and the other for text:

Which of the following qualities or elements will help to express the desired tone?

simple	loose	geometric
complex	textured	hand-made
busy	straight-forward	tints (light colors)
clean	much white space	blends
layered	not much white space	bright colors
heavy	heavy rules	subtle colors
light	light rules	harmonious colors
bold	organic	clashing colors
tight		

What other qualities or elements can you think of to help to express the desired tone?

2. Create thumbnail sketches of a nameplate

Create six very different thumbnail sketches for a nameplate that includes a title, dateline, and volume and issue numbers.

Remember to use two Pantone colors plus black. To get the best grade, use one or more of the following in ways that are creative and appropriate to the desired tone of the newsletter:

- creative typography

- illustration or photo

- appropriate subtitle or motto

3. Hand in your work

Hand in design brief and thumbnails for assessment.

Part 1 Assessment Criteria: Design Brief, Thumbnails for Nameplate

_____Completeness

_____ Execution

_____ Creativity

Procedure Part 2: Nameplate and Masthead, Due _____

1. Create and set up new document

Review the specifications listed on page 1, then:

- Create a new folder named "Nwslttr_*your last name*". Keep all elements of this project in this folder. Back up your work at the end of every session.

- Create a new document: letter size; facing pages, six columns, your choice of gutter and margins width.

- Set up the baseline grid based on the document's margins and the amount of the leading that will be used for the body text. *(For help see Skills Module 8.)*

- Save the document as "Nwslttr_*your last name*.Indd" (or ".qxd").

2. Choose colors

Choose two Pantone (uncoated) spot colors. *(See the application Skills Module 9.)* Delete all unused colors.

3. Build a nameplate

Build your nameplate at the top of page 1:

Remember to include a title, dateline, and volume and issue numbers. To get the best grade, use one or more of the following in ways that are creative and appropriate to the desired tone of the newsletter:

- creative typography

- illustration or photo

- appropriate subtitle or motto

4. Create a masthead

On page 2, create a masthead that's headed with the publication title, styled as it is in the nameplate, and includes the publisher's name, address and phone number; names of an editor, writer, photographer and/or illustrator, and designer; ISSN number; copyright notice; disclaimer; and subscription information. (See Figure 9-6.) (If any such information is missing, make it up.)

The masthead provides a good opportunity to practice a hanging indent. Select the paragraphs that the hanging indent should be applied to, then, enter a left indent measurement. Then, put the negative number in the First Line Indent field. (Tabs will automatically align with the indent.) Use contrasting type to emphasize categories. Apply space after attributes to all paragraphs.

5. Print pages 1 and 2

Print pages 1 and 2 with crop marks; select the Fit in Print Area option.

6. Collect the document

Collect or package the document, all fonts used, any linked graphics, and the report file into a folder named "P2_Nwslttr_*your last name*". (See the Application Skills Module 9.)

Open the report file and read through it to see what information is included.

7. Hand in your work

Hand in:

- B & W printout of nameplate and masthead
- P2_Nwslttr_*your last name*

Part 2 Assessment Criteria: Nameplate and Masthead

_____ B & W printout of nameplate and masthead with crop marks

_____ The document, all fonts used, any linked graphics, and the report file are submitted in a folder named "P2_Nwslttr_*your last name*"

_____ Color: Black and two Pantone uncoated spot colors **only**

Delete all unused colors.

Nameplate includes:

_____ Title

_____ Dateline

_____ Volume and issue numbers

_____ Subtitle or motto (optional)

Nameplate design:

_____ Styled to appeal to the target audience

_____ Overall quality of design

_____ Creative typography, and/or appropriate illustration or photo

Masthead includes

_____ Title styled as in the nameplate

_____ Publisher's name, address, and phone number

_____ Names of an editor, writer, photographer and/or illustrator, and designer

_____ Hanging indent applied to the elements above

_____ Contrasting type to emphasize categories

_____ ISSN number

_____ Copyright

_____ Disclaimer

_____ Subscription information

_____ Space-after attribute applied to all paragraphs

The document is free of:

_____ Spelling errors

_____ Extra tabs

_____ Extra returns

Procedure Part 3: Master Page and Library, Due _____

1. Design a master page that includes original elements that will appear on almost every page. (See the Application Skills Module.) These will include:

- Header
- Footer
- Folio

(*Optional:* Master page may include other elements such as sidebar boxes or rules.) These elements must be placed on both the recto and verso pages of the master page spread. They should be styled to appeal to the target audience.

2. Create a Library

Create a Library for the project: Go to File menu >New >Library; name it: "NL_Lib_*your last name*".

 A Library is a separate document that is used to store items that can be reused over and over. You can add an item to the Library from the document by selecting it, then dragging and dropping onto the Library. The Library saves automatically.

3. Create dummies

Imagine that you are producing a newsletter on a tight budget. Each issue contains about 20 articles. That's 20 headlines, 20 kickers, and 20 bylines. Instead of styling each of these elements one by one, you could save time by creating a reusable "dummy" that could be modified as needed. It could be a single text box, sized to fit across a text column, containing a generic sample of a headline, kicker, and byline. (See Figure 9-39.) All of the character attributes and paragraph attributes would be applied to each one. Put that dummy into the Library, then, when you start an article, just grab it and modify it as needed. Smart, huh? You'll also create dummies for other frequently used items.

 On page 2 of your document, design generic dummies for each of the following elements. Size them to fit across two grid columns, which is equal to one minimum text column. (See Figure 9-39.)

 When designing these elements, consider how to make them typographically distinct, how to make them function in a desirable hierarchy, and how to style them to appeal to the target audience.

Drag each into your Library:

a. Headline box, with a sample of a headline, kicker, and byline. When designing these elements, consider the desired hierarchy and how to make them typographically distinct.

Note

The Demo movies for Skills Module 10 may be particularly helpful for this project. They can be found on the DVD in the back of the Application Skills Module book.

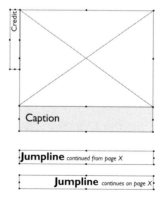

Figure 9-39 Dummies of a headline box, breakout group, photo/Illustration group, jumpline box, and continued-from box are put into the Library and then taken out and modified as needed.

- Use a first-baseline offset to create a margin between the headline and the top of the box—this will make it easier to place headlines in relation to elements that are above them.

- Apply a 1-pt. runaround (or text wrap) to the box. (See the application Skills Module.)

- Create and apply paragraph style sheets to the headline and the byline before you put the box into the Library. These will be used for the automatic table of contents function.

b. Photo/Illustration Group, consisting of a picture box, caption box, and credit box. Apply a 10-pt. runaround (or text wrap) to the picture and caption boxes, but the credit box should be placed in the gutter with no runaround.

c. Jumpline box

d. Continued-from box

e. Breakout group, including the text box with rules, frames, or other decorative elements; apply a 10-pt. runaround (or text wrap).

4. Print pages 2 and 3

Print pages 2 and 3 with crop marks; select the Fit in Print Area option.

5. Collect the document

Collect (or package) the document, all fonts used, any linked graphics, and the report file into a folder named "P3_Nwslttr_*your last name*". Put a copy of the Library ("NL_Lib_*your last name*") into the folder.

6. Hand in your work

Hand in:

- B & W printout of pages 2 and 3, including the headers, footers, folios, and all of the elements from the Library on page 2

- "P3_Nwslttr_*your last name*" folder including a copy of the Library ("NL_Lib_*your last name*") all fonts used, any linked graphics, and the report file

Part 3 Assessment Criteria: Master Page and Library

Handed in B & W printout of pages 2 and 3, with crop marks and scaled to fit in print area. Headers, footers, folios, and all of the elements from the Library are included.

Handed in "P3_Nwslttr_*your last name*" folder including a copy of the Library ("NL_Lib_*your last name*") all fonts used, any linked graphics and the report file.

Color:

_____ Black and two Pantone spot colors only.
(All unused colors are deleted.)

Master page includes:

_____ Header

_____ Footer

_____ Folio

On document page 2 and in Library

_____ Headline box with samples of headline, kicker, byline

_____ Paragraph style sheet applied to the headline, first baseline offset, and 1 pt. runaround (or text wrap) applied to the box

_____ Photo/Illustration Group: Picture box, caption box, credit box

_____ Jumpline Box

_____ Blurb box or group

The document is free of:

_____ Spelling errors

_____ Extra spaces

_____ Extra tabs

_____ Extra returns

Quality of master page and Library elements

_____ Functional hierarchy

_____ Each element is typographically distinct

_____ Elements are styled to appeal to the target audience

_____ Overall design quality of elements

PROCEDURE PART 4: STYLE SHEETS, IMPORTING TEXT AND IMAGES, LAYOUT, CREATING TOC, OUTPUT, DUE_____

1. Design layout and build page 1

Review the specifications, then

a. Design the layout of page 1

At least two articles will start on page 1; each will "jump" to another page inside the newsletter. The body copy will be provided, but all headlines, kickers, breakouts, captions, credits, and bylines will be original.

Make thumbnail sketches to design the layout of this page. Remember to use your grid! Most elements should fit in two or more columns. Consider using "umbrella" headlines to create horizontal

Part 4 Assessment Criteria: Style Sheets, Importing Text and Images, Layout, Creating TOC, Output

_____ Handed in B & W printout of pages 1– 3, with crop marks and scaled to fit in print area.

_____ Handed in "P4_Nwslttr_*your last name*" folder including a copy of the Library ("NL_Lib_*your last name*") all fonts used, any linked graphics, and the report file.

_____ Color: Black and two Pantone spot colors only.

(All unused colors are deleted.)

Paragraph styles:

Headlines:	Correct _____	Applied _____
Bylines:	Correct _____	Applied _____
Subheads:	Correct _____	Applied _____
Body text:	Correct _____	Applied_____
1st paragraphs:	Correct _____	Applied _____
Character style for lead-ins	Correct _____	Applied_____

_____ Initial caps

_____ At least two articles start on page 1 and "jump" to another page inside the newsletter; proper use of linking, jumplines, and continued-from lines

_____ Table of contents function correctly used

The document is free of:

_____ Spelling errors

_____ Extra spaces

_____ Extra tabs

_____ Extra returns

_____ Overflow icons

_____ Widows, orphans, or other unprofessional typography

Quality of layout design

_____ Layout has combination of horizontal and vertical directions

_____ Spacing of elements

_____ No dead spots in layout

Type Effects— The Good, the Trite, and the Ugly

This chapter introduces these type effects: drop shadows, text on a curved baseline, shaped boxes, text wraps around outlined pictures, distorted type, pictures used as letters, letters filled with pictures, and various other effects.

OBJECTIVES

¤ To recognize several special effects that may be used to enhance type.

¤ To understand how to employ type effects effectively.

The Designer's Judgment

Every once in a while, new technology makes it possible to do something with type that had previously been impossible—or at least very difficult. Fresh effects can grab a reader's attention, but if they are over-used they quickly go stale. Overall, the effects that survive the changing winds of fashion are those that don't overly disrupt readability. Digital technology has brought many special effects well within the reach of beginners, but once again, it is critical that the designer use visual judgment to make sure that such effects are used in desirable ways. It is crucial to understand that type effects are *not a* substitute for creativity and quality design. They need to be used in ways that reinforce the communication and not distract from it. This chapter introduces a number of effects that have become widely used over the past 25 years. It is up to you to decide how to use them—for better or for worse.

"Constructivist typographers did some amazing things with metal type in the early twentieth century, but computers give design a freedom impossible in the realm of the letterpress. The potential for creating unspeakably ugly type is practically unlimited."

—James Felici

The Complete Manual of Typography

Drop Shadows and Embossed Letters

Shadow

Figure 10-1 A bad drop shadow that makes the type hard to read; the type is too delicate, the tracking too tight, the shadow is too dark, and it falls too far from the word. (Adobe Garamond)

Shadow

Figure 10-2 Here the shadow doesn't disrupt readability. The type is bolder, the tracking looser, the shadow is lighter, and it is close enough to the letters to touch their edges. (Adobe Garamond Bold)

Shadow

Figure 10-3 A fuzzy shadow

Shadow

Figure 10-4 These letters appear to be *recessed* below the surface of the page.

Shadow

Figure 10-5 Flat white letters with a drop shadow appear embossed.

Shadow

Figure 10-6 3-D embossed letters with a drop shadow.

Drop shadows create the illusion that type is floating a little distance above the page and casting its shadow onto it. This illusion can seem to magically transform the flat surface of the page into a three-dimensional space. It can give type a monumental quality as if the type were carved in stone. But, if done without due exercise of visual judgment, drop shadows can make the type hard to read.

Unfortunately, the shapes of drop shadows can easily compete with the shapes of letter forms. For this reason, shadows behind dark type should be kept fairly light: 40% or less. This may look practically invisible on screen, but it'll work just fine on the printed page. The shadows should stay close enough to the letters to touch their edges; if they fall too far away, extra confusing shapes will be created. (See Figure 10-1.) Bolder type and relatively generous tracking will help keep things clear. (See Figure 10-2.) Fuzzy shadows are less likely to obscure letter forms than hard-edge ones. (See Figure 10-3.)

Drop shadows typically fall to the lower right of the letters; this keeps the front edge of the letters clean. If the letters are left white and surrounded by shadow, it can look as if the letters were **embossed** (pushed up from the page) instead of printed.

Text on a Curved Line

Because typography and layout are dominated by horizontal and vertical relationships, type running on a curved pen path will naturally stand out. However, once again, this effect will make it necessary to take extra time and care with fine-tuning. Tight curves can make the characters seem to lean over at odd angles. (See Figure 10-7.) (Tips for drawing more formalized paths are shown in Figure 10-8 and Figure 10-9.) Even on gentler curves, wide characters can seem to lift off the baseline. (See Figure 10-10.) This is less of a problem with condensed typefaces. In any case, the odd spacing created by curved baselines requires careful kerning.

Figure 10-7 Dangerous curves! The winding baseline can turn letters weird directions and muck up their spacing.

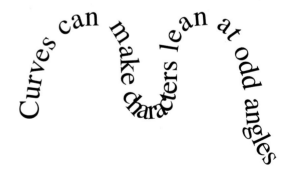

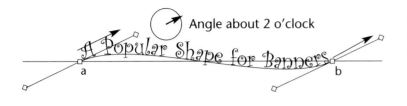

Angle about 2 o'clock

Figure 10-8 To make a path in this shape: With the Pen Tool, click on point *a* and hold while dragging toward the upper right at a shallow angle (about 2 o'clock), click on point *b* and repeat.

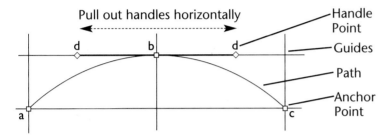

Pull out handles horizontally

Handle Point
Guides
Path
Anchor Point

Figure 10-9 To make a symmetrical curve, place guides to mark the low points (*a and c*), and at the high point (*b*). Then, click point *a* without pulling out handles, click *b* and hold while pulling out handles horizontally (*d*). Then, click *c* to complete the curve.

Figure 10-10 Even text on gentle curves requires careful kerning and slight baseline shifts as in the second example. (Minion Black)

Shaped Text Blocks

Typographers have experimented with novel shapes for text blocks almost since the origin of movable type. Of course, some shapes are easier to fill with text than others. A run of text can easily conform to the outlines of large shapes that don't have any sharp corners. But, as shapes become more narrow, careful choices of words are required to fill each line of text flush to the outline.

The problem is demonstrated in Figure 10-11. In this example, the text is set centered in a star-shaped box. Even with small 6-pt. type, the

The problem is demonstrated in this example. The text is set centered in a star-shaped box. Even at 6 pt., the edge of the shape is somewhat irregular. The outline would be smoother if the text was set with justified alignment, but then, big ugly gaps would open up between words. And then there's the problem with filling in the bottom points of the star. These problems might be fixed, more or less, with careful adjustment of spacing, adjusting the shape of the box, and some word substitutions. However, look at how the bottom lines if the text are divided by the gap between the "legs" of the star. It would be just plain mean to make a read- er jump that visual hur- dle several lines in a row.

Figure 10-11 It's difficult to fill in narrow shapes with text smoothly. Shapes that divide the text—like the legs of the star— make the text hard for readers to follow.

edge of the shape is somewhat irregular. The outline would be smoother if the text was set with justified alignment, but then big ugly gaps would open up between words. Another problem is that it's hard to get text into all the points of the star.

These problems might be fixed, more or less, with careful adjustment of spacing, adjustment of the shape of the box, and some word substitutions. But, look at how the bottom lines of the text are divided by the gap between the "legs" of the star. It would be just plain mean to make a reader jump that visual hurdle several lines in a row.

A more carefully composed text-shape can be seen in Figure 7-15. I whiled away a fair bit of time playing with those few lines. It's best to keep the shapes of text blocks fairly simple unless you enjoy playing with that sort of thing.

Text Wraps

Imagine that when some graphic object (such as a picture or a text box) is set down on top of a block of text, that the text gets pushed out from underneath it and flows around it. That's basically how a **text wrap** works. (See Figure 10-12.)

Text wraps can be thought of as an alternative way to create shaped text blocks—and they're prone to the same problems. If you create lines that are too narrow, they won't fill in evenly. And, if you disrupt the text with a shape that cuts across several lines, it will be hard for readers to follow the text. (See Figure 10-13.) When you want the text to surround the object, the best solution is usually to place it between two columns. (See Figure 10-14.) When a graphic *does* cut across a column, it should interrupt it just once. It's best to break the text mid-sentence, so the reader won't see the interruption as the end of a paragraph or end of the story. (See Figure 10-15.)

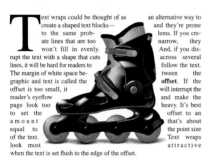

Figure 10-12 GOOD— A text wrap set with justified alignment and enough offset

Figure 10-13 BAD—The graphic cuts across several lines, so it will be hard for readers to follow the text. Also, when lines get too short, the spacing gets ugly.

Figure 10-14 GOOD—The object has been set between two columns.

Figure 10-15 GOOD—The graphic interrupts the text just once, mid-sentence, so the reader will continue.

The margin of white space between the graphic and the text is called the **offset**. If the offset is too small, the reader's eye flow is interrupted and the page may look too heavy. (See Figure 10-16.) It's usually best to set the offset to an amount that's about equal to the point size of the text. Text wraps look most attractive when the text is set flush to the edge of the offset. (See Figure 10-17.)

When creating text wraps, as in most other matters we've considered, you'll need to use visual judgement. Merely entering in the same offset measurement for all sides of an object will not guarantee equal spacing on all sides. You'll find that, because text jumps from baseline to baseline, a very small change in the vertical position of a graphic object can cause large differences in the offset spacing.

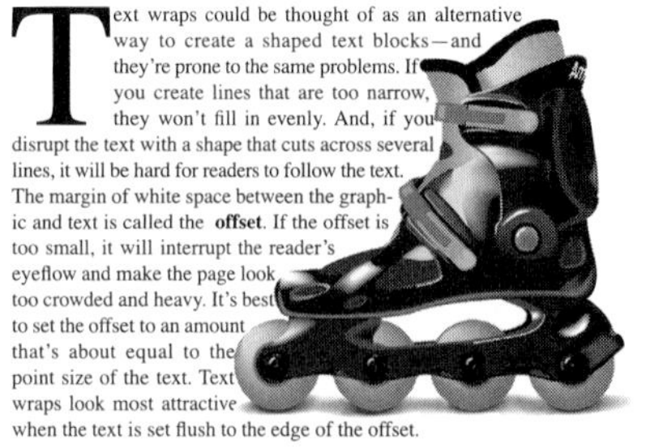

Beware of Ghosts

Traditionally, the term **watermark** referred to a faint mark that was impressed into paper when it was manufactured. (You can see one if you hold a twenty-dollar bill up to the light.) Since the advent of digital imaging, this term has become used to indicate a light image or display text that is placed beneath body text. (See Figure 10-18.) We also say that such images are "ghosted back."

A watermark of a logo may be used in a brochure to communicate company identity. A decorative image may be used to illustrate the theme of the text. Or, a watermark could convey a pervasive underlying message such as "Confidential" or "Top Secret."

Watermarks should have shapes that won't be confused with the shapes of the body type. It's usually best to keep them quite light—25% or less.

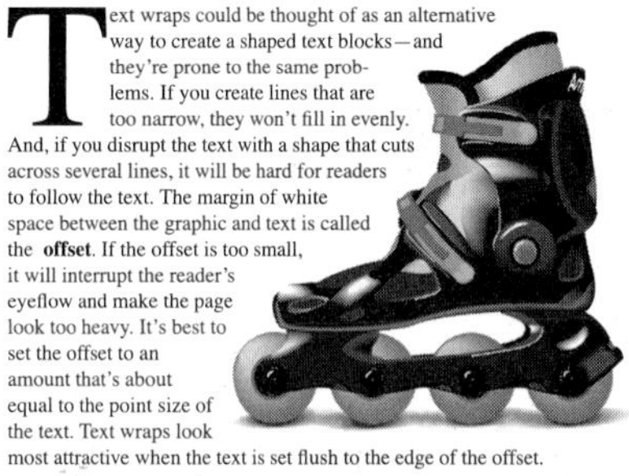

Pictorial Effects

Digital applications have made it easier to bridge the separation between text and pictures. Letters can be turned into picture boxes that can display evocative images or textures. (See Figure 10-19 and Figure 10-20.) Outlined pictures can be made to substitute for letters. (See Figure 10-22.) Photoshop and Illustrator can be used to transform type, make it appear three-dimensional, or even turn it into luminous virtual objects. (Most of these effects work best with type that has thick enough shapes to show the effect clearly.) The trend in recent years has been away from slick pictorial effects, such as fire, metal, or neon, toward effects that look hand-drawn or printed with an older process. Figure 10-19 through Figure 10-34 show examples of these various effects.

Filters and effects can radically transform the shapes of type with the push of a button. This makes them the typographic equivalent of a loaded gun. For goodness sake, be careful how you use them!

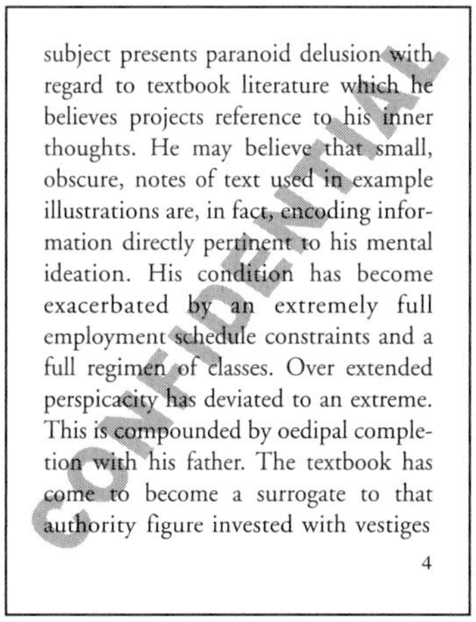

Figure 10-16 BAD—If the offset is too small, it interrupts the reader's eye flow and makes the page look too crowded and heavy.

Figure 10-17 BAD—Ragged edged wraps don't look as neat as justified edges. (*Compare Figure 10-11.*)

subject presents paranoid delusion with regard to textbook literature which he believes projects reference to his inner thoughts. He may believe that small, obscure, notes of text used in example illustrations are, in fact, encoding information directly pertinent to his mental ideation. His condition has become exacerbated by an extremely full employment schedule constraints and a full regimen of classes. Over extended perspicacity has deviated to an extreme. This is compounded by oedipal completion with his father. The textbook has come to become a surrogate to that authority figure invested with vestiges

4

Figure 10-18 A watermark

CLOUDS Wood

Figure 10-19 A word filled with a picture (Cooper Black)

Figure 10-20 A word filled with a textured surface (Arial Black)

Figure 10-21 Type can be embossed from a picture. (Marker Felt)

Figure 10-22 The linear quality of the eyeglasses is reflected in type. (Prestige Elite)

PRINT

Figure 10-23 The effect of uneven printing was created in Photoshop. (Stencil)

METAL

Figure 10-24 This chrome metal effect was also created entirely in Photoshop. (Cochin Bold)

Figure 10-26 Illustrator is capable of producing pictorial effects like this one, but it is more often used to manipulate shape and fill. (Arial Rounded Bold)

Figure 10-25 Again, Photoshop was used to make this type appear as if it was burning. (This effect is much stronger in color.) (Poplar Black)

PERSPECTIVE

Figure 10-27 The shape of this type has been distorted and the color blended to express space. (Eurostyle Bold)

Figure 10-28 Illustrator's Extrude filter (Bernard Condensed)

Pucker

Pucker

Roughen

Figure 10-29 The top example is not distorted; the others show the effects of a couple of Illustrator's many distortion filters. (Myriad)

Uglier

BETTER

Figure 10-30 My colleague Ralph Winn told me "Be sure to tell them *never* to use the *Fish* Warp effect." Nevertheless, it can be used better or worse. The bottom example has better spacing and the heavy, square, all-caps type looks less distorted and produces a cleaner outside shape. (Might work for Psychedelic retro, what do you think?)

Figure 10-31 The type is filled with a repeated pattern. (Playbill)

Sherbet

Figure 10-32 This was produced with Illustrator's Dropped Sherbet Type Graphic Style. (Modern No. 20)

Figure 10-33 These were produced with Illustrator's Scribble Graphic Styles. (Birch)

Figure 10-34 Type itself can be used to build up texture. (Bell)

Interaction of Type and Image

We say that elements have "synergy" when they work together to produce a result that is greater than the sum of their individual properties. Creative designers often create synergy between type and image by looking for cues in the image for where to place the type. Type may be placed so that it appears to be perched on an object or follow along its edge. (See Figure 10-35.) It can be placed on, or parallel, to an axis of an object. Or, it can be placed on an opposite counter-diagonal. (See Figure 10-36.) Type can be fit in around objects or follow them into space. (See Figure 10-37.) These kind of unusual placements call special attention to the type, so fine-tuning will be especially important.

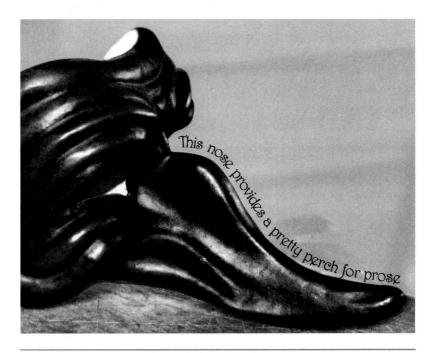

Figure 10-35 Type placed along a curved edge

Figure 10-36 Type placed parallel to an axis and on a counter-diagonal

Figure 10-37 Type following the surface of an object into space

Chapter Summary

This chapter introduced a number of effects that have become widely used over the past 25 years. It is crucial to understand that such type effects are *not a* substitute for creativity and quality design. They need to be used in ways that reinforce the communication and not distract from it. It is up to you to decide how to use them—for better or for worse. The related Skills Modules show how to create some of these effects.

Design Concepts Study Guide Chapter 10

After you have read the previous chapter, fill in the blanks with the letter of the correct answer within each section.

1. _____ Drop shadows should be kept

2. _____ Embossed type looks like it is

3. _____ When text is set on a tight curve

4. _____ Shapes are easiest to fill with text when they

5. _____ If you disrupt the text with a shape that cuts across several lines

A. are fairly simple and don't have any sharp corners

B. it will be hard for readers to follow the text

C. pushed up from the flat surface of the page

D. 40% or less

E. characters often lean over at odd angles

○ ○

6. _____ When you want a text wrap to surround an object, the best solution is usually to

7. _____ It's usually best to set a text wrap offset to an amount that's

8. _____ Text wraps look most attractive when

9. _____ A light image or display text that is placed beneath body text is called

10. _____ Most pictorial type effects work best with type

11. _____ It's usually best to tint a watermark

A. the text is set flush to the edge of the offset

B. that has thick enough shapes to show the effect clearly

C. watermark or ghosted back

D. 35% or less

E. about equal to the point size of the text

F. place it between two columns

○ ○

Exercises

Directions for the type effects in this chapter are given in the Skills Modules.

Off the Page—Type in New Media

This chapter describes problems and solutions for using type effectively in digital presentations and the World Wide Web.

OBJECTIVES

- ¤ To recognize problems inherent to type on screen and learn strategies for getting readable results
- ¤ To learn strategies for effective type in presentations
- ¤ To learn basic type elements used in Web design
- ¤ To understand basics of styling type for the Web
- ¤ To get an overview of type in Adobe Acrobat and Macromedia Flash
- ¤ To learn a basic process for using type in designing a Web site

Type On Screen— Through the Glass, Haphazardly

The human mind has a marvelous capacity to look past distractions and find meaningful information. This capacity can be appreciated if we take a close look at how text type is displayed on screen. What most people accept as normal letter shapes are actually crude approximations. However, although readers may not *consciously* recognize the distortions, almost everyone will acknowledge that reading from the screen is harder than reading from paper. Studies have verified that on average it's 10% to 20% slower.

As explained in Chapter 1, digital typefaces (except bitmap and screen fonts) are drawn as vector outlines. When type is output, the characters are rasterized into shapes made up of square dots. The resolution for

> "Digital
>
> communications design is far more conceptual than traditional graphic design and requires a much deeper understanding of the communications process. This is not just making nifty images on a computer."
>
> —Katherine McCoy,
>
> *Digital Communications Design in the Second Computer Revolution*, 1998

Handgloves Handgloves **Handgloves**
Handgloves Handgloves **Handgloves**

Figure 11-1 The word "Handgloves" is commonly used to display characteristics of type because it combines a good sample of letters. The top row shows 12-pt. Times Roman; the second row is set in Georgia at the same size. The type in the left-hand column is rendered at normal print resolution. In the other two columns, the type is rendered at screen resolution of 72 dpi. Anti-aliasing was applied to the type on the right, but not to the type in the middle.

Figure 11-2 Samples of 12-pt. Georgia rendered at 72 dpi are shown here magnified 2 times. At top, type without anti-aliasing is shown with the character outlines superimposed. You can see how much the font's hinting instructions have changed the shapes of the characters. Below, you can see how anti-aliasing uses shades of gray to create the *impression* of shapes that don't fit on the grid. The anti-aliased type required less hinting, so the type is set with tighter tracking.

Figure 11-3 Uppercase characters can be drawn at a minimum height of 5 pixels. Lowercase letters require 9 pixels to describe the counters, the ascenders, and the descenders.

screen display is usually between 72 and 85 dots per inch (dpi). Compare that to the much finer resolution of the print output for publications, typically between 1200 and 2400 dpi. The difference in rendering can be seen in Figure 11-1 and Figure 11-2.

The thinnest line that can be shown on screen is 1 pixel wide. That means that at 72 dpi, no letter strokes can be thinner than 1 pt. wide. Wider strokes are constrained to expand in multiples of 1 pt. As can be seen in Figure 11-2, this means that *all* of the strokes in a 12-pt. roman type, including hairline serifs, will be displayed at the same weight. Curved lines are impossible at that size. Fine-tuning of the space between characters is impossible because the smallest increment of adjustment is a coarse jump of 1 pt.

To keep type legible at low resolutions, type designers program instructions into fonts called **hints**. Hints change the shapes of characters so that they will fit into the pixel grid as legibly as possible. (See Figure 11-2.) As explained in Chapter 1, **anti-aliasing** can create the impression of smooth curves, but the resulting effect of blurriness can, be wearing on the eyes. Anti-aliasing shouldn't be applied to type below 10 pt.

As you can see, the limitations of screen display will encourage bigger type and more spacing. While normal size for text on paper is 9 or 10 pt., on screen type will render much better at 14 pt. Extra tracking will help most typefaces. The norm for leading should be increased to 130%, or even more with wide column measures.

It's best to use narrow line measures on screen. About 35 to 40 characters is a good column width. However, the benefits of added spacing and narrow columns must be balanced against the consequence that readers will be required to scroll more to get through longer texts. Scrolling may be eliminated in certain situations by setting lists or relatively short texts in side-by-side columns but only if the text is short enough to fit entirely on one screen—scrolling multiple columns is a drag (literally!).

If you need to show type at the smallest possible size, an uppercase character can be depicted at a minimum height of five pixels. Nine pixels are needed to describe the counters, ascenders, and descenders in lowercase alphabets. (See Figure 11-3.)

When all other variables are equal, type will look about one-third larger in Windows OS than on a Mac. That's because screen resolution is calculated in Windows at 96 pixels per inch, whereas Macs work at 72 ppi. Because most monitors actually display at 72 to 85 dpi, the Mac display will be the same size or smaller than the actual measurement, whereas the size in Windows will be exaggerated.

It's important to realize that some typefaces are more legible on screen at text size than others. Generally, the faces that work best have large, open counters, simple shapes that are free of decoration or subtlety, and minimal curves and diagonals. As seen in Figure 11-2, the thickness of hairline serifs become exaggerated on text type, so they tend to become clunky and distracting. Slab-serif faces will reproduce more accurately, but the simplicity of sans-serif faces have made them the most popular choice.

Several typefaces have been designed to work well at screen resolutions. The most popular is Verdana, a sans serif created by Matthew Carter in 1996. (See Figure 11-4.) Carter also designed an effective serif typeface named Georgia. Lucida was originally designed by Chuck Bigelow and Kris Holmes for low-resolution printing. It has been enlarged into an extensive family of screen-friendly faces that includes several distinct styles.

Italic text, with its oblique and curving strokes, does not display well on screen. Likewise, script faces should be avoided. But, if you *do* use one, look for one with simple, open, and sturdy shapes.

Bold type can also be a problem at text sizes because it can only be drawn by doubling the width of the vertical strokes. (See Figure 11-5.) The contrast between thick and thin strokes can look particularly clunky at smaller sizes.

A change of color or shade can be a very effective alternative way to create emphasis on particular words or to differentiate blocks of type. (It's best to change color [hue] and shade together so the difference won't be lost on readers with color blindness.) One distinct advantage that screen display has over printing is that it doesn't cost extra to use color. Screens can display over 16 million different colors. However, if colored type is overused, the design can look too busy or garish. On Web sites, the colors blue, red and violet are often used for indicating links to other pages, so those colors shouldn't be used for other text.

Many people find bright white backgrounds harsh and wearing on the eyes. Backgrounds of soft earth tones or light grayish colors are more gentle. Clean, light tints can give a festive feeling. Dark backgrounds with light type can work for texts of moderate length. With the wide range of tones that can be produced on screen, it's possible to find background colors that will accommodate both dark and light type colors at the same time.

It can be very attractive to use colors that share a hue in common while contrasting in brightness and saturation. For example, orange type over a dark orange/brown background, or a light blue type over a warm dark purple. If you place type over a texture or a picture, be careful that the background doesn't interfere with readability. Watermarks can be too distracting unless they are very subtle.

At display sizes, greater variety and nuance of type styles and spacing can be rendered. Because type tools are so limited in presentation and Web software, it's often best to create titles and other display type in Photoshop and import them as image files.

Handgloves
Handgloves
Handgloves

Figure 11-4 Verdana at 10 pt. and 14 pt. without anti-aliasing, and, at bottom, 14 pt. with anti-aliasing. Note the changes in the proportions of letters.

Handgloves
Handgloves
Handgloves
Handgloves

Figure 11-5 The top row shows Verdana at 14 pt. without anti-aliasing. The second row shows Verdana Bold. You can see that the weight of the vertical strokes has been doubled. Anti-aliasing was applied to the type in row three. The last row shows Verdana bold at 10 pt. The strokes are the same thickness as they are in the larger type, so they look proportionally much heavier.

Andale Mono

Arial Black

Comic Sans

Georgia

Impact

Trebuchet MS

Verdana

Figure 11-7 These fonts are widely available because they have been bundled with Internet Explorer.

Figure 11-8 A splash page is entirely dominated by a signature graphic or an animation.

Figure 11-9 This home page shares a large logo and a generous amount of space with a mission statement and several links.

size, resolution, and the way they show color. A Web page may call for certain fonts, but the browser can only use the fonts that are installed on the user's computer. Some files cannot be seen unless the user takes the time to install an additional software plug-in. Differences in users' Internet connections and the speed of their computers can make big differences in the speed that pages build. (See Figure 11-7.)

Although most designers have large monitors, fast connections, all the newest software, and extensive font collections, as a rule, it's best to *design for the average user*. At the same time, a good designer also plans so that users with even less optimal set-ups, and those with special needs, will be able to access all information in the best way possible.

The discussion that follows provides an overview of typographic design for the Internet. Detailed explanation of how to create Web sites is beyond the scope of this book, but several excellent resources are listed in the bibliography.

Type Elements in Web Design

Many of the principles of page design that were covered in Chapter 9 are just as important for Web design—maybe even more important. Internet users are, if anything, *less* patient than print readers. This is partly because of the lower quality of on screen type, but also because users know that the very instant they get bored, a quick click or two of the mouse can take them away to something new. To hold users' interest and to stand out from the competition, it's vital that Web pages instantly convey a distinctive identity, get readers involved with the text, and help them to find the information they're looking for.

Technically, each Web page is a separate document. However, the need for clear and accessible presentation puts a limit on how much information can be put on a single page. Therefore, several pages are usually linked together to create a **Web site**. The separate pages of a Web site are held together by two things: one is the **hyperlinks** (or **links**) that take users from one page to the next. The other, which is just as important, is the designer's use of type, layout, and other design elements to create a cohesive identity for the site.

Some designers introduce a Web site with a **splash page**. Its sole purpose is to announce the identity of the site with a large signature graphic or an animation. (See Figure 11-8.) However, many designers have come to feel that splash pages add an unnecessary extra step between the user and the content.

The splash page, when there is one, leads directly to the heart of the Web site: the **home page**. If the site has no splash page, a large portion of the home page may be taken up with a signature graphic. (See Figure 11-9.) However, the home page's main function is to provide the central means for accessing the site's contents. The home page is the

Web's equivalent of a table of contents, consisting of short descriptions of the site's contents and hyperlinks (or links) to their locations.

Web pages can be any length, but studies have shown that, about half of the time, users don't bother to scroll down below the first screen they see. Although most users' screens can display an area 800 pixels wide by 600 pixels deep, nearly 10% of that space will get used up by the browser. A safe estimate for the area that can be used to display the contents of a page without scrolling is just 760×540 pixels (10.5" × 7.5")—or even *less* if an ad is included on the page. That means that the space on the opening screen on the home page is precious. The content must be described in brief and general terms, sorted into clear categories, and prioritized. More important items should be placed closer to the top of the page. Links are used to take users to more lengthy and detailed information on other pages. Ideally, the user should be able to get the content they're looking for with three clicks or fewer.

Many designers choose to conserve screen space and download time by limiting the signature graphic to a small area in the page header. (See Figure 11-10.) Usually, the site's identity is promoted by repeating the same graphic at the top of *all* of the site's pages. The repeated use of the same graphic saves download time because, once a graphic has been downloaded, the user's browser temporarily saves it for immediate reuse in a special folder called a **"cache"** on the user's hard drive.

In addition to the signature graphic, the header also usually contains a **navigation bar** (or **navbar**) that contains concise links to several main features of the Web site. Often, these will include site tools, such as a search utility. The navbar generally will be kept the same throughout all of the site's pages. On the other hand, a **sidebar** column, usually placed on the left side, lists links that require more description or change with the context of different pages. At the bottom of the page, the footer may have additional links, as well as a copyright and other legal notices. In pages that are more than one screen long, a link back up to the top might be included. Consistent treatment of navigation and identity elements throughout a Web site will make the site more recognizable and easier to use.

The Look of Links

Links are often represented as underlined text; usually the text is colored blue and changes to violet after the link has been used. Virtual buttons can also be used. A **rollover** is an image that changes when the user's cursor is moved over it and can be clicked like a button link. **Image maps** use areas within pictures as links. Links can be listed in menus. **Cascading menus** open to show submenus that contain lists of links.

Forms are used to gather information from users. They can be made up of radio buttons, check boxes, pop-up lists, and text entry fields. A button labeled "Submit" sends the information back to the server.

Figure 11-10 This home page conserves screen space by limiting the logo to a small area in the page header.

Live Text vs. Type Images

Now, let's turn our attention away from larger layout considerations to the nuts and bolts of using type over the Internet. There are two kinds of online type: live text and type images. **Live text** is written content that comes to the user's computer with a list of requested type attributes. It is set by the user's browser, using fonts from the local hard drive. Live text can be read by a search engine (such as Google) or the user's Find tool. It can be copied and pasted into another text document. Because it can be updated almost immediately, new live text can be received from a dynamic source such as an online database.

On the other hand, a **type image** is set by a designer, using an application such as Photoshop, and saved as an image file. It's a *picture* of set type, so it can no longer be recognized as text by the computer. If the designer wants to change a word, the graphic will have to be completely redone.

Designers have much less creative control over live text than type images. First, Internet browsers don't support fine-tuning of kerning or alignment. But the main thing is, for the reasons outlined in in the first section of this chapter, with live text you can never be sure what font or size will show up on the user's screen. On the other hand, a type image can be set in any font that designers choose. It can be fine-tuned or artfully modified to their heart's content. When it's absolutely perfect, it can be optimized so that it has a low file size and saved as a Gif or PNG-8 file (if it's made up of flat colors) or a JPEG (if it has complex blends or pictorial effects).

Gif and PNG-8 graphics can download quite quickly. For example, a one-color 84-pt. title that's 8 inches long can be anti-aliased and saved as a 4-bit (16-color) Gif, and its file size will only be about 2K. On a 56.6-Kbps (kilobits per second) modem it would only take about 2 seconds to download. Even so, it would obviously be impractical to use type images for running of body text. They are not usually used for subheads or even for headlines. But type images are very useful for the stable elements that define the look and feel of the site, such as signature graphics, department headings, and navigational elements.

However, there's a few problems that should be considered. First, some users with slow modems choose not to receive images to save download time. Other users may have text-only devices. Likewise, blind users won't be able to access the text. And, of course, neither will search engines or utilities. All of these problems can be solved with a simple bit of HTML coding: the text information can be inserted with an ALT (alternative) tag so that it only shows up when the picture doesn't. This is a good example of the kind of contingency planning that is required to make a Web site accessible to diverse users.

Applying Attributes to Live Text

The type attributes of live text are controlled with **cascading style sheets (CSS)**. CSS function much like the style sheets in QuarkXPress or InDesign. The designer chooses different sets of type attributes for text of various functions such as body type, headlines, or subheads. Then, each CSS can be applied to the appropriate text with simple commands. It is possible to set up CSS so that changes to any attribute can automatically be applied throughout the entire Web site.

Font choices for live text should be limited to the common fonts listed in Figure 11-6 and Figure 11-7. Even so, there's no guarantee that any particular font will actually be installed on all users' computers. Again, this problem calls for contingency planning. The best solution is to list several font choices in order of preference. The font attribute could be written like this:

```
P {font-family: Verdana, Geneva, Helvetica, Arial, "sans serif"}
```
                                    or,
```
B {font-family: Georgia, "New Times Roman", Times, serif}
```

The user's browser will try to use the fonts in the order that they are listed. When it can't find one choice it will go on to the next. The last choice should be a broad generic category. (Note that when a font name is more than one word, it must be bound with quotes.)

The size attribute can be defined in several ways. The traditional pt. units can be used, but, as we've seen, the results will be very different on the Mac platform than on the PC. Results will be more predictable if size is defined in pixels (as in: `P {font-size: 14px}`). However, because browsers give users the ability to choose the preferred size for body type, why not base the sizes of type on this preference? This approach will make the text accessible for those with special needs. In CSS, an **em** unit is defined as equal to the default size for body type. Subheads could be defined as, say, 1.3 em and headlines, perhaps, could be 2 em or more.

Em units can also be used to define the widths of text columns. This will create a predictable relationship between text size and column width. An ideal column width of 35 to 40 characters would be about 18 to 20 em wide. Alternatively, column widths can be defined as a percentage of the browser window. These *relative* measures are responsive to users' individual differences. In contrast, *absolute* measurements, such as points, picas, inches, millimeters, or pixels, cannot respond to such differences. CSS can also be used to position text on the page.

Web browsers don't support hyphenation, so justified body text tends to develop lots of gaps and rivers. Flush left/ragged right is usually a better choice for running text.

Older browsers occasionally have problems interpreting some CSS commands. This can be a problem on *InternetExplorer:mac* because Microsoft stopped upgrading it in 2003. I've also experienced minor

STYLES FOR DIVERSE MEDIA

Cascading style sheets (CSS) can be configured to adapt text styles to different output media on the fly. Choices include: screen, projection, handheld devices, print, TV, TTY terminals, Braille, or aural. This can help to make Web content accessible to users with diverse needs.

errors in a recent version of Apple Safari. Nevertheless, at this point CSS is quite broadly supported and will only continue to be more so.

Print-Friendly Web Content

If you're designing a document that users will want to print, it's safest to keep it to a maximum width of 560 pixels.

If quality is important, you might consider offering users the option of downloading an alternative document saved in the Adobe Acrobat PDF format. PDFs can be made from documents created in QuarkXPress, InDesign, Illustrator, or other programs. They generally reproduce the original document very accurately. File sizes are quite reasonable because images are compressed and type is saved as live text. All type attributes from the original document are preserved (except when there are errors). Any typeface may be used because Acrobat **embeds** the fonts into the PDF document. This means that, instead of using the end user's fonts, font information can be incorporated into the document itself. PDF documents can be opened for viewing or printing on either Mac or PC platforms with Adobe Reader, which can be downloaded free of charge. Hyperlinks can be placed into PDF documents to help readers navigate through the document or to connect to outside Web sites.

Type in Flash Animations

Macromedia Flash is a vector-based program used to create interactive "movies" for the Web and other purposes. As discussed in Chapter 1, vector graphics are very economical in terms of file size. This makes it possible to create full-screen motion graphics with very small file sizes. Type and other graphic elements can dance across the screen and weave in and out of space. Flash movies can also integrate sound and video clips. Movies can be configured for many varieties of user interaction. Text can be updated from user input or an online source. Content is protected from copying or printing unless the designer chooses to allow it.

Flash can access fonts from the user's computer, or they may be embedded into the movie for more control and variety. However, each embedded font will significantly increase the file size.

Flash's control of type attributes is not up to par with current browsers. Basic CSS commands have been supported since version MX_2004. Superior control over anti-aliasing was introduced with Flash 8. But, when fine-tuned display type is desired, it is best to set the type in a vector program, such as Adobe Illustrator, then convert the type to outlines and import the paths into Flash.

To view Flash movies, users must have the Flash Player plug-in installed on their hard drive. This isn't a severe limitation because Macromedia estimates that 98% of all Web users have it. Anyone who doesn't can download it free of charge.

Designing a Web Site

Without a clear planning process, a Web site can easily degenerate into a tangled morass. The key to planning is, once again, the design brief. The brief should begin with descriptions of these factors:

- The **brand identity** of the site's sponsor: make note of graphic elements that will express this identity, such as a logo or other signature graphics, certain typefaces, or a particular color scheme.

- The demographics and shared interests of the site's target users.

- The communication goals of the site: whether its main purpose is to entertain, inform, generate sales, or to gather responses from users.

- An appropriate **tone** that will make the sponsor's content appeal to the site's users: make note of graphic elements that may help to express this tone.

Next, organize the site's content. It can be convenient to begin by writing short descriptions of the items that will be regularly featured on the site. Look for similarities between items and organize them into overarching categories. Other categories can be developed for short-term features. Some items might be arranged in sequences that branch out in response to user choices. Descriptions of content and categories can become the basis for the links that users click on to get to the content. Some categories won't have titles, but instead they'll be unified and set apart by graphic devices such as grouping, position, color, and type. The links and categories should be sorted by level of importance to determine where they will be placed on the Web site.

For an example, look at the home page for the United States Post Office Web site (www.usps.gov). (See Figure 11-11.) It has about three

Figure 11-11 This home page conserves screen space by limiting the logo to a small area in the page header. (*www.usps.com screenshot © United States Postal Service. Used with permission. All rights reserved. Written authorization from the Postal Service is required to use, reproduce, post, transmit, distribute, or publicly display this image.*)

dozen links. This could make a terrible mess, but instead it's neat and well organized. The links are divided into four main groups: the header, the footer, a sidebar, and the center of the page. These groups are broken down into subcategories. For instance, the center group has three subcategories: Shipping Tools, Mailing Tools, and Receiving Your Mail. Each of these categories has four related links listed below it. The categories make it easy for users to find what they want.

Content should be evaluated to determine in general terms:

- The range of lengths of text
- The number of images and their sizes
- What information will be requested from users
- What other media may be used in the Web site, such as Flash or MPEG movies or PDFs

Use the information that you've collected to help decide **specifications** for the site. For instance, if a site is targeted to a younger audience, it is probably safe to expect that they have newer software and faster connections. An older audience may appreciate larger body text. Make preliminary decisions for text attributes for elements such as body text, headlines, subheads, and navigation elements. Decide on an overall limit for the total file size for a page (30 Kb is a good maximum size for a site that that will be frequented by users with dial-up modems). Consult the suggestions outlined earlier in this chapter and define as many other parameters as you can. The design brief will change and grow as you develop the project.

When you've completed an early version of your design brief, begin to design the overall structure of the site. Decide which links will be represented on the home page. Then, sketch a branching diagram that represents the linked pages. Linked pages may, in turn, contain links to other pages, but generally the structure shouldn't be more than three pages deep. (See Figure 11-12.)

Now you'll be ready to start the design of the home page. It's usually easiest to begin with paper and pencil sketches. The site's signature graphic (or logo) is usually placed in the upper-right corner of the page. Decide what else will be included in the header and the footer. Decide if a sidebar will be used and, if so, which side it will be on and what will be in it. You may need to reserve space for advertising. Decide which kinds of links will be used and where to place them. And you will also have to decide where the other content will be placed. The most important items should be placed near the top of the page where they will load first. Plan how to use typography and other graphic elements to create a functional and distinctive hierarchy.

As the design of the home page is established, you can adapt it to make a general template for the other pages on the site. Keeping the pages similar will help users to navigate the site and give it a cohesive identity.

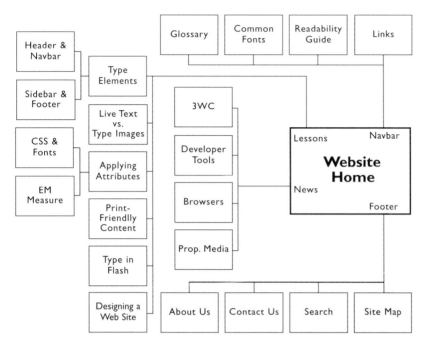

Figure 11-12 This is a diagram for the home page in Figure 11-10.

As you collect and develop the graphic content for the site, you can start to develop a **prototype** (or model) of the home page in Photoshop or another application. Keep graphic elements on separate layers, so that when they are ready they can be exported and optimized for the Web site. Test out your design by showing it to several different people from the targeted user group. See how they read its tone and identity and how quickly they can find their way to various links. After the Photoshop prototype is completed, you can use Web-authoring software, such as Dreamweaver, Adobe GoLive, or QuarkXPress to build the Web site in HTML (Hypertext Markup Language). After the first version of the Web site is complete, it should be tested on as many computers and with as many browsers as possible.

Chapter Summary

This chapter described problems and solutions for using type effectively in digital presentations and the World Wide Web. You were shown problems that are inherent to the presentation of type on screen and taught strategies for getting readable results. Several rules of thumb for using type effectively in digital presentations were outlined. The basic typographic elements used in Web design were introduced with suggestions of how to style them. We also looked at use of type in Adobe Acrobat and Macromedia Flash. The chapter concludes by outlining a process to design a Web site. The exercises guide you in analyzing home pages to learn from them and designing a home page.

Design Concepts Study Guide Chapter 11

After you have read the previous chapter, fill in the blanks with the letter of the correct answer within each section.

Type On Screen—Through the Glass, Haphazardly

1. _____ Studies have shown that reading type on screen is on average

2. _____ At 72 dpi all of the strokes in a 12-pt. roman type, including hairline serifs, will be

3. _____ Fine-tuning of the space between characters on screen is impossible because

4. _____ Instructions programmed into fonts to change the shapes of characters so that they will fit into the pixel grid as legibly as possible are called

5. _____ Anti-aliasing shouldn't be applied to type below

6. _____ The norm for leading body text on screen should be

7. _____ A good column width for body text on screen is

A. 130% or even more with wide column measures

B. 10 pt.

C. 10% to 20% slower

D. the same weight

E. the smallest increment of adjustment is a coarse jump of 1 pt.

F. about 35 to 45 characters

G. hints

○ ○

8. _____ An uppercase character can be depicted at a minimum height of

9. _____ The minimum height to depict the counters, ascenders, and descenders in lowercase alphabets is

10. _____ When all other variables are equal, type will look about one-third larger in

11. _____ Type faces that are legible on screen generally have

12. _____ The most popular choice for body text on screen is

13. _____ Italic text, with its oblique and curving strokes, does not

A. large open counters, simple shapes that are free of decoration or subtlety, and minimal curves and diagonals

B. 9 pixels

C. display well on screen

D. Windows OS than on a Mac

E. 5 pixels

F. sans-serif faces

○ ○

14. _____ The Rule of Six is

15. _____ Headlines should be above

16. _____ The minimum type size used for unimportant details, or legalities such as credits or copyright notices, should be

17. _____ Other text can range from

18. _____ Readability is helped by using

19. _____ should not be used because they're distracting and hard to read.

20. _____ Don't use more than two different

21. _____ Consider setting bullets

22. _____ Ready-made templates for slide layouts can be found by going to

23. _____ Don't let backgrounds, clip-art, sounds, motion, or transition effects

A. distract attention from the content

B. bold type with generous tracking and leading

C. 20 pt. to as much as 32 pt.

D. script faces

E. smaller than the text, or perhaps, in a color with less contrast

F. type families on a slide

G. 12 pt.

H. View menu > Formatting Palette > Add Objects

I. use no more than three to six words for an entry and put no more than three to six entries on a slide

J. 28 pt. and may be more than twice that size

Type Elements in Web Design

24. _____ The separate pages of a Web site are held together by the links and

25. _____ The purpose of a splash page is

26. _____ The home page's main function

27. _____ Users don't bother to scroll down below the first screen they see

28. _____ 760 by 540 pixels is

29. _____ On the home page, content must be described in brief and general terms, sorted into clear categories, and

30. _____ Ideally, the user should be able to get the content they're looking for

31. _____ The user's browser saves downloaded graphics for immediate reuse in

32. _____ A row of links to site tools and other main features of a Web site that is kept the same on the headers of all the site's pages is called

33. _____ A column that usually contains links that require longer description or change with the context of different pages is called

34. _____ Consistent treatment of navigation and identity elements throughout a Web site will

A. a safe estimate for the area that can be used to display a page without scrolling

B. about half of the time

C. to provide the central means for accessing the site's contents

D. reinforce the site's identity and make it easier for users to find what they want

E. more important items should be placed closer to the top of the page

F. navbar

G. with three clicks or less

H. a special folder on the user's hard drive called a cache

I. the designer's use of type, layout, and other design elements to create a cohesive identity for the site

J. sidebar

K. to announce the identity of the site with a large signature graphic or an animation

○ ○

Live Text vs. Type Images

35. _____ Type set by a designer using an application such as Photoshop and saved as an image file is called

36. _____ Written content that comes to the user's computer with a list of requested type attributes and is set by the user's browser using fonts from the local hard drive can be called

37. _____ Text that can be copied, searched, and updated from a dynamic source is called

A. Live text (use twice)

B. ALT

C. JPEG

D. Type Images (use twice)

E. Gif or PNG-8

38. _____ These are not usually used for body text, subheads, or even for headlines, but are very useful for the stable type elements that define the look and feel of the site.

39. _____ File format(s). that are good for type images made up of flat colors are called

40. _____ File format(s). that are good for type images with complex blends or pictorial effects are called

41. _____ The HTML tag that can be used to make text show up when the picture doesn't is

° °

Applying Attributes to Live Text

42. _____ Type attributes of live text are controlled with

43. _____ It's best if the font attribute lists

44. _____ In CSS, an em unit is defined as

45. _____ An ideal column width of 35 to 40 characters would be about

46. _____ Measurements based on ems or percentages are

47. _____ Measurements, such as points, picas, inches, millimeters, or pixels, that cannot respond to contextual differences are

48. _____ Because Web browsers don't support hyphenation, the best choice for alignment of body text is

49. _____ If you're designing a document that users will want to print, it's safest to keep it to a maximum width of

50. _____ A file format that can be used to send print quality documents over the Web is called

51. _____ Font information incorporated into a document is said to be

52. _____ A vector-based program used to create interactive "movies" for the Web and other purposes is called

A. Adobe Acrobat PDF

B. Cascading Style Sheets (CSS)

C. relative measurements

D. several choices in order of preference

E. 18 to 20 em wide

F. equal to the default size for body type

G. Macromedia Flash

H. flush left/ragged right

I. embedded

J. 560 pixels

K. absolute measurements

° °

Exercises

These exercises were designed to reinforce the concepts that were presented in Chapter 11.

Analyzing Home Pages

OVERVIEW

You will find three distinctly different examples of Web site home pages and critique them.

SPECIFICATIONS

Screen captures of home pages will be printed at 70%. The student will develop a clear system of call outs and text for explanations and critique of the page.

OBJECTIVE

- To think analytically and critically about the use of type and other graphic elements in the design of home pages and Web sites

PROCEDURE FIND EXAMPLES OF HOME PAGES

1. Find examples of home pages

Find three good examples of Web site home pages that are distinctly different in terms of communication goals and tone.

2. Make screen captures

Make screen captures of each (Mac keystroke: ⌘ 3).

3. Use questionnaire to analyze home pages

Place each screen capture onto a separate page at 70%. Type the answers to the following questions below each. Use call outs as needed to clarify your points.

a. What type and graphic elements express the brand identity of the site's sponsor? What makes them effective? Can you think of ways they may be improved?

b. What, do you think, are the communication goals of the site? What makes the page effective for these functions? Can you think of elements that may be improved?

c. What seems to be the overall tone of the page? Make note of type and other graphic elements that help to express this tone.

d. Describe what you think the demographics and shared interests of the site's target users are. What clues led to your conclusion?

e. Describe how type, placement, and other graphic elements create a visual hierarchy from the most emphasized items and groups to the least emphasized. Describe how each group is unified. What do items within groups have in common?

Assessment Criteria

____ Distinctive examples

____ Completeness

____ Neatly labeled

Creating a Home Page

OVERVIEW

You will create a prototype for a home page for a Web version of an existing magazine or newsletter. This page should be developed *without looking* at any Web site that the magazine may have (and so the design will be significantly different).

SPECIFICATIONS

Prototype home pages will be 760px × 540px at 72 ppi (10.5" × 7.5"). Photoshop has become generally accepted as a major tool for building prototypes, but you may use QuarkXPress, Illustrator, or InDesign if you like.

The total combined area of all type images shouldn't exceed approximately one-quarter of the area of the page. No more than one picture image will be used with a maximum size of 216px × 216px (3" × 3").

For each font chosen for live text, three alternatives and a last resort generic category will be chosen.

OBJECTIVES

• To practice analyzing and organizing content for a Web site

• To creatively apply what you have learned about structuring information in a Web page through typography and layout

PROCEDURE

1. Choose a magazine

Choose a magazine for which to develop a prototype home page. (Note: Do not visit the magazine's Web site; your design should reflect independent development.)

2. Develop a design brief

Develop a design brief for the Web site:

a. Note graphic elements that can be used to express the magazine's identity on the Web site. (Of course, a logo based on the magazine's nameplate would be an important element.)

b. Describe what you think the demographics and shared interests of the magazine's target readers are. What clues led to your conclusion?

c. Describe the communication goals of the magazine. What new goals can be added to the Web site?

d. Describe the overall tone of the magazine. What type and graphic elements can be adapted express this tone on the Web site?

3. Organize the content

Organize the site's content. One major category will list current feature articles. The magazine's regular departments will be a consistent category. Other items may include a mission statement, staff listings, contact information, and subscription information. Write short descriptions of items that should appear. Categorize them and list them in order of importance. (Specifications will be as listed above).

4. Design structure of the site

Design the overall structure of the site. Finalize the names of the links that will be represented on the home page. Then, sketch a branching flowchart that represents the linked pages. Linked pages may, in turn, contain links to other pages, but generally the structure shouldn't be more than three pages deep. (See Figure 11-12.)

5. Draw thumbnail sketches

Draw several thumbnail sketches to design the home page. Decide the size and placement of the logo. Decide which kinds of links will be used and where to place them. Decide where the other content will be placed. Plan how to use typography and other graphic elements to create clear and functional groupings and hierarchy.

6. Create the home page

Review the specifications, then create a document to build the prototype home page. The site's logo should be adapted from the magazine's nameplate. As you collect and develop the graphic elements for the site, keep them on separate layers.

   Use live text as much as possible to keep the file size of the site small. (Certainly, it will be used for text that must be updated frequently.) Choose type attributes for live text. For each font chosen, choose three alternatives and a last resort generic category. Test each alternative on a separate layer.

7. Test your design

Test out your design by showing it to several different people from the targeted user group. See how they read its tone and identity and how quickly they can find their way to various links.

Assessment Criteria

_____ Completeness of design brief

_____ Organization of the site's content

_____ Flowchart

_____ Several thumbnail sketches

_____ Layout has clear groupings and hierarchy; information easy to find

_____ Follows specs: doc size; size of types image and picture (if used); appropriate alternatives chosen for live text fonts

_____ Appropriate and effective logo and other identity elements

_____ Appropriate use of live text and type images

_____ Appropriate use of layers

_____ Creativity, aesthetics, and craftsmanship

A Closer Look at Type Design

As you have worked through this book, you've been exposed to many different typefaces and put them to work in functional and creative designs. You've mastered a good deal of vocabulary and have had the chance to see how such words can improve your powers of observation and your understanding. Now you're ready to go in for a closer look at the fundamentals of type design.

OBJECTIVES

- ◻ To expand vocabulary used to describe parts of letterforms
- ◻ To understand optical adjustments in typefaces
- ◻ To observe fine points of design in letters
- ◻ To learn a process for designing a set of capital letters

Detailed Anatomy of Letterforms

The following list will add to the terms that were introduced in Chapter 12. Learning to identify these features will help you recognize the fine points of font design. (See Figure 12-1.)

"The making of letters in every form is for me the purest and greatest pleasure, and at many stages of my life it was to me what a song is to a singer, a picture to a painter, a shout to the elated, or sigh to the oppressed— it was for me the most happy and perfect expression of my life."

—Rudolf Koch

Term	Definition
Apex	The point where strokes join at the tops of letters such as *A*, *M*, or *N*
Arm	A stroke that is attached to a vertical stem at one end and projects horizontally or at an upward angle
Bar or **Crossbar**	A stroke that runs horizontally between stems or across a stem
Bowl	A curved stroke that encloses a counter
Eye	The counter in the lowercase *e*
Flex	A slight calligraphic bend in a stroke
Juncture	Where strokes join
Nick	A sharp indentation
Shoulder	The downward curving stroke on *h*, *m*, and *n*
Spine	The central stroke in an *S*
Spur	A small pointed stroke that pokes out from a curved stroke
Tail	A curved or diagonal stroke that reaches downward from a bowl or a stem as in *j*, *K*, *Q*, or *R*
	The tail on a *K* or *R* may be called a "leg"
Terminal	End of any stroke that doesn't have a serif; varieties of terminal include angled, ball, beak, cupped, hook, square, tapered (finial), tear
Vertex	The point where strokes join at the bottoms of *V* or *W*

Features of the two-story lowercase "g":

Term	Definition
Ear	A short stroke that sticks out from the upper right of the bowl
Loop	The lower bowl
Link	Stroke that reaches from the bowl to the loop

Figure 12-1 All letters are set in Adobe Garamond except the *I*, which is in Trajan, and the *a*, which is Bodoni.

Figure 12-2 The stem on the first *T* looks thinner than the crossbar, but they are the same. The second *T*, set in Futura Bold, has a heavier stem, which gives the letter a sturdy feeling. The gray rectangles are identical, so they can be used to compare widths of the strokes.

Optical Adjustments in Typefaces

Throughout this guidebook, I've stressed that designers can't rely on rules or measurement, but, instead, they must be sensitive to the *feel* of their design. A close look at the design of letters will reveal more evidence that, as the painter Henri Matisse said, "Accuracy is not truth."

For an example, look at the first *T* shown in Figure 12-2. The vertical stem is exactly the same width as the horizontal crossbar, but I think you'll agree that the stem looks too light. On the second *T*, the stem looks decidedly heavier, giving the letter a satisfyingly sturdy feeling. The first letters in Figure 12-2, Figure 12-3, and Figure 12-4 are also monoweight constructions. The second letters in all three of these examples are Futura Bold. It's instructive to see how much variation can be found in the strokes of a monoweight typeface!

Figure 12-3 Again, a monoweight construction is compared to an *O* set in Futura Bold. Notice how the weight of the stroke shifts in the second example.

Figure 12-4 Note how the second *V*'s strokes taper toward the vertex.

'R' You Seein' the Type?

You can learn a lot about a typeface by looking closely at its capital *R*. This letter combines many of the most characteristic features in type design: main stem, bowl, serifs, and usually a bar. And oh, let's not forget the leg—even though this element is only used on a couple of the alphabet's letters—it is, along with the spine of the *S*, usually one of the most sensual features in a typeface. As you compare the several examples of *R* in Figure 12-5, you'll find that each expresses its own distinctive personality.

Our sample begins majestically with an *R* set in Trajan. This character's upright posture contrasts decisively with the languorous fall of its leg. Compare that calligraphic stroke with the solid square-toed strut of the Palatino *R*. But, the rest of the Palatino *R* isn't rigid by any means. See how the flex and play of the other strokes create springy energy? The open juncture reinforces that feeling.

The bowls on both of those *R*s lift upward. In contrast, Cochin's bowl droops down like a beer belly. Other *R*s have bowls that push forward confidently.

The type in the first row is classified as old style roman because the characters have moderate contrast between thick and thin strokes and sturdy bracketed serifs. Adobe Caslon, in the second row, can also be included in this category. But Big Caslon, next door, was designed to be a display face. It has more robust thick strokes, more delicate thin strokes, and pointed serifs. These characteristics make it a transitional face (see Chapter 6). Look at how the legs of both versions flow forward from their junctures. Baskerville's does too.

Look at how wide Baskerville's serif is...well, unless you compare it to the elephantine feet on Wide Latin! (**Latin** is a relatively rare category of type with triangular serifs.)

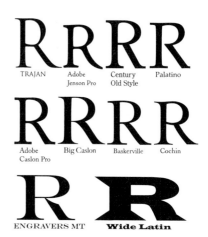

Figure 12-5a Can you tell which samples are old style roman and which are transitional?

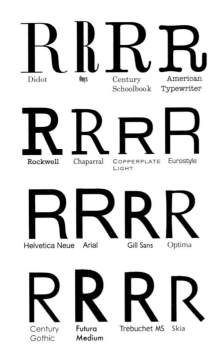

Didot   Onyx   Century Schoolbook   American Typewriter

Rockwell   Chaparral   COPPERPLATE LIGHT   Eurostyle

Helvetica Neue   Arial   Gill Sans   Optima

Century Gothic   Futura Medium   Trebuchet MS   Skia

Figure 12-5b Can you tell which samples are modern, which are slab serif, grotesque, humanist sans serif, or geometric sans serif?

Have you noticed that many of the serifs aren't symmetrical? Which do you prefer, cupped serifs or flat? Did you notice that many of the *R*s have a slight dent above the stem? How do you think such details affect the way the letters feel?

Didot's *R* has a split personality. Its straight and square parts give it a dignified bearing, but the bowl and leg sprout forth like spring leaves. Doesn't the finial on the leg look like it wants to reach out and tickle the next letter? American Typewriter takes the upturned finial to the max! Check out its rounded slab serifs.

You can see square-cornered slab serifs in Rockwell. Its solid monoweight construction gives it a no-nonsense character. On the other hand, Chaparral has refined variation in its stroke; it looks like a cross between Rockwell and Caslon.

Copperplate's serifs almost disappear, but not quite. The structure of this letter is quite square, but not so much as Eurostyle. Eurostyle is the only *R* that doesn't take even the smallest step forward. Even so, its large counters, restrained curves, and the slight variation in its strokes gives it a fresh modern feeling. Its designer, Aldo Novarese, may have been influenced by Helvetica, the foremost exemplar of Swiss style. The double curve in the leg of the Helvetica *R* is a holdover from the 19th century **grotesques** it was based on.

Arial is often used interchangeably with Helvetica. Their proportions are quite similar. But, in contrast, Arial's leg flows forward like the transitional *R*s. This is a common characteristic of many humanist sans serifs. It can also be seen in Gill Sans. Optima does not have this particular feature, but the flex in the strokes of make it a humanist sans serif, too. Compare the humanist faces to the first three examples in the last row. These are **geometric** sans serifs. They look quite monoweight, but subtle variations of thickness can still be found in their strokes.

Pages of observation could be written about these characters, but it seems best to turn you loose to make your own discoveries. Eventually, you will come to recognize that each character in each typeface is in itself a small work of art. To find beauty in such small and common things can be tremendously enriching.

A Close Look at serifs

Figure 12-6 shows close-ups of the outlines of serifs from a variety of typefaces. This gives you the opportunity to observe subtleties of construction. Compare the shapes of brackets and the shapes of the points. Notice how cupping and subtle asymmetry gives several examples a calligraphic feeling. Observing the positions of anchor points and handles will help you learn to draw outline paths for these shapes.

Chapter Summary

This book concludes with a close look at the fundamentals of type design. This chapter expanded your vocabulary of terms used to describe parts of letterforms. You were shown optical adjustments that are necessary to make type look balanced and you were given the opportunity to observe other fine points of design in letters. After the Study Guide, a process for designing a set of capital letters will be described. The Illustrator Skills Tutorial goes over some important points relating to drawing type to produce a font.

Thanks for the time you spent with this guide. I hope it helped you to appreciate the type you see around you every day, and I hope its lessons help you design with attractive and inventive typographic communication. Best of luck with your career!

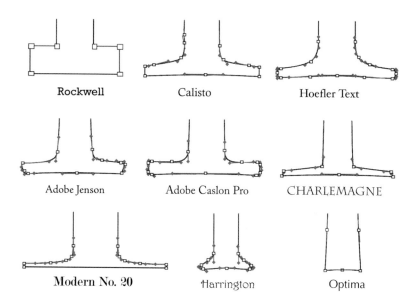

Figure 12-6 Outlines of serifs from a variety of typefaces.

Design Concepts Study Guide Chapter 12

After you have read the previous chapter, fill in the blanks with the letter of the correct answer.

1. _____
2. _____
3. _____
4. _____
5. _____
6. _____
7. _____
8. _____
9. _____
10. _____
11. _____
12. _____
13. _____
14. _____
15. _____
16. _____
17. _____
18. _____
19. _____
20. _____
21. _____
22. _____
23. _____

A. loop

B. crossbar

C. vertex

D. bowl

E. eye

F. beak terminal

G. flexed stem

H. juncture

I. spur

J. arm (use twice)

K. ear

L. shoulder

M. tail

N. link

O. nick

P. spine

Q. apex

R. tear terminal

S. cupped serif

T. leg

U. finial

V. pear terminal

Exercise

This exercise was designed to reinforce the concepts that were presented in the preceding chapter.

Designing an Uppercase Alphabet

Overview

Designing an entire typeface with uppercase and lowercase alphabets, the figures *0* through *9*, punctuation, ligatures, and other special characters is an extensive project that requires a level of commitment that may be beyond many students. However, attacking the 26 uppercase letters alone is a much more manageable exercise and can be quite enlightening. Making decisions about shapes, proportions and spacing will make you more sensitive to those characteristics in other typefaces. A serif typeface is a good choice for this initial experience because it will give you the opportunity to make choices about a wide range of typographic features. If you find that you enjoy type design and want to develop expertise in this field, excellent resources are listed in the Bibliography.

Objective

- To creatively apply what you have learned about type design.

Specifications

You will design an alphabet of 26 original capital letters with serifs. Each letter will be drawn on a grid measuring 10 × 10 cm. This exercise may be executed in Adobe Illustrator or on paper with pencil and ink.

Procedure

1. Write a design brief

It may be helpful to begin by writing a short *design brief* that envisions the end purpose of your typeface and the tone you would like it to express. You may wish to find examples of type that your design might be influenced by in some way.

2. Prepare em grids

It's best to draw letters large because it's easier to see subtleties of shape. Also, small irregularities in large drawings tend to become less noticeable when the drawing is scaled down

You'll draw each of the letters on identical square grids. This square will represent the typeface's em square. (It's height and width are identical to the body-height of the typeface.) Type designers divide the em square into small units. One thousand units per em is a commonly used

**ABCDEFGHI
JKLNOPQRS
TUVWXYZ
ABCDeFGHi
JKLNOPQRS
TUVWXYZ.,!?"
1234567890**

Figure 12-7 Leslie Cabarga, author of the excellent *Logo, Font and Lettering Bible*, based his typeface BadTyp on the worst examples of sign painting and amateur lettering that he collected over a period of years. This is the work of a highly trained and talented professional— kids, for goodness sake, don't try to make anything this ugly yourself!

increment. For this exercise, percent (0.01) divisions will be sufficient. A grid of 10 × 10 cm will be convenient. At this scale, 1 mm will be equal to 1% of an em. If you are using Illustrator, directions for setting up the em grids are in ISM 12. If you are drawing by hand it is recommended that you use graph paper.

3. Draw guidelines

You'll recall that a typeface's body-height includes small spaces above and below the letters' ascenders and descenders:

Place a horizontal guideline about 7 mm below the top of the em square—this will be the cap height.

Place (or draw) a horizontal guideline about 2 mm above the cap height guideline. This will be used to mark the "overshoot" guideline. Apexes and round tops of capital letters will reach this level.

4. Place baseline and center guides

Place the baseline guide. This will determine the proportion between the cap-height and the size of descenders. The baseline would typically be about 20% (2 cm) from the bottom of the em grid.

Mark the center with a vertical guideline.

5. Draw an *I*

Draw a capital *I* centered on the baseline. Take your time. This letter will be the model for all vertical stems in the alphabet. Its serifs will be the basis for all other serifs.

How thick should you make the stem? This is a decision that will have a strong influence on the tone of your alphabet. For comparison's sake, I'll tell you that the width of Times roman's stem is about 10% new of its em (1 cm on our grid).

Another consideration is size and shape of the serifs. (Times' serifs are almost three times the width of the stem. They have a flat pad that's about 2% [2 mm] thick. Their gentle brackets join the stems about 5% above. **Don't copy these dimensions or the shapes, but instead, react to them to find an alternative solution.**)

Consider putting flex in the stem and/or cupping the bottom of the serif.

6. Draw an *H*

Next, you'll draw an *H* on a new em grid.

Copy the *I* twice, to use for the stems. (You might, however, consider slimming their width slightly.)

Decide how far apart to space the stems. This will establish the pattern for the set width of many characters. (Times has a somewhat narrow set width that's 68% of the em.)

Decide on the height of the crossbar. It's usually, but not always, slightly higher than ½ the cap height. You can use this height to determine the height of bars and junctures in several other letters.

Decide the thickness of the cross-stroke. This will determine the thickness of the other thin strokes. (Times' thin strokes are about 43% of the thickness of its thick strokes. Didot's are only 14%.)

Place vertical guides to mark the set width of the *H*. Place horizontal guides for the thickness of the serifs and the brackets, and for the crossbar. (See Figure 12-8.) You will copy this grid for each new letter. Each letter will be centered on the baseline.

7. Draw a *V*

The *V* will give you a chance to reevaluate the ratio of thick/thin contrast that you chose.

Begin with the top serifs of the *H*. The thickness of the left stroke will be based on the *I* stem; the right stroke will be based on the crossbar. Both will be somewhat heavier at the top and narrow as they approach the vertex. Adjust the widths of serifs as needed. Note that the vertex goes slightly below the baseline—about 2mm. Use the same baseline overshoot for all vertexes and bottoms of round characters. Be careful not to make the inner angle of the vertex too narrow—it can fill up with ink. (See Figure 12-9.)

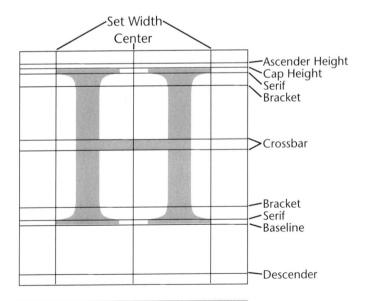

Figure 12-8 Em-square grid with an *H* (shown at 50% scale).

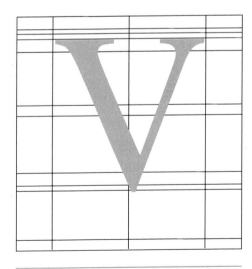

Figure 12-9 Grid with an *V* (shown at 50% scale).

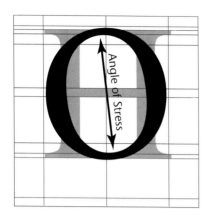

Figure 12-10 Grid with an *O* (shown at 50% scale). Note its proportions in relation to the width of the *H*. Also note the angle of stress.

8. Draw an *O*

The *O* will provide the prototype for all curved strokes. Consider its proportions in relation to the width of the *H*.

Remember, the outer oval will overshoot the baseline and the cap height. Its shape can range from round to somewhat square.

The inner oval will be concentric with the outer. It will be more oblong than the outer, so that the wide point of the side strokes is somewhat thicker than the *H* stems and the top and bottom are a little thinner than the crossbar. If you wish, rotate the inner oval counter-clockwise to create the **angle of stress to a diagonal**. (See Figure 12-10.) (If you are using Illustrator, directions for rotating the inner oval are given in the Skills Module.)

9. Evaluate your letters

Copy the letters that you've made so far and put them in a row. Evaluate their design both individually and as a group. These four letters will form the basis of the other 22, so you'll want to be sure they look good before you go on.

10. Draw *E, F, L,* and *T*

E, F, L, and *T* are easily derived from the *H*, but there is some room for creativity in developing the terminals of the arms.

11. Draw a *Z*

Use the arms you created above to create a *Z*.

12. Draw round characters

Next, let's do some round characters.
Q is simply derived from the *O* by adding a tail—have fun with this!
C is a partial *O* with terminals (maybe related to your *E*?).

13. Draw a *D* and *G*

D and *G* can be modeled by borrowing from the *I* and the *O*. Take the *G*'s terminal from the *C*. What about a spur?

14. Draw a *P*

P is derived from *I* and *O*, but it will need more adjustment. Its bowl may not close at the bottom.

15. Draw an *R* and *B*

When the *P* looks good, copy it to begin the *R* and the *B*. The upper bowls on these characters may be somewhat smaller than the *P*'s.

16. Draw a *K*

The stem and leg of the *R* can be copied to begin the *K*, however the legs may be treated differently. The arm and leg of the *K* are often at right angles to each other.

17. Draw an *A*

Angled characters are of course based on the *V*. To make an *A*, rotate the *V* 180% and add a crossbar. The crossbar may be lower than the one on the *H*. Open the Font Book Special Characters Palette and look at all the *A*s to get ideas for the treatment of the apex. Remember that the apex will overshoot the cap height

18. Draw an *X*

Make an *X* by taking the feet from the *A* and put them below the tops of the *V* then connect them crosswise.

19. Draw a *Y*

For *Y* use the top of the *X* and the bottom of an *I*.

20. Draw a *W*

W is derived from two *V*s. This is generally the widest letter in the alphabet. Open the Font Book Special Characters Palette to get ideas for the treatment of the central juncture.

21. Draw an *M*

The *M* is not an upside-down *W*. It's closer to a thin *I* and a thick *I* with a *V* hanging between them. Sometimes the outer strokes incline inward somewhat.

22. Draw an *N*

The *N* is two thin *I*s connected by a thick diagonal stroke that can be borrowed from a *V*.

23. Draw a *U*

The *U*, like its cousin the *V*, has a thick stroke and a thin stroke. It can be made from thick *I* and a thin *I* joined by a round bottom.

24. Draw a *J*

The top of the *J* is made from an *I*. Open the Font Book Special Characters Palette to get ideas for the treatment of the hook.

25. Draw an *S*

S is probably the most challenging letter in the alphabet. It can be drawn by stacking two ellipses; the lower one can be somewhat larger than the top one. Then, create the *S* by winding the stroke around the ellipses as in Figure 12-11.

Figure 12-11 An *S* formed by drawing over two ellipses

26. Evaluate your letters

Look carefully at all the letters as a group. Make sure that they are balanced in weight and look compatible before you continue.

27. Set the sidebearings

Sidebearings are the boundaries at the left and right sides of a character. Poorly designed sidebearings can make an otherwise good font practically unworkable because kerning problems become colossal. Good sidebearings cannot be decided by measurement alone—they require careful visual judgment.

> Start by lining up four copies of your *H* side by side. Experiment to find the best spacing for these letters. Try for a feeling of balance between the spaces within the letters and the space between the letters.

Remember that the spacing between large letters looks looser than proportional spacing for smaller scale type—so don't go too tight.

Sidebearings are measured as one-half of the distance between adjacent letters' stems (*not* the distance between serifs). On symmetrical letters, the left and right sidebearings will be the same.

> Sandwich other letters between the *H*s to find their sidebearings. The straight-sided figures *I*, *N*, and *U* (and maybe *M*) will probably have similar values to the *H*. The values for the straight sides of *B*, *D*, *E*, *F*, *J*, *K*, *L*, *P*, and *R* will probably be similar, too.
>
> The spacing for *O* will probably be somewhat tighter than *H*. Its values will probably be repeated by *Q* and the round sides of *C*, *D*, *G*, and *P*.
>
> Next, try the *A*. Its diagonal sides makes it one of letters that have the tightest spacing. *T*, *V*, *W*, *X*, and *Y* will be similar. So will the right sides of *K*, *L*, and *R*, and the left side of *J*.
>
> Last, use your best judgment to decide the spacing of *S* and *Z*.

27. Adjust kerning

Make sure that you are confident of all your sidebearings before you begin to adjust kerning. This will save you more than 75% of the work. Figure 12-12 shows pairs of capital letters that generally need some adjustment.

28. Test your typeface

Lastly, test your typeface by forming words with it. The word *HAMBURGEFONTS* is often used for this purpose.

Leslie Cabarga compiled a list of words that uses practically every kerning pair in the alphabet. He calls it Kern King. It's a great tool for diagnosing kerning problems. It can be copied from his Web site at www.logofontandlettering.com.

Congratulations! I'm sure you've learned a lot in this project. If you wish to create punctuation for this set, it could be used as titling font. It can be a great feeling to see your own creation used in many different configurations.

A complete typeface may have more than 10 times this many characters. I'm sure that after this you'll never take for granted the creativity that goes into a typeface! Once again, if you find that you enjoy type design and want to develop expertise in this field, excellent resources are listed in the Bibliography.

AC	AG	AO	AQ	AT	AU	AV	AW	AY
BT	BV	BW	CC	CG	CO	CQ	CT	CV
CW	CY	DA	DJ	DV	DY	FA	FG	FJ
FO	FT	FV	FW	FY	GY	KC	KG	KO
KQ	LO	LT	LV	LW	LY	LA	LC	LG
LO	LQ	LT	LU	LV	LW	OA	OT	OV
OW	OX	OY	PA	PT	PV	PW	PY	QA
QT	QU	QV	QW	QX	QY	RC	RG	RO
RQ	RT	RU	RV	RW	RX	RY	TA	TC
TG	TO	TQ	TT	TX	TY	VA	VC	VG
VO	VQ	WA	WC	WG	WQ	WT	XC	XG
XO	XQ	YA	YC	ZA	ZC	ZG	ZO	ZQ

Figure 12-12 These pairs of capital letters generally need some adjustment of kerning.

Adobe Garamond

During the early 16th century, Claude Garamond was the first to specialize in creating the punches used to make type molds. His output was so prolific, and of such high quality, that it played a major role in the transition from Gothic textura to roman type. Garamond's work was based on the type that Francesco Griffo created for the famous Venetian publisher Aldus Manutius. However, Garamond's work is lighter, with greater contrast between thick and thin strokes (but not so much as the later Caslon). Its tall ascenders and long descenders give the type an aristocratic bearing. The small x-height of this type makes it very economical because more letters can fit on a line—but this same characteristic also makes it less legible at small sizes. The small bowls on the *a* and the *e* are distinctive features.

Several typefaces that have been named Garamond are in fact based on later work by Jean Jannon, which has a more irregular structure. *Adobe Garamond* was created in 1989 by Robert Slimbach. The *italic*, which was based on a mid-16th-century design by Robert Granjon, has a lively loose-scripted quality.

ABCDEFGHIJKLMNOPQRSTUVWXYZ
abcdefghijklmnopqrstuvwxyz
1234567890 !?()&.,:;•“”’$€

ABCDEFGHIJKLMNOPQRSTUVWXYZ
abcdefghijklmnopqrstuvwxyz
1234567890 !?()&.,:;•“”’$€

ABCDEFGHIJKLMNOPQRSTUVWXYZ
abcdefghijklmnopqrstuvwxyz
1234567890 !?()&.,:;•“”’$€

10/12 × 18p FL/RR:

To the Reader; Giambattista Bodoni, 1818:
Printing is the final outcome of man's [sic] most beautiful, ingenious and useful invention: that I mean, of writing: and its most valuable form where it is required to turn out many copies of the same text. This applies still more where it is important to ensure uniformity, and more readable form for the enjoyment of posterity. When we consider the range of usefulness *of printing, together with the long series of devices which have brought us from the first discovery of letters to our*

8/9.6 × 18p FL/RR:

To the Reader; Giambattista Bodoni, 1818:
Printing is the final outcome of man's [sic] most beautiful, ingenious and useful invention: that I mean, of writing: and its most valuable form where it is required to turn out many copies of the same text. This applies still more where it is important to ensure uniformity, and more readable form for the enjoyment of posterity. When we consider the range of usefulness of printing, together with the long series of devices which have brought us from the first discovery of letters to our present power of printing thousands of *sheets of fine laid paper words no longer evanescent but fixed with sharper outlines than the articulation of lips can give them, the thought of such surpassing achievement compels admiration at the force of the human intellect.*

Adobe Jenson

Nicolas Jenson was a Frenchman who learned the art of type founding in Germany, perhaps from Johan Gutenberg himself. Later, he settled in Venice and created early roman typefaces of exceptional quality. His work has been long admired for its clear letter shapes and balance between form and space, resulting in even color throughout blocks of text. Jenson's type and other early roman faces are sometimes classified as humanist because they show influences from the flat-nib pen calligraphy of early Renaissance manuscripts. The sloping bar on the lowercase *e* is an obvious characteristic of this subcategory.

This version, created by Robert Slimbach, is somewhat heavier than the original, but retains its calligraphic quality. There is considerable flex in its strokes and distinctive flattening in the round strokes near their stress. The asymmetrical serifs are blunt and heavily bracketed. There is moderate contrast in the weight of strokes. The lowercase letters are short with a low x-height. Slimbach based the robust italic on the late 15th century calligraphy of Ludovico degli Arrighi. Note the crimped tails on the lowercase letters.

ABCDEFGHIJKLMNOPQRSTUVWXYZ
abcdefghijklmnopqrstuvwxyz
1234567890 !?()&.,:;•""$€

ABCDEFGHIJKLMNOPQRSTUVWXYZ
abcdefghijklmnopqrstuvwxyz
1234567890 !?()&.,:;•""$€

ABCDEFGHIJKLMNOPQRSTUVWXYZ
abcdefghijklmnopqrstuvwxyz
1234567890 !?()&.,:;•""$€

10/12 × 18p FL/RR:

To the Reader; Giambattista Bodoni, 1818: **Printing is the final outcome of man's [sic] most beautiful, ingenious and useful invention: that I mean, of writing: and its most valuable form where it is** required to turn out many copies of the same text. This applies still more where it is important to ensure uniformity, and more readable form for the enjoyment of posterity. When we consider the range of usefulness of *printing, together with the long series of devices which have brought us from the first discovery of letters to our present power of printing thousands of sheets of fine laid*

8/9.6 × 18p FL/RR:

To the Reader; Giambattista Bodoni, 1818: Printing is the final outcome of man's [sic] most beautiful, ingenious and useful invention: that I mean, of writing: and its most valuable form where it is required to turn out many copies of the same text. This applies still more where it is important to ensure uniformity, and more readable form for the enjoyment of posterity. When we consider the range of usefulness of printing, together with the long series of devices which have brought us from the first discovery of letters to our present power *of printing thousands of sheets of fine laid paper words no longer evanescent but fixed with sharper outlines than the articulation of lips can give them, the thought of such surpassing achievement compels admiration at the force of the human intellect.*

Times New Roman

About 1930, Stanley Morison wrote an article criticizing the typographic standards of *The Times of London*. The newspaper responded by putting Morison in charge of developing a new typeface, which was drawn by Victor Lardent. Since its debut in 1932, Times New Roman has become one of the most popular typefaces of all time. It was designed for legibility, economy of space, and printability. Morison based the design on Platin, Frank Pierpont's 1916 revival of a 16th century typeface by Robert Granjon, and he was also influenced by Eric Gill's Perpetua of 1925.

Times New Roman is built from robust strokes with moderate contrast. Its large x-height makes letters easy to recognize despite their condensed widths. Their short ascenders and descenders permit tight leading. In all other respects this typeface is a model of moderation, free of eccentricity. The strokes of the italic are fluid and even. It is somewhat lighter than the *roman* weight. The *bold* face would properly be classified as transitional, or perhaps even modern, because of its greater contrast between thick and thin strokes, the vertical axis of stress in the round letters, and flat upper serifs on the ascenders of lowercase letters.

ABCDEFGHIJKLMNOPQRSTUVWXYZ
abcdefghijklmnopqrstuvwxyz
1234567890 !?()&.,:;•""'$€

ABCDEFGHIJKLMNOPQRSTUVWXYZ
abcdefghijklmnopqrstuvwxyz
1234567890 !?()&.,:;•""'$€

ABCDEFGHIJKLMNOPQRSTUVWXYZ
abcdefghijklmnopqrstuvwxyz
1234567890 !?()&.,:;•""'$€

10/12 × 18p FL/RR:

To the Reader; Giambattista Bodoni, 1818: **Printing is the final outcome of man's [sic] most beautiful, ingenious and useful invention: that I mean, of writing: and its most valuable form** where it is required to turn out many copies of the same text. This applies still more where it is important to ensure uniformity, and more readable form for the enjoyment of posterity. When we consider the *range of usefulness of printing, together with the long series of devices which have brought us from the first discovery of letters to our present power of*

8/9.6 × 18p FL/RR:

To the Reader; Giambattista Bodoni, 1818: **Printing is the final outcome of man's [sic] most beautiful, ingenious and useful invention: that I mean, of writing: and its most valuable form** where it is required to turn out many copies of the same text. This applies still more where it is important to ensure uniformity, and more readable form for the enjoyment of posterity. When we consider the range of usefulness of printing, together with the long series of devices which have brought us from the first discovery of letters to our present power of printing thousands of sheets of *fine laid paper words no longer evanescent but fixed with sharper outlines than the articulation of lips can give them, the thought of such surpassing achievement compels admiration at the force of the human intellect.*

Adobe Caslon

William Caslon's type dominated printing in the English language during the 18th century. The first official printings of the *Declaration of Independence* and the *Constitution* were set in this type. Caslon's popularity stemmed from its sturdy, open letterforms, flavored with slight eccentric irregularities that create a subtle jaunty rhythm in lines of text. For instance, notice the weight of the upper serifs on *h, j, k* and *l*.

Many revivals of Caslon were created in the early 20th century. More recently, designer Carol Twombly based this digital version on Caslon's specimens from 1734 through 1770. Examining specimens of different sizes, she found significant variations in their designs. From these sources she interpolated a typeface that is handsome at any scale. Matthew Carter's Big Caslon is a version designed to be set at display sizes only. Twombly's design has subtle flex in the strokes and cupping in the serifs that produces an attractive calligraphic quality. The italic is fluid and energetic with long descenders and several fancy details. *Caslon Pro* is an OpenType font family that includes handsome ligatures and ornate decorative Pi characters.

ABCDEFGHIJKLMNOPQRSTUVWXYZ
abcdefghijklmnopqrstuvwxyz
1234567890 !?()&.,:;•""'"$€

ABCDEFGHIJKLMNOPQRSTUVWXYZ
abcdefghijklmnopqrstuvwxyz
1234567890 !?()&.,:;•""'"$€

ABCDEFGHIJKLMNOPQRSTUVWXYZ
abcdefghijklmnopqrstuvwxyz
1234567890 !?()&.,:;•""'"$€

10/12 × 18p FL/RR:

To the Reader; Giambattista Bodoni, 1818:
Printing is the final outcome of man's [sic] most beautiful, ingenious and useful invention: that I mean, of writing: and its most valuable form where it is required to turn out many copies of the same text. This applies still more where it is important to ensure uniformity, and more readable form for the enjoyment of posterity. When we consider the range *of usefulness of printing, together with the long series of devices which have brought us from the first discovery of letters to our present power of printing thousands of*

8/9.6 × 18p FL/RR:

To the Reader; Giambattista Bodoni, 1818:
Printing is the final outcome of man's [sic] most beautiful, ingenious and useful invention: that I mean, of writing: and its most valuable form where it is required to turn out many copies of the same text. This applies still more where it is important to ensure uniformity, and more readable form for the enjoyment of posterity. When we consider the range of usefulness of printing, together with the long series of devices which have brought us from the first discovery of letters to our present power of printing *thousands of sheets of fine laid paper words no longer evanescent but fixed with sharper outlines than the articulation of lips can give them, the thought of such surpassing achievement compels admiration at the force of the human intellect.*

Century Schoolbook

This typeface had it genesis in 1917, when a textbook publisher asked Morris Fuller Benton of American Type Foundry (ATF) to design type for children's schoolbooks. Benton's design, based on the legibility research of his day, is clear and precise but not cold.

The letters have open counters and the lowercase has high x-height. Set widths are very consistent. The letterspacing is generous. There is moderately strong contrast between the weight of its strokes, but the thin strokes aren't too light. Its thick, square-cornered serifs join to the thick strokes with little bracketing, but those connected to the thin strokes have heavy bracketing. The thick serifs make it possible to categorize this face as a clarendon.

The strokes have no flex and the angle of stress is vertical, but the generous curves in this type help it avoid a mechanical feeling. The high-waisted capitals and the oversized tear and beak terminals make its proportions seem a bit child-like.

From its release in 1923 up through the mid-1960s, this typeface was used in early reading primers, so it has literally been regarded as the model of legibility for generations. It is not very economical of space, but this can be helped a little by setting it with tightened tracking and word spacing.

ABCDEFGHIJKLMNOPQRSTUVWXYZ
abcdefghijklmnopqrstuvwxyz
1234567890 !?()&.,:;•""'$€

ABCDEFGHIJKLMNOPQRSTUVWXYZ
abcdefghijklmnopqrstuvwxyz
1234567890 !?()&.,:;•""'$€

ABCDEFGHIJKLMNOPQRSTUVWXYZ
abcdefghijklmnopqrstuvwxyz
1234567890 !?()&.,:;•""'$€

10/12 × 18p FL/RR:

To the Reader; Giambattista Bodoni, 1818: **Printing is the final outcome of man's [sic] most beautiful, ingenious and useful invention: that I mean, of writing: and its most** valuable form where it is required to turn out many copies of the same text. This applies still more where it is important to ensure unifomity, and more readable form for the enjoyment of *posterity. When we consider the range of usefulness of printing, together with the long series of devices which have brought us from the first*

8/9.6 × 18p FL/RR:

To the Reader; Giambattista Bodoni, 1818: **Printing is the final outcome of man's [sic] most beautiful, ingenious and useful invention: that I mean, of writing: and its most valuable form** where it is required to turn out many copies of the same text. This applies still more where it is important to ensure uniformity, and more readable form for the enjoyment of posterity. When we consider the range of usefulness of printing, together with the long series of devices which have brought us from the first discovery *of letters to our present power of printing thousands of sheets of fine laid paper words no longer evanescent but fixed with sharper outlines than the articulation of lips can give them, the thought of such surpassing achieve-*

Georgia

This is a "pixel font" designed to be legible even at small sizes on a computer monitor. Mathew Carter created it in 1996, drawing primarily from the design of Richard Austin's early 19th century Scotch Roman, which in turn was adapted from Didot. Georgia's debit to those faces is most visible in the almost flat top serifs on lowercase *b, d, h, k,* and *l.* Closer comparison will reveal many other similarities of construction. The overall proportions of the capital letters are quite similar. But many differences are also apparent. The delicate hairline strokes of Didot have been beefed up considerably. The stubby serifs are reinforced with brackets. These factors make Georgia's type color heavier and its spacing appear more dense. Carter has opened up the letters by raising the x-height and the ascenders project above the cap height. In general, the nuanced details found in the models have been simplified and exaggerated. However, Carter added a delicate lilting curve to the legs of *k, K,* and *R.* The italic is fairly heavy, with open shapes and rigorously parallel orientation.

ABCDEFGHIJKLMNOPQRSTUVWXYZ
abcdefghijklmnopqrstuvwxyz
1234567890 !?()&.,:;•""$€

ABCDEFGHIJKLMNOPQRSTUVWXYZ
abcdefghijklmnopqrstuvwxyz
1234567890 !?()&.,:;•""$€

ABCDEFGHIJKLMNOPQRSTUVWXYZ
abcdefghijklmnopqrstuvwxyz
1234567890 !?()&.,:;•""$€

10/12 × 18p FL/RR:

To the Reader; Giambattista Bodoni, 1818: **Printing is the final outcome of man's [sic] most beautiful, ingenious and useful invention: that I mean, of writing: and its** most valuable form where it is required to turn out many copies of the same text. This applies still more where it is important to ensure uniformity, and more readable form for the enjoyment *of posterity. When we consider the range of usefulness of printing, together with the long series of devices which have brought us from the*

8/9.6 × 18p FL/RR:

To the Reader; Giambattista Bodoni, 1818: **Printing is the final outcome of man's [sic] most beautiful, ingenious and useful invention: that I mean, of writing: and its most valuable form where** it is required to turn out many copies of the same text. This applies still more where it is important to ensure uniformity, and more readable form for the enjoyment of posterity. When we consider the range of usefulness of printing, together with the long series of devices which have brought us from the first discovery of letters to our present power of printing thousands of sheets of fine laid paper words no *longer evanescent but fixed with sharper outlines than the articulation of lips can give them, the thought of such surpassing achievement compels admiration at the force of the human intellect.*

Hoefler Text

Jonathan Hoefler is a self-proclaimed "armchair type historian" who often finds inspiration outside of the classical canon. This face was based on early 20th-century revivals of 17th-century creations: *Linotype Garamond No. 3*—which is actually an interpretation of work by Jean Jannon—and *Linotype Janson Text 55*—which was actually based on the type of Nicholas Kis. Hoefler declared, "I wanted to create a typeface that didn't feel like a digital font. At the time I felt like straight lines meant digital, and digital meant cold." In result, this font has calligraphic features such as bowed arms and cupped serifs with heavy brackets that flow to blunt points. The tail on the capital *J* has a distinctive leftward thrust ending with a heavy pear terminal. While the vertical axis of stress and moderately strong contrasts of weight in this typeface argue for its classification as *transitional*, it doesn't have the lightness and precision typical of this style. Instead, like Caslon, Hoefler Text is full-bodied and energetic. The *italic* has fluid shapes with strokes that tilt in a syncopated variety of directions. It is slightly heavier than the regular weight, which helps it stand out. *Hoefler Text* is an extensive family of 27 fonts and a related titling face.

ABCDEFGHIJKLMNOPQRSTUVWXYZ
abcdefghijklmnopqrstuvwxyz
1234567890 !?()&.,:;•""$€

ABCDEFGHIJKLMNOPQRSTUVWXYZ
abcdefghijklmnopqrstuvwxyz
1234567890 !?()&.,:;•""$€

ABCDEFGHIJKLMNOPQRSTUVWXYZ
abcdefghijklmnopqrstuvwxyz
1234567890 !?()&.,:;•""$€

10/12 × 18p FL/RR:

***To the Reader*; Giambattista Bodoni, 1818: Printing is the final outcome of man's [sic] most beautiful, ingenious and useful invention: that I mean, of writing: and its most** valuable form where it is required to turn out many copies of the same text. This applies still more where it is important to ensure uniformity, and more readable form for the enjoyment of *posterity. When we consider the range of usefulness of printing, together with the long series of devices which have brought us from the first discovery of letters to our*

8/9.6 × 18p FL/RR:

***To the Reader*; Giambattista Bodoni, 1818: Printing is the final outcome of man's [sic] most beautiful, ingenious and useful invention: that I mean, of writing: and its most valuable form where it is required** to turn out many copies of the same text. This applies still more where it is important to ensure uniformity, and more readable form for the enjoyment of posterity. When we consider the range of usefulness of printing, together with the long series of devices which have brought us from the first discovery of letters *to our present power of printing thousands of sheets of fine laid paper words no longer evanescent but fixed with sharper outlines than the articulation of lips can give them, the thought of such surpassing achievement compels admiration at the force of the human intellect.*

Didot

The modern roman style was developed during the late 18th century more or less simultaneously in Parma, Italy, by Giambattista Bodoni, and in Paris by Firmin Didot ("dee-doe"). Their typefaces were the ultimate typographic expression of the Age of Enlightenment's value for clarity and precision. They feature rigorously vertical letters with extreme contrast between thick and thin strokes and serifs that are reduced to mere hairlines that have little or no brackets. All of this contributes to the feeling that these letters are creations of mind and machine rather than the hand. These typefaces were constructed out of repeated shape modules; this anticipates the way of thinking that led to industrial mass production in the 19th century. But, it has often been observed that the dazzling contrast in the letters distracts from their readability. These faces are more successfully employed as display type than for running text.

ABCDEFGHIJKLMNOPQRSTUVWXYZ
abcdefghijklmnopqrstuvwxyz
1234567890 !?()&.,:;•"""$€

ABCDEFGHIJKLMNOPQRSTUVWXYZ
abcdefghijklmnopqrstuvwxyz
1234567890 !?()&.,:;•"""$€

ABCDEFGHIJKLMNOPQRSTUVWXYZ
abcdefghijklmnopqrstuvwxyz
1234567890 !?()&.,:;•"""$€

Modern

10/12 × 18p FL/RR:

To the Reader; Giambattista Bodoni, 1818:
Printing is the final outcome of man's [sic] most beautiful, ingenious and useful invention: that I mean, of writing: and its most valuable form where it is required to turn out many copies of the same text. This applies still more where it is important to ensure uniformity, and more readable form for the enjoyment of posterity. *When we consider the range of usefulness of printing, together with the long series of devices which have brought us from the first discovery of*

8/9.6 × 18p FL/RR:

To the Reader; Giambattista Bodoni, 1818:
Printing is the final outcome of man's [sic] most beautiful, ingenious and useful invention: that I mean, of writing: and its most valuable form where it is required to turn out many copies of the same text. This applies still more where it is important to ensure uniformity, and more read-able form for the enjoyment of posterity. When we consider the range of usefulness of printing, together with the long series of devices which have brought us from the first dis-covery of letters to our present power of printing thousands *of sheets of fine laid paper words no longer evanescent but fixed with sharper outlines than the articulation of lips can give them, the thought of such surpassing achievement compels admiration at the force of the human intellect.*

Chaparral

This slab-serif family created by Carol Twombly looks like a cross between typewriter type and oldstyle roman. Its construction is almost monoweight, but subtle tapering in the strokes and slight diagonal stresses in the round characters give it a warm feeling. The structure of the letters is very open—with the unfortunate exceptions of the capital *E* and *F*. The large x-height of the lowercase is matched by ascenders that are taller than the cap height. The regular weight is a clean and readable alternative to use for body text, with good type color and economy of space.

At display size, the regular weight looks rather spindly. The bold looks bloated and its counters look cramped. Fortunately, a handsome semibold is available. The italic is an interesting translation of calligraphic strokes into crisp, restrained lines. Chaparral Pro is an OpenType font family that has a handsome *Th* ligature and playful Pi fonts.

ABCDEFGHIJKLMNOPQRSTUVWXYZ
abcdefghijklmnopqrstuvwxyz
1234567890 !?()&.,:;•""$€

ABCDEFGHIJKLMNOPQRSTUVWXYZ
abcdefghijklmnopqrstuvwxyz
1234567890 !?()&.,:;•""$€

ABCDEFGHIJKLMNOPQRSTUVWXYZ
abcdefghijklmnopqrstuvwxyz
1234567890 !?()&.,:;•""$€

10/12 × 18p FL/RR:

To the Reader; Giambattista Bodoni, 1818:
Printing is the final outcome of man's [sic] most beautiful, ingenious and useful invention: that I mean, of writing: and its most valuable form where it is required to turn out many copies of the same text. This applies still more where it is important to ensure uniformity, and more readable form for the enjoyment of posterity. When we consider the *range of usefulness of printing, together with the long series of devices which have brought us from the first discovery of letters to our present power of printing*

8/9.6 × 18p FL/RR:

To the Reader; Giambattista Bodoni, 1818:
Printing is the final outcome of man's [sic] most beautiful, ingenious and useful invention: that I mean, of writing: and its most valuable form where it is required to turn out many copies of the same text. This applies still more where it is important to ensure uniformity, and more readable form for the enjoyment of posterity. When we consider the range of usefulness of printing, together with the long series of devices which have brought us from the first discovery of letters to our present power of printing thousands of sheets of fine laid paper *words no longer evanescent but fixed with sharper outlines than the articulation of lips can give them, the thought of such surpassing achievement compels admiration at the force of the human intellect.*

Rockwell

Slab-serif typefaces were originally developed for advertising posters in the early 19th century. Their heavy strokes and thick square-cornered serifs made them more legible from a distance. Napoleon's troops used slab serif characters on signboards that relayed orders on the battlefield.

Rockwell was created under the supervision of Frank Pierpont for Monotype and released in 1934. It differs from 19th-century slab serifs by virtue of its geometric structure. For instance, the letter O is almost a perfect circle. Only the slightest adjustments have been made to its shape and the thickness of its stroke to make it appear perfectly round. Other subtle variations in stroke weight can be found, most notably at the junctures between bowls and stems, but the effect these adjustments is to maintain a rigorously geometric and monoweight appearance. The unbracketed square-cornered serifs are just as thick as the stems. The lilting tail on the Q is the only relief from stringent geometry. Despite its large x-height and wide-set widths, the short extenders on the lowercase take away from its readability. The space demanded by its thick serifs make it not very economical of space. However, Rockwell sets with very even color and could be used for short runs of text when its dense and mechanical flavor enhances the expressive tone of the message. The so-called italic is merely an oblique version of the regular type.

ABCDEFGHIJKLMNOPQRSTUVWXYZ
abcdefghijklmnopqrstuvwxyz
1234567890 !?()&.,:;•""''$€

ABCDEFGHIJKLMNOPQRSTUVWXYZ
abcdefghijklmnopqrstuvwxyz
1234567890 !?()&.,:;•""''$€

ABCDEFGHIJKLMNOPQRSTUVWXYZ
abcdefghijklmnopqrstuvwxyz
1234567890 !?()&.,:;•""''$€

10/12 × 18p FL/RR:

To the Reader; Giambattista Bodoni, 1818: Printing is the final outcome of man's [sic] most beautiful, ingenious and useful invention: that I mean, of writing: and its most valuable form where it is required to turn out many copies of the same text. This applies still more where it is important to ensure uniformity, and more readable form for the enjoyment of *posterity. When we consider the range of usefulness of printing, together with the long series of devices which have brought us from the first*

8/9.6 × 18p FL/RR:

To the Reader; Giambattista Bodoni, 1818: Printing is the final outcome of man's [sic] most beautiful, ingenious and useful invention: that I mean, of writing: and its most valuable form where it is required to turn out many copies of the same text. This applies still more where it is important to ensure uniformity, and more readable form for the enjoyment of posterity. When we consider the range of usefulness of printing, together with the long series of devices which have brought us from the first discovery of letters *to our present power of printing thousands of sheets of fine laid paper words no longer evanescent but fixed with sharper outlines than the articulation of lips can give them, the thought of such surpassing achievement compels*

Futura

Created by Paul Renner and released by the German Bauer Type Foundry in 1928, Futura is the most successful realization of the typographic ideals of the Bauhaus and Jan Tschichold's New Typography. It is a geometric sans serif built from unembellished circles, triangles, and rectangles. Subtle adjustments were made only to maintain the optical effect of regularity. Looking at the medium weight (top), notice the circularity of C, G, O, and Q. Letters with triangular shapes have apexes and vertexes that are sharpened to fine points. The terminals end with clean verticals, horizontals, or 45 diagonals.

The x-height of the lowercase is quite high but seems almost dwarfed by ascenders that tower above the cap height—they make the normal leading of 120% feel a bit cramped. The sledge hammer *bold* weight has a higher x-height and shorter ascenders.

The lack of a hook on the lowercase *j* puts it in some danger of being mistaken for an *i*. In other respects, however, this type in this family is quite legible, but not very economical of space. It has the advantage of a very extensive range of styles and weights. The so-called italic is actually an oblique version of the regular type.

ABCDEFGHIJKLMNOPQRSTUVWXYZ
abcdefghijklmnopqrstuvwxyz
1234567890 !?()&.,:;•""$

ABCDEFGHIJKLMNOPQRSTUVWXYZ
abcdefghijklmnopqrstuvwxyz
1234567890 !?()&.,:;•""$

ABCDEFGHIJKLMNOPQRSTUVWXYZ
abcdefghijklmnopqrstuvwxyz
1234567890 !?()&.,:;•""$

10/12 × 18p FL/RR:

***To the Reader;* Giambattista Bodoni,1818: Printing is the final outcome of man's [sic] most beautiful, ingenious and useful invention: that I mean, of writing: and its** most valuable form where it is required to turn out many copies of the same text. This applies still more where it is important to ensure uniformity, *and more readable form for the enjoyment of posterity. When we consider the range of useful-ness of printing, together with the long series of*

8/9.6 × 18p FL/RR:

***To the Reader;* Giambattista Bodoni, 1818: Printing is the final outcome of man's [sic] most beautiful, ingenious and useful invention: that I mean, of writing: and its most valuable form** where it is required to turn out many copies of the same text. This applies still more where it is important to ensure uniformity, and more readable form for the enjoyment of posterity. When we consider the range of usefulness of printing, together with the long series of devices which have *brought us from the first discovery of letters to our present power of printing thousands of sheets of fine laid paper words no longer evanescent but fixed with sharper outlines than the articulation of lips can give them, the thought of such*

Sans Serif

Gill Sans

Eric Gill was a designer who mixed innovation with deep reverence for tradition. Gill Sans, released in 1928, offered a warmer alternative to the geometric faces that were being formulated in Germany. It is one of the earliest examples of humanist sans-serif type, so called because their forms and proportions reflect the influence of oldstyle roman type.

The shapes of the capital letters are, overall, remarkably similar to Caslon. The descender on capital *J* is an oldstyle feature that hadn't been seen in previous sans serifs. The widths of *C, D, G, O,* and *Q* are majestic. *O* and *Q* are actually wider than they are tall. It is also unusual that capital *M* is the same width as *N*. The high central junction of *M* opens up its interior space.

In the lowercase, the double-story structure of *a* and *g* resemble oldstyle prototypes. The x-height is slightly larger than Caslon's, but the extenders are much shorter.

Subtle calligraphic details can be seen in the leg of the *R*, the spreading tail on *Q*, the bowl of *a*, and the arm of *r*. This type family features a true italic with several calligraphic elements.

Gill Sans is clean, eye-friendly, economical of space, and sets with good type color—a good choice for body type.

ABCDEFGHIJKLMNOPQRSTUVWXYZ
abcdefghijklmnopqrstuvwxyz
1234567890 !?()&.,:;•""'$?

ABCDEFGHIJKLMNOPQRSTUVWXYZ
abcdefghijklmnopqrstuvwxyz
1234567890 !?()&.,:;•""'$?

ABCDEFGHIJKLMNOPQRSTUVWXYZ
abcdefghijklmnopqrstuvwxyz
1234567890 !?()&.,:;•""'$?

10/12 × 18p FL/RR:

To the Reader; Giambattista Bodoni, 1818:
Printing is the final outcome of man's [sic] most beautiful, ingenious and useful invention: that I mean, of writing: and its most valuable form where it is required to turn out many copies of the same text. This applies still more where it is important to ensure uniformity, and more readable form for the enjoyment of posterity. When we *consider the range of usefulness of printing, together with the long series of devices which have brought us from the first discovery of letters to our present power of* printing

8/9.6 × 18p FL/RR:

To the Reader; Giambattista Bodoni, 1818:
Printing is the final outcome of man's [sic] most beautiful, ingenious and useful invention: that I mean, of writing: and its most valuable form where it is required to turn out many copies of the same text. This applies still more where it is important to ensure uniformity, and more readable form for the enjoyment of posterity. When we consider the range of usefulness of printing, together with the long series of devices which have brought us from the first discovery of letters to our present *power of printing thousands of sheets of fine laid paper words no longer evanescent but fixed with sharper outlines than the articulation of lips can give them, the thought of such surpassing achievement compels admiration at the force of the human intellect.*

Neue Helvetica

In the mid-1950s, Edouard Hoffman and Max Miedinger revised the 19th-century Akzidenz Grotesk to produce Helvetica, the most popular sans serif of all time. Named after the Latin word for Switzerland, the clarity of this typeface made it an emblem of the Swiss style. Unfortunately, the other faces in the Helvetica family were created by different designers, so they did not coordinate well. In 1983, Linotype resolved the problem with the release of the Neue Helvetica family, which contains 51 systematically coordinated faces of differing weights and proportions.

The outstanding characteristic of this type is its large x-height. This makes the type very legible, but less economical of space. The capital letters have quite consistent proportions that tend toward a width-to-height ratio of 3 to 4. Curved strokes are somewhat flattened to maintain this shape. This helps open up the counter spaces in the round letters. Conversely, the mouths of open bowls almost close shut.

The vertical leg of the *R* also conforms to the rectangular pattern, but its languorous double-curve stands out from the prevailing geometric simplicity. The double-story *a* is another standout feature. These humanizing details stand in opposition to the square dots on *i* and *j*, and in the punctuation. As in most other sans serifs, the so-called italic is actually an oblique version of the regular type.

ABCDEFGHIJKLMNOPQRSTUVWXYZ
abcdefghijklmnopqrstuvwxyz
1234567890 !?()&.,:;•""''$€

ABCDEFGHIJKLMNOPQRSTUVWXYZ
abcdefghijklmnopqrstuvwxyz
1234567890 !?()&.,:;•""''$€

ABCDEFGHIJKLMNOPQRSTUVWXYZ
abcdefghijklmnopqrstuvwxyz
1234567890 !?()&.,:;•""''$€

10/12 × 18p FL/RR:

To the Reader; Giambattista Bodoni, 1818: Printing is the final outcome of man's [sic] most beautiful, ingenious and useful invention: that I mean, of writing: and its most valuable form where it is required to turn out many copies of the same text. This applies still more where it is important to ensure uniformity, and more readable form for the enjoyment of *posterity. When we consider the range of usefulness of printing, together with the long series of devices which have brought us from*

8/9.6 × 18p FL/RR:

To the Reader; Giambattista Bodoni, 1818: Printing is the final outcome of man's [sic] most beautiful, ingenious and useful invention: that I mean, of writing: and its most valuable form where it is required to turn out many copies of the same text. This applies still more where it is important to ensure uniformity, and more readable form for the enjoyment of posterity. When we consider the range of usefulness of printing, together with the long series of devices which have brought us from the first discovery of letters to our present power of printing thousands of sheets *of fine laid paper words no longer evanescent but fixed with sharper outlines than the articulation of lips can give them, the thought of such surpassing achievement compels admiration at the force of the human intellect.*

News Gothic

This workhorse was designed by Morris Fuller Benton in 1908, but the bold weight was not added until 50 years later. The capital letters have quite consistent proportions that tend toward a very condensed width-to-height ratio of nearly 1 to 2. It is distinctly lighter than its cousin, Helvetica, and quite a bit more economical of space. The bowls are more oval shaped and the openings don't close as tight. Its x-height is so large that it can be set a half point or more smaller than most other faces. However, short ascenders and even shorter descenders make it somewhat less readable. The clear, monoweight structure, and the square dots on the *i*, *j* and in the punctuation, give it a no-nonsense quality. The double-story *a* and *g* stand out from the prevailing geometry. The *bold* face makes strong and concise headlines, but at text sizes it benefits from a little extra tracking. Like most sans serifs, this family has an oblique face instead of a true italic.

ABCDEFGHIJKLMNOPQRSTUVWXYZ
abcdefghijklmnopqrstuvwxyz
1234567890 !?()&.,:;•""$€

ABCDEFGHIJKLMNOPQRSTUVWXYZ
abcdefghijklmnopqrstuvwxyz
1234567890 !?()&.,:;•""$€

ABCDEFGHIJKLMNOPQRSTUVWXYZ
abcdefghijklmnopqrstuvwxyz
1234567890 !?()&.,:;•""$€

10/12 × 18p FL/RR:

***To the Reader**; Giambattista Bodoni, 1818:* **Printing is the final outcome of man's [sic] most beautiful, ingenious and useful invention: that I mean, of writing: and its most** valuable form where it is required to turn out many copies of the same text. This applies still more where it is important to ensure uniformity, and more readable form for the enjoyment of *posterity. When we consider the range of usefulness of printing, together with the long series of devices which have brought us from the first*

8/9.6 × 18p FL/RR:

***To the Reader**; Giambattista Bodoni, 1818:* **Printing is the final outcome of man's [sic] most beautiful, ingenious and useful invention: that I mean, of writing: and its most valuable form where it is required to turn out** many copies of the same text. This applies still more where it is important to ensure uniformity, and more readable form for the enjoyment of posterity. When we consider the range of usefulness of printing, together with the long series of devices which have brought us from the first discovery of letters to our present power of printing thousands of sheets of fine laid paper words *no longer evanescent but fixed with sharper outlines than the articulation of lips can give them, the thought of such surpassing achievement compels admiration at the force of the human*

Optima

Created by Hermann Zapf in 1958, Optima is a sprightly humanist sans serif of outstanding clarity. It bears strong structural resemblance to Palatino, Zapf's oldstyle *roman* of 1950. If you eliminated Palatino's serifs, the set widths of both typefaces would be virtually identical. Like Palatino, the round capitals in Optima are wide and slightly square. However, Optima has a lighter and more regular overall appearance than Palatino. Its lowercase has higher x-height and the ascender heights are uniform. Its thin strokes are more delicate and the flow of the strokes is more fluid.

The degree of calligraphic play in this typeface's strokes was unprecedented in previous sans serifs. It has considerable flex in the stems and vertical stress in the bowls. Its flared, cupped terminals are distinctive. Zapf referred to his creation as "a serif-less roman." Despite the innovative hybrid features of its roman (regular) face, Zapf did not develop a true italic for this family.

This type is exceptionally legible and sets with even color. It can be set smaller than most other faces, but likes looser leading. The bold weight makes an elegant and distinctive display type.

ABCDEFGHIJKLMNOPQRSTUVWXYZ
abcdefghijklmnopqrstuvwxyz
1234567890 !?()&.,:;•""$€

ABCDEFGHIJKLMNOPQRSTUVWXYZ
abcdefghijklmnopqrstuvwxyz
1234567890 !?()&.,:;•""$€

ABCDEFGHIJKLMNOPQRSTUVWXYZ
abcdefghijklmnopqrstuvwxyz
1234567890 !?()&.,:;•""$€

10/12 × 18p FL/RR:

To the Reader; Giambattista Bodoni, 1818: **Printing is the final outcome of man's [sic] most beautiful, ingenious and useful invention: that I mean, of writing: and its most valuable form** where it is required to turn out many copies of the same text. This applies still more where it is important to ensure uniformity, and more readable form for the enjoyment of posterity. When we consider *the range of usefulness of printing, together with the long series of devices which have brought us from the first discovery of letters to our present*

8/9.6 × 18p FL/RR:

To the Reader; Giambattista Bodoni, 1818: **Printing is the final outcome of man's [sic] most beautiful, ingenious and useful invention: that I mean, of writing: and its most val-**uable form where it is required to turn out many copies of the same text. This applies still more where it is important to ensure uniformity, and more readable form for the enjoyment of posterity. When we consider the range of usefulness of printing, together with the long series of devices which have brought us from the first discovery of letters to our present power of printing thousands of sheets of fine laid paper *words no longer evanescent but fixed with sharper outlines than the articulation of lips can give them, the thought of such surpassing achievement compels admiration at the force*

CHARLEMAGNE BOLD
ABCDEFGHIJKLMNOPQRSTUVWXYZ
1234567890 !?()&.,:;·""$€

Cooper Black
ABCDEFGHIJKLMNOPQRSTUVWXYZ
abcdefghijklmnopqrstuvwxyz
1234567890 !?()&.,:;·""$€

COPPERPLATE BOLD
ABCDEFGHIJKLMNOPQRSTUVWXYZ
ABCDEFGHIJKLMNOPQRSTUVWXYZ
1234567890 !?()&.,:;•""$€

Curlz
ABCDEFGHIJKLMNOPQRSTUVWXYZ
abcdefghijklmnopqrstuvwxyz
1234567890 !?()&.,:;·""$€

ENGRAVERS BOLD
ABCDEFGHIJKLMNO
PQRSTUVWXYZ
1234567890 !?0&.,:;·" "$€

Harrington
ABCDEFGHIJKLMNOPQRSTUVWXYZ
abcdefghijklmnopqrstuvwxyz
1234567890 !?()&.,:;•""'$€

Playbill
ABCDEFGHIJKLMNOPQRSTUVWXYZ
abcdefghijklmnopqrstuvwxyz
1234567890 !?()&.,:;•""$€

ROSEWOOD
ABCDEFGHIJKLMNOPQRSTUVWXYZ
1234567890 !?()&.,:;•""$€

Viva Bold
ABCDEFGHIJKLMNOPQRSTUVWXYZ
abcdefghijklmnopqrstuvwxyz
1234567890 !?()&.,:;""$€

Wide Latin
ABCDEFGHIJKLMN
OPQRSTUVWXYZ
abcdefghijklmn
opqrstuvwxyz
1234567890 !?()&.,:;•""$€

Abadi Condensed Extra Bold
ABCDEFGHIJKLMNOPQRSTUVWXYZ
abcdefghijklmnopqrstuvwxyz
1234567890 !?()&.,:;•""''$€

Bauhaus 93
ABCDEFGHIJKLMNOPQRSTUVWXYZ
abcdefghijklmnopqrstuvwxyz
1234567890 !?()&.,:;•""''$€

Braggadocio
ABCDEFGHIJKLMN
OPQRSTUVWXYZ
abcdefghijklmnopqrstuvwxyz
1234567890 !?()&.,:;•""''$€

Britannic Bold
ABCDEFGHIJKLMNOPQRSTUVWXYZ
abcdefghijklmnopqrstuvwxyz
1234567890 !?()&.,:;•""''$€

DESDEMONA
ABCDEFGHIJKLMNOPQRSTUVWXYZ
1234567890 !?()&.,:;•""''$€

Gill Sans Ultra Bold
ABCDEFGHIJKLMNOPQRSTUVWXYZ
abcdefghijklmnopqrstuvwxyz
1234567890 !?()&.,:;•""''$€

Impact
ABCDEFGHIJKLMNOPQRSTUVWXYZ
abcdefghijklmnopqrstuvwxyz
1234567890 !?()&.,:;•""''$€

Kino
ABCDEFGHIJKLMNOPQRSTUVWXYZ
abcdefghijklmnopqrstuvwxyz
1234567890 !?()&.,:;•""''$€

LITHOS BLACK
ABCDEFGHIJKLMNOPQRSTUVWXYZ
1 2 3 4 5 6 7 8 9 0 !?()&.,:;•"" $ €

Poplar Black
ABCDEFGHIJKLMNOPQRSTUVWXYZ
abcdefghijklmnopqrstuvwxyz
1234567890 !?()&.,:;•""''$€

Brush Script
ABCDEFGHIJKLMNOP2RSTUVWXYZ
abcdefghijklmnopqrstuvwxyz
1234567890 !?()&.,:;•""''$€

Caflisch Script
ABCDEFGHIJKLMNOPQRSTUVWXYZ
abcdefghijklmnopqrstuvwxyz
1234567890 !?()&.,:;•""$€

Edwardian Script
ABCDEFGHIJKLMNOPQRSTUVWXYZ
abcdefghijklmnopqrstuvwxyz
1234567890 !?()&.,:; •""$€

Giddyup
ABCDEFGHIJKLMNOPQRSTUVWXYZ
abcdefghijklmnopqrstuvwxyz
1234567890 !?()&.,:;•""$€

HERCULANUM
ABCDEFGHIJKLMNOPQRSTUVWXYZ
1234567890 !?()&.,:;•""$€

Arm A stroke that is attached to a vertical stem at one end of a letter and projects horizontally or at an upward angle.

Art Deco The popular commercial design style of Modernism of the 1920s and 1930s.

Art file Originally derived from the term *line art*, which meant an illustration without blending, this term now is now used for any vector illustration document. Compare to *Continuous tone.*

Art Nouveau A highly fashionable international style that began about a decade before the end of the 19th century that featured elegantly flowing lines.

Arts and Crafts Movement A design movement of the late 19th and early 20th centuries that sought to elevate design and craftsmanship, and raise the status of workers to that of artists,

Ascender The tall stem that reaches upward on lowercase letters such as *b, d,* or *l.*

Asymmetrical balance When the weight of elements on one side of the composition are compensated by different elements on the other side. Also called *informal balance.*

Auto-kerning Information about kerning that is encoded into a digital font where it can be automatically applied by layout programs.

Axis of stress The direction of an implied line that passes through the thin parts of the round shapes in letters.

B

Balance The principle of compensation between elements.

Banner See *Nameplate.*

Bar A stroke in a letter that runs horizontally between stems or across a stem.

Baseline The implied line on which most letter characters rest.

Bauhaus German school of art and design with a curriculum that brought together ideas from all early 20th century avant-garde movements.

Benefits Fulfillment of the customer's basic needs and desires.

Big Idea see *New Advertising.*

Bit The smallest storage unit of information; the choice between two alternatives.

Bit map 1) An alternative term for raster images. 2) A strictly two-color mode for raster images (usually black and white without any shades of gray).

Black A weight of type heavier than bold.

Bleed The extra printed area beyond the trim lines.

Bounce A quality in letters designed with baselines shifting up and down.

Bowl A curved stroke that encloses a counter.

Bracket A curve from the serif to the main stroke.

Brand identity A description of who the client is and how the client would like the public to think of them.

Breaker head See *Subhead.*

Breakout A short, provocative, extract from an article set in display type. It may be placed beside the body text, or the text can wrap around them. Also known as *callouts, liftouts,* or *pull quotes.*

Browser Software to access the World Wide Web.

Byline The listing of the name of an article's author.

Byte A row of eight bits, which can create 256 possible alternatives.

C

Calligraphic Lines that vary between thick and thin.

Callout A label that points out some element in an illustration with a line or an arrow. Also, a synonym for *Breakout*.

Cap height The height of capital letters in a particular typeface. Note that this may be different than the height of the ascenders.

Caption Explanatory note attached to a picture.

Cascading menus Menus that open to show submenus containing lists of links.

Cascading Style Sheets (CSS) CSS function for Web browsers much like style sheets function in QuarkXPress or InDesign. The designer can choose different sets of type attributes for text of various functions such as body type, headlines, or subheads. Then, each CSS can be applied to the appropriate text with simple commands. A change to any CSS can automatically be applied throughout an entire Web site.

CD-R A compact disk that can record information once only.

CD-RW A compact disk that may be re-recorded hundreds of times.

Cell A unit in a table that can contain an entry.

Center stop Defines a point on which characters that come after a tab, but before a return or new tab, will be centered.

Centered alignment When each line of type is balanced from the midpoint.

Chancery A style of fancy calligraphic script, also called *cancellaresca,* originally developed for correspondence and documents in the Church, business, and government during the Renaissance.

Clarendon A category of slab-serif faces with bracketed serifs and moderately contrasting thick and thin strokes.

Clarendon Slab-serif faces with bracketed serifs and moderately contrasting strokes; also known as *Egyptian* or *Ionian*.

Click-drag To click with the mouse on some object or command, and continue to hold down while moving the cursor across the screen to a certain place before releasing.

Click on To position the cursor over some object or command, then press down with the mouse and immediately release it.

Closure The mind's tendency to seek completeness.

Clothesline A dominant horizontal guideline that has several elements "hanging" from it.

Column A vertical area that is filled with running body text.

Compact disk A plastic recording medium that uses a laser to "burn" information onto it.

Composition To put separate parts together to create a new whole.

Condensed type A style of type that is narrower than regular.

Connecting letters A style of geometricized cursive characters that was developed to be molded as a single piece of chromed metal brightware to be used on cars and appliances.

Constructivism An elemental approach to design that tried to clear "away the old rubbish in preparation for a new life" of Soviet Communism from about 1917 to 1930.

Continued-from line Informs readers that the following text is continued from an article that began earlier in the publication.

Continuous tone (c.t.) A raster image, usually photographically based, that contains blended colors or tones.

Contrast Differences between elements or qualities.

Counter A shape inside of a letter.

Creative Revolution See *New Advertising*.

Crossbar A stroke in a letter that runs horizontally between stems or across a stem.

Cuneiform The first written language, developed by the Sumerians in Mesopotamia.

D

Dada An international movement, about 1916 to 1925, characterized by absurdity, chance, and free improvisation with extreme contrasts in typography and bizarre juxtapositions of type and images.

Dazzle A somewhat aggressive quality in body type created by too much contrast between thick and thin strokes in letters.

De Stijl The Dutch of design established by Theo van Doesburg to spread Piet Mondrian's elemental formal vision throughout society.

Deck A sentence or two placed near an article's headline that introduces the article and stirs readers' interest. Also called *kicker*.

Deconstruction Philosopher Jacques Derrida's practice of exposing contradictions in communication and opening up alternative meanings.

Decorative type A category that includes any of a large number of typefaces with novel characteristics designed to give special flavors to display text.

Defamiliarization The concept propounded by Constructivists that forms of representation must be "made strange" or they remain invisible.

Default The option that is automatically chosen by the computer software unless the user chooses a different option.

Demibold A weight of type between regular and bold.

Demographic profile Information about the age, sex, ethnic background, education level, or income of a group of people.

Department headings A heading designed to help magazine readers find sections that are devoted to particular topics.

Descender The part of a lowercase letter that extends below the baseline on letters like *p* or *q*.

Design brief A document that communicates the client's identity, and the purpose, content, audience, tone, and specifications of a prospective design.

Desktop The background screen for the computer monitor where users can put objects that they are working with.

Dialog box Small windows that give information or ask for it.

Discretionary hyphen A hyphen that is inserted manually, but will automatically hide itself if the text reflows so that it is no longer needed. Also known as *dischy* for short.

Disk drive An electromechanical storage device that writes information onto a spinning piece of metal or plastic.

Display type Large type (usually 14 pts. and larger) that stands out on the page, such as titles, headlines, and subheads.

Document Any digital file that is produced or modified by an application.

Dot extension See *File name extension*.

Dots per inch (dpi) Unit for measuring resolution of input devices, such as scanners, and output devices, such as printers.

Double-click To press and release the mouse two times quickly.

Down-style Headline format where only the first letter of the first word and proper names are capitalized; also known as *sentence style*.

Drop cap An large initial cap that drops down and displaces some number of lines of body text and is usually large enough to come up at least even with the top of the text block.

Drop shadow The illusion that type is floating a little distance above the page and casting its shadow onto the page.

Dynamic Relationships of elements that create a feeling of energetic movement by placing elements in diagonal orientation, or through contrasts in direction, or in off-center placements.

E

Ear On a two-story lowercase *g*, a short stroke that sticks out from the upper right of the bowl.

Egyptian 19th-century name for slab-serif faces with bracketed serifs and moderately contrasting strokes; also known as *Clarendon* or *Ionian*.

Elements Term used to describe the parts used in a design.

Ellipsis (…) A character of three dots that indicates that something has been left out or that an incomplete message will be continued. It is best formed by three periods with thin spaces between them.

Em dash (option-shift-hyphen) A long dash used to break up a sentence, as in "I will—hey wait!"

Em A proportional unit that is as wide as the point size of the type. In Cascading Style Sheets (CSS) an em unit is defined as equal to the *default* size for body type.

Embedded fonts Instead of using the end user's fonts, font information can be incorporated into the document itself.

Emboss Slightly raising letters or a design off the surface of the page.

En dash (option-hyphen) A moderately long dash used between ranges of numbers as in "4–6 weeks."

En A proportional unit that is one half the width of an em.

End mark A small icon that signifies the conclusion of a magazine article.

Extended type A style of type that is wider than regular.

Extenders Ascenders and descenders.

Extrabold A weight of type heavier than bold.

Eye The counter in the lowercase *e*.

F

Fat face Category of type that has thick strokes that may be as wide as one-half of the cap height.

Faux type styles When an application restyles a regular font into a simulated bold or italic style.

File name extension A short code consisting of a period followed by between two and four letters (usually three). It is appended to the end of a file name to identify its file format.

Flag See *Nameplate*.

Flash drive A small, inexpensive storage device that works without any moving parts. Instead, they save information onto a solid-state chip.

Flex A slight calligraphic bend in a letter stroke.

Flow line A strong horizontal division that is repeated from page to page in a publication to promote a feeling of unity.

Flush-left alignment When the beginnings of lines of type in a text block align along the left edge.

Flush-right alignment When the ends of lines of type in a text block align along the right edge.

Folder An icon that resembles a file folder that's used in an office. Used to hold related items together and keep them organized.

Folios Page numbers and the graphic elements used to style them.

Font (digital) The encoded information that describes the entire typeface and the digital file that contains this information.

Font editing and creation programs Applications used to change font specifications and convert formats, change characters or add new ones, or create an entirely new font set.

Foot margin Margin at the bottom of the page.

Footer Any combination of elements at the bottom of most the pages of a publication or a Web site.

Formal balance See *Symmetry*.

Formal elements The parts used to create all kinds of visual design, such as line, shape, plane, form, etc. Also called *abstract elements*.

Formalism A doctrine that gives highest value for honesty to the nature of media and how the principles of design are used in a work of art or design.

Format The outside shape, size, and proportion of the design composition.

Forms Used to gather information from users.

Functionalism The idea that design decisions should be based on the product's end purpose.

Futurism An Italian movement that celebrated the innovations of the machine age. Its founder, poet Filippo Marinetti, created a new typography style of energy and expressive force that he called "words in liberty" with extreme contrasts of scale, direction, color, and typeface.

G

Geometric Smooth and regular quality of shape or line.

Geometric Sans Serif A category of typefaces without serifs that were systematically constructed from geometric forms, without regard for traditional forms of type.

German Expressionism Contrary to the mechanistic trend in Modernism, this movement celebrated intense emotions with graphics that had a rugged, hand-hewn look.

Gigabyte (GB) 1024 MB.

Golden mean A proportion of roughly 0.618 to 1 (close to 3:5).

Gothic A common 19th-century name for sans-serif type in the United States. See *Grotesque.*

Grid A system of nonprinting guidelines that make clear implied relationships of alignment and proportion.

Grotesque A common European name for 19th-century sans-serif type. Generally distinguished by condensed letterforms with heavy monoweight strokes that thin at junctions. The vertical sides of round shapes are often straightened to make the set widths of letters consistent. An unusual feature of this quite geometric style is the languorous double-curve of the leg of the capital *R.*

Grouping Bringing related items close together so they become one visual unit.

Grunge Typefaces that looked as though they had been scraped, smashed, burnt, blurred, or run through the wash too many times.

Gutter The space between columns, or the inside margin of a two-page spread.

H

Hanging punctuation When a punctuation mark extends out beyond the text block's edge of alignment.

Hard disk A large capacity rewriteable recording device for digital information.

Hardware The physical components of a computer.

Head margin Margin at the top of the page.

Header Any combination of elements that appear at the top of most pages of a publication or a Web site.

Heading An entry at the top of a column in a table that identifies the variables listed below.

Headline The most important typographic element for enticing readers into a story.

Headline style Headline format where all the major words are capitalized but not the prepositions, articles, and any conjunctions that have four letters or fewer; also known as *leading caps* or *up-style.*

Hierarchy Giving the most important and general information the most contrast, and other elements are given less contrast in order of importance.

Hieroglyph *Priestly writing;* ancient Egyptian writing with naturalistic pictographic characters.

Hints Instructions programmed into fonts to change the shapes of characters so that they will fit into a low-resolution pixel grid as legibly as possible.

Home page A Web site's equivalent to a table of contents, consisting of short descriptions of the site's contents and links to them. A large portion of a home page may be taken up with a signature graphic and other identity elements.

Humanist Sans Serif A category of typefaces without serifs that have some characteristics of oldstyle roman type.

Hybrid typeface A typeface that combines characteristics from different categories of type.

Horizontal alignment A paragraph attribute that controls how the right and left ends of sequential lines of type align. See also *flush-left alignment, flush-right alignment, center alignment, and justified alignment.*

Hyperlink On a Web page, underlined words or a symbol that users can click to get to new content. Also called *link.*

Hyphen A short dash used to break up words at the ends of lines and to join compound words.

I

Icon A small graphic symbol that represents an application, storage device, network server, document, folder, or tool.

Ideograph A symbol that is conventionally used to represent an idea.

Illustration programs Vector-based applications, such as Adobe Illustrator and Macromedia Freehand. These applications were originally developed to create what was traditionally called *line art*: hard-edge spot illustrations or logos made up of flat colored shapes. Since that time, many enhancements have made these tools capable of producing far more sophisticated images.

Image editing programs Raster-based applications, such as Adobe Photshop, used to change colors in images, take parts of images out of their original context and recombine them, or create special effects with digital filters.

Image map A way of making certain areas within pictures behave as Internet links.

Implied line When different elements line up.

Indexes Lists that help readers find particular items of information.

Informal balance When the weight of elements on one side of the composition are compensated by different elements on the other side. Also called *asymmetrical balance.*

Initial cap An enlarged letter at the beginning of a paragraph.

Interlocking letters Typefaces where parts of some characters extend above or below others.

International Typographic Style The mature phase of Modern design that stressed clear, orderly, and impersonal communication; most designers commonly refer to it as *Swiss style.*

Ionian Slab-serif faces with bracketed serifs and moderately contrasting strokes; also known as *Clarendon.*

Issue number Tells how many issues have been published in the current volume of a periodical.

Italic type Typefaces that have calligraphic qualities of cursive writing.

J

Jumpline A note at the end of the first part of an article that tells readers the page where it will be continued.

Juncture Where strokes in letters join.

Justified alignment When both the left and right edges of a text block align.

K

Kerning The adjustment of how a letter fits together with its immediate neighbor.

Kicker A sentence or two placed near an article's headline that introduces the article and stirs readers' interest. Also called *deck.*

Kilobyte (K) 1024 bytes.

L

Landscape format A horizontal format.

Latin A relatively rare category of type with triangular serifs.

Lead-in A distinctive type treatment at the beginning of body text.

Leading caps Headline format where all the major words are capitalized, but not the prepositions, articles, and any conjunctions that have four letters or less; also known as *up-style* or *headline-style*.

Leading The distance between lines of type, measured from baseline to baseline.

Left stop Defines a point where a tab will push the next character that comes after it.

Leg The tail on a *K* or *R*.

Letterspacing When type is set with very wide spacing (or *tracking*) between letters.

Liftout See *Breakout*.

Ligature Two or more letters that have been redesigned to join together into a compound character. This usually is done to avoid clumsy fitting between characters. Many applications can automatically substitute ligatures for certain letter combinations.

Lining figures Numeral characters that stand up above the baseline, like capital letters.

Link 1) In typography: the stroke that reaches from the bowl to the loop on a two-story lowercase *g*. 2) On a Web page: underlined words, or a symbol, or an area in an image, that users can click on to get to new content. Also called *hyperlink*.

Lithography A printing process where an image on a plate is created with oil-based crayon or ink. Then, the surface of the plate is flooded with water. The water is repelled from the oily areas. When ink is applied to the surface, it only sticks to the oily areas—it is repelled from the wet areas. Last, paper is pressed onto the inked plate to receive the impression.

***Littera antiqua* (ancient letters)** Writing style based on the Carolingian minuscule adopted by humanist scholars during the Renaissance for secular manuscripts; later became the basis of roman lowercase letters.

Live text Written content that comes to the user's computer with a list of requested type attributes and is set by the user's browser using fonts from the local hard drive. It can be copied, searched, and updated from a dynamic source.

Logo See *Logotype* and *Nameplate*.

Logotype An emblem that is used to create a recognizable and expressive graphic identity for a person, product, or organization.

Loop The lower bowl of a two-story lowercase *g*.

Luxury margins Wide margins.

M

Macromedia Flash A vector-based program used to create interactive "movies" for the Web and other purposes.

Margin lines Invisible lines for aligning the elements that are closest to the perimeter edges of the layout and marking the "live area" that will contain most of the type.

Masthead A box headed with the publication title, containing business-related information such as a list of the staff and contributors, contact and subscription information, the copyright, and other legalities.

Measure The width of a column of type.

Megabyte (MB) 1024 K.

Menu A hidden list of commands to the computer software that can be opened by clicking on a word or a symbol.

Modern roman Style of serif type characterized by dazzling contrast between thick stems and hairline thin strokes, unbracketed serifs, and vertical axis of stress in round strokes.

Moderne See *Art Deco*.

Monoweight Lines that do not vary in thickness.

Mouse A piece of computer hardware that is the virtual substitute for the user's hand in the digital environment. The user holds the mouse in one hand and drags it over a flat surface to move a pointer (or *cursor*) across the screen. One or more push-buttons on the mouse can be used to control the computer software.

N

Nameplate The main expression of a publication's identity. Placed on the cover, it shows the title and often a small descriptive subtitle or a motto that concisely expresses the publication's mission. If the publication is affiliated with an organization, its name will be included. Sometimes, a distinctive illustration helps to express the publication's tone and content. The nameplate also usually includes the date of publication, a volume number and issue number, and the price. Also known as a *logo, flag,* or *banner.*

Navbar or **navigation bar** A row of links on a Web site's header that leads to site tools and other main features of the site.

Navigation devices Elements used to remind readers of where they are and to help them find what they're looking for.

Negative leading When leading is set so tight that descenders and ascenders may touch.

Negative shapes Shapes between and within the shapes of figures.

New Advertising The new approach to advertising that took shape in New York City in the 1950s that featured unexpected combinations of strong visuals and clever copy to grab readers' attention. Also known as *The Creative Revolution* or *The Big Idea*.

Nick A sharp indentation in the shape of a letter.

Nonbreaking hyphens A special hyphen that won't break at the end of a line; should be used for telephone numbers.

Nonbreaking space A special space that won't break at the end of a line.

O

Oblique A style of type with tilted letters (often confused with *italic*).

Oblong Longer in one direction.

Offset Margin of white space between the graphic and the text.

Oldstyle figures Number characters that have ascending and descending elements. Also called Non-lining figures.

Oldstyle roman Style of serif type that goes back to the Renaissance, characterized by moderate calligraphic contrast between thick and thin strokes, diagonal axis of stress in round strokes, and bracketed serifs.

Opener A page that announces the beginning of a new article.

Organic Shapes that have the irregular and flowing quality of living things.

Orphan A line from the beginning or end of a paragraph that is left stranded at the top or bottom of a column.

Overlap Placing elements so that they partly cover one another.

P

Page layout programs Applications, such as QuarkXPress or Adobe InDesign, primarily used for preparing documents for print. They can place type, images, and other graphic elements with great precision. They have the best tools for working with type and many tools that can automate production of multiple-page documents.

Paint programs Raster-format applications, such as Corel Painter, that simulate traditional painting and drawing media.

Phoenicians Semitic seafaring traders that spread the phonetic alphabet (which later became the basis of the Hebrew, Arabic, Greek, Cyrillic, and Roman alphabets) throughout the eastern Mediterranean about 1500 BCE.

Photo or illustration credit A listing that acknowledges the picture's creator.

Phototypesetting System for setting type that was widely used from the late 1950s until the ascendancy of digital type in the 1980s. It worked by projecting images of characters onto photosensitive film or paper.

Pi character A nonalphabetic character designed to be used as a symbol or decoration.

Pica A unit used equal to twelve points or ⅙ inch.

Pictograph A picture symbol.

Pixels per inch (ppi) An increment for measurement of resolution in raster images.

Point A unit used to measure type equal to 0.0138 inch—just a smidgen less than 1/72 inch.

PostScript point Exactly 1/72 inch.

Portable Document format (PDF) See *Adobe Acrobat Portable Document format*.

Portrait format A vertical format.

Postmodern A recent phase of design that has generally sought to challenge readers by disrupting the flow of information and calling attention to graphic style itself as part of the message.

Prepress house A professional agency that prepares designer's layout documents for printing.

Presentation programs Applications such as Microsoft PowerPoint that are primarily used to create slide shows to accompany lectures and presentations. These shows can integrate some animation and other audiovisual elements.

Principles of design Ideas about how visual elements work together.

Prototype A model for a design such as a Web page.

Psychedelic Design from the "hippie" counter-culture of the late 1960s that adapted elements from numerous sources including Victorian design, Art Nouveau, Secession Style, Surrealism, Pop Art, and Op-Art.

Pull quote See *Breakout*.

Q

Qualities Adjectives used to describe the "feel" of elements.

R

Ragged When the beginnings or ends of lines of type in a text block don't align.

RAM (Random Access Memory) The "live" or "short-term" memory that's held in the circuitry of the computer.

Raster A graphic format in which the image is broken up into a mosaic of squares called picture elements or pixels. Pixels are arranged side by side in a grid; the image is formed by assigning different color values to each pixel.

Raster image processing (RIP) Translation of page layout documents (or other vector documents) into *raster* images made up of dots that can be output from a printer, image setter, or plate maker.

Rasterize To convert a vector image into a raster image.

Rebus Combinations of different pictures used to sound out an unrelated word.

Recto An odd numbered, right-hand page of publication.

Repetition Reusing similar visual elements in a composition.

Resolution The size of the pixels in an image relative to the size of the output, measured in increments such as pixels per inch (ppi).

Resolution independent Ability of vector images to be scaled to any size without loss of quality.

Retro The term used by designers for quotations of popular styles from the past, usually with nostalgic or ironic connotations.

Reversed type Letters printed as white shapes against a dark background.

Rhythm The organization of elements to create visual interest by establishing intervals of both repetition and variety.

Right stop Defines an endpoint where characters that come after a tab, but before a return or new tab, will be pushed to.

River A distracting white line that can form in a block of body type when gaps between words line up.

Rococo The ornate style of aristocratic luxury in the 1700s.

Rollover An image that changes when the user's cursor is moved over it and that can be clicked like a button link.

Romain du Roi The first transitional roman typeface; developed in the late 17th century for French King Louis XIV's Royal Printing Office.

Rule A straight line.

Rule of Six Use no more than three to six words for an entry and put no more than three to six entries on a slide.

S

Save A command to record the current state of an active document.

Sans serif Any typeface that has no serifs.

Scale Size.

Script type A category that includes any typeface that looks hand-lettered with any tool—pen, brush, or pencil.

Scroll bar An image beside a window of a slider on a track. The slider can be click-dragged to move hidden items into view.

Selling points Advantages or attractive qualities that an advertised product or service promises to potential customers.

Semibold A weight of type between regular and bold.

Sentence style Headline format where only the first letter of the first word and proper names are capitalized; also known as *down-style*.

Serif A small cross-stroke at the ends of the main strokes of a letter.

Service bureau A professional agency that prepares designer's layout documents for printing.

Set solid When the measurement for leading is equal to the point size of the type.

Set width The width of a character.

Shape A two-dimensional area that is separated from those around it by differences in color or by outlines.

Shoulder A downward curving stroke in letters such as *h*, *m*, and *n*.

Sidebar In print publications: a box, usually on the outside of the page, that contains a short commentary that enlarges on the main story. On Web sites: a column off to one side that usually contains links that require several words of description or that change with the context of different pages.

Sidebearings The boundaries of space around the left and right sides of a character.

Signature graphic A distinctive graphic expression of identity.

Slab serif A category of typefaces with thick square serifs, just as thick as the stem stroke, and usually unbracketed. Typically the characters are monoweight, open, with wide-set widths and large x-height.

Small caps Special characters that are designed to replace lowercase letters with capitals that are sized close to the x-height.

Smart quotes Quotation marks which in roman typefaces are curled, like this: "", as opposed to the straight quotation marks that look like this: "; also known as *6s & 9s* or *typesetter's quotation marks*.

Software The digital information that the computer hardware uses to create virtual tools.

Specifications Information about where a design product will appear, its size, and how it will be produced.

Spine The central stroke in an *S*.

Splash page A Web page that introduces a Web site with a large signature graphic or an animation.

Spread Two facing pages in a publication.

Spur A small pointed stroke that pokes out from a curved letter stroke.

Square capitals Basis of the oldstyle roman capital letters that we use today.

Stacked type Display type broken up into two or more lines.

Standing cap An initial cap that rises up from the first baseline.

Static Relationships of elements that imply stability or lack of movement through central placement, symmetry, parallel shapes, horizontal or vertical orientations, or placing elements at right angles.

Staub column The first column of a table that contains entries that identify or explain the entries in the other columns in the table.

Stem The main stroke of a letter.

Straddle entry A single entry that replaces two or more repeated entries in adjacent columns or rows.

Straddle headings Headings that run over two or more subheadings to show that they share something in common.

Subhead A small heading that interrupts running text to advise the reader of the content of the next section. Also called a *breaker head.*

Swash A decorative extension at the beginning or end of a letter.

Swipe file A collection of examples of cool design that you can turn to for inspiration.

Swiss style The mature phase of Modern design that stressed clear, orderly, and impersonal communication; called by art historians the *International Typographic Style.*

Syllabary Characters conventionally used to stand for the phonetic sounds of syllables.

Symmetry Arrangement so that each element on one side of the central axis of the composition is echoed by a similar element at an equal distance on the other side.

T

Tab entries The data in a table at the intersections of the rows and columns.

Table function A special grid for creating tables that is available in many graphics applications.

Table of contents (TOC) A key navigation device in publications, the TOC lists each chapter's title or each article's headline, its page number, and often the author. It may also include short enticing descriptions of feature stories. Excerpts of pictures from articles might also be displayed.

Tail A curved or diagonal stroke that reaches downward from a bowl or a stem as in *j, K, Q,* or *R.*

Terminal End of any stroke that doesn't have a serif. Varieties of terminal include angled, ball, beak, cupped, hook, square, tapered (finial), and tear.

Text blocks The general shapes made by an area of body text.

Text wrap When text flows around a graphic object (such as a picture or a text box).

Textura (or blackletter) Style of script that began during the 12th century Gothic period that is dominated by thick, closely spaced, vertical strokes topped with pointed serifs.

Texture The surface quality of a shape or line.

The Glasgow School A style that rejected the fluidity of Art Nouveau for styles of greater simplicity, symetry, geometric form, and modular repetition.

Thinspace A nonbreaking narrow space.

Tone 1) Lightness, darkness, or value. 2) The overall feeling that is evoked by the ideas, wording, type, images, style, and layout in a design; also called *voice.*

Transitional roman A category of roman typeface that differed from the earlier oldstyle and anticipated many features of the later modern roman. Has strong contrast in weights of strokes, vertical or nearly vertical axis of stress, and bracketed serifs.

Tracking The overall adjustment of letter spacing throughout entire words and longer runs of text.

Trim lines The outside boundaries of a full-page composition, identical with the edge of the document.

Type color The tone or density of a block of type.

Typeface Each alternative style within a type family.

Type family A set of related typefaces that share a common name.

Type image Type set by a designer using an application such as Photoshop and saved as an image file. Not usually used in Web sites for body text, subheads, or even for headlines, but very useful for the stable type elements that define the look and feel of a site.

Type structure Difference in the vocabulary of elements used to construct different typefaces; for instance, the difference between roman and italic, or serif and sans-serif.

Type weight The difference between heavier type (with thicker strokes) and lighter type (with thinner strokes).

Typesetter's quotation marks Quotation marks which in roman typefaces are curled, like this: ""; also known as *6s & 9s* or *smart quotes.*

U

Uncial The rounded style of manuscript letters that developed in the 3rd century AD, which are the ancestors of lowercase letters.

Unity When separate parts tie together to make up a whole.

Up-style Headline format where all the major words are capitalized, but not the prepositions, articles, and any conjunctions that have four letters or fewer; also known as *leading caps* or *headline-style.*

Utilitarianism See *Functionalism.*

Utilities Small applications that help you perform specific tasks, such as managing fonts or printing.

V

Vector A force applied to a line segment to bend it into a curve.

Vector graphic Images described as geometric relationships of points and line segments that run between them. The outlined shape can be filled with any color, or a combination of blended colors, or a pattern.

Verso An even-numbered, left-hand page of a publication.

Vertex The point where strokes join at the bottoms of letters such as *V* or *W.*

Vienna Secession A early 20th-century style that rejected the fluidity of Art Nouveau for styles of greater simplicity, geometric patterning, and modular repetition.

Voice The overall feeling that is evoked by the ideas, wording, type, images, style, and layout in a design; also called *tone*.

Volume number A new volume of a periodical publication is begun annually, so this number tells how many years the periodical has been published. Usually listed in the *nameplate*.

Watermark A faint mark impressed into paper.

Web page A document for presentation on the World Wide Web.

Web page development programs Applications, such as Dreamweaver, that are used to create pages for the Internet.

Web site A collection of separate Web pages held together by hyperlinks that take users from one page to the next and by the use of type, layout, and other design elements to create a cohesive identity for the site.

White space Negative shapes between elements on a page.

Widow A line at the end of a paragraph that looks too short.

Window A rectangular area that appears to hold icons or other content, usually surrounded by a frame with navigation controls.

Wood type Nineteenth-century display type cut from hard wood with a router.

x-height The height of most of the lowercase letters in a particular typeface (excluding the height of the ascender). The line of the top of the x-height is called the *mean line* or *waist line*.

Selected Bibliography

Designing with Type

Bringhurst, Robert. *The Elements of Typographic Style.* Hartley and Marks Publishers (2004)—Thorough and authoritative

Carter, Rob; Day, Ben; Meggs, Philip. *Typographic Design: Form and Communication.* John Wiley & Sons (2002)—Has a great survey of student projects

Elam, Kimberly. *Grid Systems.* Princeton Architectural Press (2004)—Guide to using Swiss grid

Felici, James. *The Complete Manual of Typography.* Adobe Press (2002)—Clear guide covering both technical and design aspects

Heller, Steven (Editor); Meggs, Philip (Editor). *Texts on Type: Critical Writings on Typography.* Allworth Press (2004)—Essays by many foremost practitioners

Krause, Jim. *Idea Index: Graphic Effects and Typographic Treatments.* North Light Book (2000)—Demonstrates a wide compendium of display type treatments

Lupton, Ellen. *Thinking With Type: A Critical Guide for Designers, Writers, Editors, & Students.* Princeton Architectural Press (2004)— Basic principles from a critical perspective that can enhance creativity

Spiekermann, Erik; Ginger, E. M. *Stop Stealing Sheep & Find Out How Type Works.* Adobe Press (2002)—Great at showing how type is related to everyday experience

Tschichold, Jan. *The New Typography: A Handbook for Modern Designers.* University of California Press; Reprint edition (1998)—The classic formulation of the principles of modern typography

Wheeler, Susan G.; Wheeler, Gary S. *TypeSense: Making Sense of Type on the Computer.* Prentice Hall (2000)—Has a terrific section on logotypes

White, Alexander. *Type in Use: Effective Typography for Electronic Publishing.* W. W. Norton & Company (1999) —Great for type in publication design

Williams, Robin. *The Non-Designer's Type Book.* Peachpit Press (1998)—A witty and enlightening introduction

Typeface Design

Cabarga, Leslie. *Logo Font & Lettering Bible: A Comprehensive Guide to the Design, Construction and Usage of Alphabets and Symbols.* How Design Books (2004)—Stuffed full of inspiring examples and detailed explanation

Goudy, Frederic. *Alphabet and Elements of Lettering.* Dorset Press (1989)—Detailed introduction by one of the great type designers of the early 20th century

Heller, Steven (Editor). *The Education of a Typographer.* Allworth Press (2004)—Essays by many foremost practitioners

Moye, Stephen. *Fontographer: Type by Design.* Mis Pr (1995)—Find this out-of-print gem for detailed and practical advice on type design

Perfect, Christopher. *The Complete Typographer.* Prentice Hall (1992)—Great detailed and annotated type specimens

History and Theory

Blumenthal, Joseph. *Art of the Printed Book, 1455–1955: Masterpieces of Typography Through Five Centuries from the Collections of the Pierpont Morgan Library, New York.* David R. Godine Publisher (1994)—Has spectacular reproductions

Carter, Sebastian. *Twentieth-Century Type Designers.* W. W. Norton & Company (1995)—A very informative survey

King, Emily. "New Faces: Type Design in the First Decade of Devise-Independent Digital Typesetting" (unpublished PHD thesis; available at www.typotheque.com)—Essential for understanding the recent history of type design

Lupton, Ellen; J. Abbott Miller. *Design Writing Research.* Phaidon Press (1999)—A thought-provoking series of essays

Meggs, Philip (Editor); McKelvey, Roy (Editor). *Revival of the Fittest: Digital Versions of Classic Typefaces.* RC Publications, Inc. (2000)—Stimulating and informative

Meggs, Philip. *A History of Graphic Design.* John Wiley & Sons (1998)—The best broad survey of graphic design

Tschichold, Jan. *Treasury of Alphabets and Lettering: A Source Book of the Best Letter Forms of Past and Present for Sign Painters, Graphic Artists, Commercial Artists.* W. W. Norton & Company (1995)—Source of exceptional examples and strong opinions

Web Sites

Font Sources

chank.com

emigre.com

dafont.com (shareware and free fonts)

fonts.com

fontdiner.com

itcfonts.com

linotype.com

myfonts.com

stonetypefoundry.com

store.adobe.com/type

Journals, Forums, and Information

abc26.de

abc.planet-typography.com

creativepro.com/author/home/951.html

www.itcfonts.com/ulc/4011/index.htm

jeff.cs.mcgill.ca/~luc

just.letterror.com/ltrwiki

omniglot.com/writing

typeculture.com

typeworkshop.com

typographer.org

typographi.com

typophile.com

microsoft.com/typography

woodtype.org

Web Type

w3.org (World Wide Web Consortium)

usability.gov/guidelines

webstyleguide.com

Font Software

Fontlab.com

Index

3-D programs, 11

A

Abadi Condensed Extra Bold typeface, 269
Adobe Caslon typeface, 252
Adobe Garamond typeface, 248
Adobe Illustrator, 10
Adobe InDesign, 10
Adobe Jenson typeface, 249
Adobe Photoshop, 9
advertising, 108
Aldine Press, 85
Aldus Corporation, 113
alignment
    centered, 43
    composition and, 32
    fine-tuning, 44–45
    flush-left, 42–43
    flush-right, 43
    justified, 43
    punctuation and, 44–45
    ragged, 43
alleys, columns, 135
animation and interactive design
  programs, 10
anti-aliasing, 212
apex, letterforms, 234
applications. See software
Aramaic phonetic alphabet, 76
arm, letterforms, 234
Art Deco, 104

art files, 10
Art Nouveau, 97
Arts and Crafts movement, 95–96
ascender, 18
asymmetrical balance, 33
Austin, Richard, 257
auto-leading, body type, 136
axis of stress, 18

B

balance, 31
bar, letterforms, 234
Basel School of Design, 111
baseline, 18
    Greek alphabet and, 77
    phonetic alphabet and, 77
Baskerville typeface, 254
Baskerville, John, 89, 254
Bauhaus typeface, 101, 269
Bayer, Herbert, 101
Bell typeface, 355
Bell, John, 255
benefits, communication and, 155
Benton, Morris Fuller, 256, 265
bit map color, 8
bits, 7
black faces, 19
bleed, trim lines, 158
blocks of text. See text blocks
Bodoni, Giambattista, 89, 259
body type
    auto-leading, 136
    leading, 136

bold faces, 19
    screen resolution and,
      212–213
book faces, 19
bowl, letterforms, 234
boxes enclosing text, 46
bracket, 18
Braggadocio typeface, 269
Brainder, Paul, 113
brand identity, 155
breaker heads, 177
breakouts, 176
brightware, 106
Britannic Bold typeface, 269
Brody, Neville, 113
Brush Script, 271
bullets, PowerPoint, 214
bylines, 176
bytes, 7

C

Caflisch Script typeface, 271
Calisto typeface, 250
calligraphic qualities, 30
callouts, 176
cancellaresca, 86
cap height, 18
capitalization
    down-style, 45
    formats, 45
    headline style, 45
    leading caps, 45
    sentence style, 45

small caps, 141
up-style, 45
captions, 178
Carpenter, Ron, 250
Carson, David, 113
Carter, Matthew, 116, 257
Caslon, William, 89, 253
CD-R disks, 5
CD-RW disks, 5
cells, tables, 163
center tab stop, 161
centered alignment, 43
Century Schoolbook typeface, 256
chancery, 86
Chaparral typeface, 260
character parts, 18
Charlemagne typeface, 81, 267
Chinese brush calligraphy, 75
clicking with mouse, 3
clothesline, 161
color, 134–135
bit map, 8
columns, 135–136
alleys, 135
gutters, 135
reflowing text, 139
tables, 162
commands
dialog boxes, 4
executing, 4
menus, 4
communication
demographic profile, 156
design and, 154–156
compact disks, 5
composition, 31–32
alignment, 32
asymmetrical balance, 33
formal balance, 33
format, 31
static relationships, 33
symmetrical arrangement, 33
text blocks, 32
unity, 32
white space, 32
condensed faces, 19
Constructivists, 101
context, 16
continued-from lines, 183

contrast, 30
Cooper Black typeface, 267
Copperplate Bold typeface, 267
Corel Painter, 9
counter, 18, 29
crossbar, letterforms, 234
CSS (cascading style sheets), Web
pages, 219–220
cuneiform, 74
Curlz typeface, 267
curved line letters, 202

D

Dada movement, 99
dazzle, 88
De Stijl, 101
Decorative type, 61
demibold faces, 19
demographic profile, 156
department headings,
magazines, 180
descender, 18
Desdemona typeface, 269
design, 29
brand identity, 155
communication and, 154–156
composition, 31–32
demographic profile, 156
grid, 156–161
letterforms, 29–31
PowerPoint, 214
specification, 155
swipe file, 156
tabs, 161
Web pages, 216–217
Web sites, 221–223
design brief, 155
desktop, 2
dialog boxes, 4–5
Diderot, Denis, 89
Didot typeface, 259
Didot, Firmin, 259
discretionary hyphens, 138
reflowing text and, 139
disk drive, 5
backups, 6
CD-R disks, 5
CD-RW disks, 5
compact disk, 5

DVD drives, 5
flash drives, 6
hard disks, 5
removable disks, 5
display type, 41–42
alignment, 42–45
capitalization, 45
kerning, 50–52
letterspacing, 46–48
linespacing, 48
stacked, 42
text in boxes, 46
documents, 2
dollar bill, typeface on, 93
down-style capitalization, 45
dpi (dots per inch), 7
drag and drop, 3
dragging mouse, 3
Dreamweaver, 10
drop caps, 181, 182
drop shadows, 202
DVD drives, 5

E

ear, letterforms, 234
Eckmann, Otto, 97
Edwardian Script typeface, 271
elements
formal, 28
letterforms, 29–31
ellipsis (…), 138
em dashes, 138
embossed letters, 202
emotions, 16–17
tied to workds, 27–28
emphasis, 140–141
ems, 62
en dashes, 138
end marks, 183
Engravers Bold typeface, 267
executing commands, 4
expanded faces, 19
extended faces, 19
extrabold faces, 19
eye, letterforms, 234

F

fat faces, 92
faux styles, 21

figures, 142
    oldstyle, 142
filenames, extensions, 7
files
    art files, 10
    organization, 3–4
Flash animations, 220
flash drives, 6
flex, letterforms, 234
flow line, 184
flush-left alignment, 42–43
flush-right alignment, 43
folders, 3
font editing/creating programs, 11
FontLab, 11
Fontographer, 11
fonts, 19
    names, 20
footers, 175
formal balance, composition, 33
formalism, 95
format, grid, 157
formats
    capitalization, 45
    landscape, 31
    portrait, 31
    text in boxes, 46
Fournier le Jeune, Pierre Simon, 88
Freehand. *See* Macromedia
  Freehand
functionalism, 95
Futura typeface, 262
Futurism, 99

G

Garamond, Claude, 87, 248
GB (gigabytes), 7
geometric qualities, 30
geometric sans-serif typefaces,
  102, 236
Georgia typeface, 257
German Expressionism, 99
Giddyup typeface, 271
gigabytes (GB), 7
Gill Sans typeface, 263
Gill Sans Ultra Bold typeface, 270
Gill, Eric, 96, 104, 263
Glasgow School, 98
golden mean, 159
Gothic typeface, 92

Goudy, Frederic, 96
Granjan, Robert, 87
Greek alphabet, baseline and, 77
Greeks, phonetic alphabet and, 77
Greiman, April, 114
grid, 156–157
    bleed, 158
    clothesline, 161
    format, 157
    margin lines, 158
    publications, 184–185
    trim lines, 158
Griffo, Francesco, 85
Gropius, Walter, 101
Grotesques, 92
grouping, 153
grunge typefaces, 115
Gutenberg, 83–84
Gutenberg Forty-two Line Bible,
  82, 83
gutters, columns, 135, 162

H

Haley, Allan, 90
half uncials, 78
hard disk, 5
hardware, 1–2
Harrington typeface, 268
head margin, 158
headers, 175
headings, tables, 162
headline style capitalization, 45
headlines, 176
    PowerPoint, 214
    stacked type, 42
hearing type, 15–17
Helvetica, development, 106
Herculanum typeface, 271
hierarchy, 153
hieroglyph, 75
hints, 212
Hoefler Text typeface, 258
Hoefler, Jonathan, 258
Hoffman, Edouard, 106, 264
home pages, Web pages, 216
humanist scholars, 82
hyperlinks, Web pages, 216
hyphens, 138. *See also* ellipsis (...)
    discretionary, 138
    em dashes, 138

en dashes, 138
nonbreaking, 138

I

icons, 3
ideographs, 74
    Chinese, 75
illustration programs, 10
Illustrator. *See* Adobe Illustrator
image editing applications, 9
images
    continuous tone, 9
    interaction with type, 208
    raster graphic format, 7
Impact, 270
InDesign. *See* Adobe InDesign
    kerning, 51
initial caps, 180
    drop caps, 181
    standing caps, 181
interaction of type and
  images, 208
International Typographic
  Style, 106
italic faces, 20
    Aldus Manutius and, 86
    emphasis and, 141
    screen resolution, 212–213
ITC (International Typeface
  Corporation), 109

J

Jenson, Nicolas, 85, 249
jumplines, 183
juncture, letterforms, 234
justified alignment, 43

K

K (kilobytes), 7
kickers, 176
kilobytes (K), 7
Kimo typeface, 270
Koch, Rudolf, 96

L

landscape format, 31
lateral router, 92
layout, early, 80
lead-ins, 180, 181, 182

leading, 48
    body type, 136
leading caps, 45
left tab stop, 161
letterforms, 76–79
    apex, 234
    arm, 234
    bar, 234
    bowl, 234
    crossbar, 234
    ear, 234
    elements, 29–31
    eye, 234
    flex, 234
    juncture, 234
    link, 234
    loop, 234
    nick, 234
    principles of design, 29–31
    qualities, 29–31
    shoulder, 234
    spine, 234
    spur, 234
    tail, 234
    terminal, 234
    vertex, 234
letterspacing, 46–48
    early, 80
Licko, Zuzana, 114
liftouts, 176
ligature, 19
light faces, 19
line breaks, 42
line length, 62
linespacing, 48
lining figures, 142
link, letterforms, 234
Lissitzky, El, 101
lists, 142–143
lithography, 93
Lithos Black typeface, 270
littera antiqua, 84
live text, Web pages
    attributes, 219–220
    type images and, 218
logotypes, 63–65
loop, letterforms, 234
Louis XIV of France, 88–91

M

machine age, 98–106
Macromedia Freehand, 10
magazines, department
    headings, 180
manuscripts, copying in
    monasteries, 80–82
Manutius, Aldus, 85
margin lines, 158
    head margin, 158
margins, ragged, 138
Marker Felt Wide typeface, 272
masthead, 175
Matura Script typeface, 272
MB (megabytes), 7
measurement
    body height, 62
    column width, 62
    ems, 62
    line length, 62
    picas, 62
    points, 61
    proportional, 62
    spec abbreviations, 62
megabytes (MB), 7
memory, 5–6
menus, 4
    dialog boxes, 4
Microsoft PowerPoint. See
    PowerPoint
Miedinger, Max, 106, 264
Mistral typeface, 272
modern roman style, 89
Modern type, 60
monasteries, manuscript copying,
    80–82
Mondrian, Piet, 101
monoweight, 30
Morris, William, 95
mouse, 2–3
    clicking with, 3
    drag and drop, 3
    dragging, 3
Mucha, Alphonse, 97
Muller-Brockmann, Josef, 106

N

nameplate, 174–175
naming fonts, 20

navigation, 2
    paths, 4
navigation bar, Web pages, 217
negative shapes, 29
Neue Helvetica typeface, 264
News Gothic typeface, 265
nick, letterforms, 234
nonbreaking hyphens, 138
numbers, 142

O

oblique faces, 20
oldstyle figures, 142
Oldstyle type, 60
openers, 176
Optima typeface, 266
organic qualities, 30
organization, 6
    grouping, 153
    hierarchy, 153
orphans, 139

P

page layout programs, 10
Page Spinner, 10
PageMaker, 113
paint programs, 9
Painter. See Corel Painter
Palatino typeface, 251
Palatino, Giambattista, 251
Pannartz, Arnold, 84
papyrus, 75
paragraphs, 80
    indents, 140
paths, navigation, 4
pens, Romans, 77
Phoenicians, phonetic alphabet
    and, 76
phonetic alphabet, 76–79
Photoshop. See Adobe Photoshop
phototypesetting machines,
    108–109
picas, 62
pictographs, 73
pictorial effects, 205–206
pictures, type over, 22
Pierpont, Frank, 261
pixels, 212
Playbill typeface, 268

points, 61
  PostScript, 61
Poplar Black typeface, 270
portrait format, 31
postmodern typography, 110–117
PostScript, points, 61
PowerPoint, 11
  bullets, 214
  design, 214
  headlines, 214
  Rule of Six, 214
ppi (pixels per inch), 7
presentation programs, 11
priestly writing, 75
proofreader's marks, 144
proportional measurement, 62
publications
  footers, 175
  grid, 184–185
  headers, 175
  introduction, 173–174
  mastheads, 175
  nameplate, 174–175
  navigation
    continued-from lines, 183
    department headings, magazines, 180
    end marks, 183
    initial caps, 180
    jumplines, 183
    lead-ins, 180
    table of contents, 179
  breaker heads, 177
  breakouts, 176
  bylines, 176
  callouts, 176
  captions, 178
  headlines, 176
  kickers, 176
  liftouts, 176
  openers, 176
  pullquotes, 176
  subheads, 177
pull quotes, 176
punctuation
  alignment and, 44–45
  early, 80

Q

qualities, 29
  letterforms, 29–31
QuarkXPress, 10
  kerning, 51

R

ragged alignment, 43, 138
RAM (Random Access Memory), 5–6
raster graphic format, 7
rasterization, 9
rebus, 75
reflowing text, 139
regular faces, 19
removable disks, 5
Renner, Paul, 262
repetition, 30
resolution, 7, 212–213
  dpi, 7
  hints, 212
  ppi, 7
  vector graphics format, 8
rhythm, 30–31
right tab stop, 161
RIP (raster image processing), 9
Rockwell typeface, 261
Rodchenko, Alexander, 101
Romain du Roi, 88
roman faces, 19, 20
  modern, 89
  origins, 84–88
  transitional roman, 88
Romans
  Greek alphabet adaptation, 77
  pens, 77
  serifs and, 78
  square capitals and, 77
Rosewood typeface, 268
rows, tables, 162
rules, tables, 162

S

sans-serif
  geometric, 102, 236
  versus serif, 20
Sans-serif type, 60
screen legibility, 212–213
Script type, 61
scriptoria, 80

scroll bars, 3
selling points, 155
semibold faces, 19
sentence style capitalization, 45
serif
  origins, 78
  Roman alphabet and, 78
  versus sans serif, 20
serifs, 236
  slab serif faces, 92
  symmetry, 236
  uncial, 78
set width, 18
shaped text blocks, 203–204
shoulder, letterforms, 234
size, 135
slab-serif type, 60, 92
Slimbach, Robert, 116
small caps, emphasis and, 141
soft return, reflowing text and, 139
software, 1–2, 2
  3-D programs, 11
  animation and interactive design, 10
  font editing/creating programs, 11
  illustration programs, 10
  image editing, 9
  page layout programs, 10
  paint programs, 9
  presentation programs, 11
  utilities, 11
  Web page development programs, 10
spacing
  kerning, 50–52
  letterspacing, 46–48
  linespacing, 48
  lists, 143
  tracking, 46–48
  word spacing, 136–137
spine, letterforms, 234
splash pages, Web pages, 216
spur, letterforms, 234
square capitals
  Greek letters and, 77
  Romans, 77
stacked display type, 42
standing caps, 181
static relationships, 33

staub columns, 162
stem, 18
Stone, Sumner, 116
stories
    breaker heads, 177
    breakouts, 176
    byline, 176
    callouts, 176
    captions, 178
    headlines, 176
    kicker, 176
    liftouts, 176
    openers, 176
    pull quotes, 176
    subheads, 177
straddle headings, tables, 162
stylus, 74
subheads, 177
swash, 18
Sweynheym, Conrad, 84
swipe file, 156
Swiss style, 106
syllabary, 75
symmetrical arrangement, 33

T

tab entries, tables, 162
table of contents, 179
tables, 162–163
tabs, 161
    tables, 162–163
tail, letterforms, 234
Tatlin, Vladimir, 101
terminal, letterforms, 234
text, in boxes, 46
text blocks, 32
    shaped, 203–204
text wraps, 204–205
textura, 81–82
texture, 30

Times New Roman typeface, 252
titles, stacked type, 42
TOC (table of contents), 179
tone, 155
Tory, Geoffrey, 86
tracking, 46–48, 136–137
    reflowing text and, 139
transitional roman, 88
trim lines, 158
    bleed, 158
true lines, 30
Tschichold, Jan, 104–105
Twombly, Carol, 116, 260
type families, 19–20
type images, Web pages, 218
type structure, categories, 60–61
typefaces, 19. *See also* individual
    typefaces
        compounded, 20
        optical adjustments, 235
        selecting, 133–134

U

ultra light faces, 19
uncial, 78
units of measure, 7
unity, composition and, 32
up-style capitalization, 45
uppercase text, emphasis and, 141
utilities, 11

V

van de Velde, Henri, 97
Van Doesburg, Theo, 101
VanderLans, Rudy, 114
vector graphics format, 8
vectors, definition, 8
Venturi, Robert, 112
vertex, 234

Victorian type, 91–94
Vienna Secession, 98
Viva Bold typeface, 268
voice, 155

W

watermarks, 205
Web page development pro-
    grams, 10
Web pages, 215–216
    design, 216–217
    Flash animations, 220
    live text
        attributes, 219–220
        type images and, 218
    printing and, 220
Web sites, design, 221–223
Weingart, Wolfgang, 41, 111–112
Weisert, O., 97
white space, composition and, 32
Wide Latin typeface, 268
widows, 139
windows, 3
wood type, 92
woodblock printing, 83
word spacing, 136–137
wrapping text, 204–205
written language, development
    of, 74

X

x-height, 18

Z

Zapf, Hermann, 251, 266
Zapfino typeface, 272